Drama A to Z

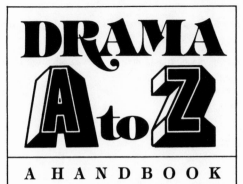

A HANDBOOK

Jack A. Vaughn

FREDERICK UNGAR PUBLISHING CO.

NEW YORK

Copyright © 1978 by Frederick Ungar Publishing Co., Inc.
Printed in the United States of America

Library of Congress Cataloging in Publication Data

Vaugh, Jack A   1935–
    Drama A to Z.

    Bibliography: p.
    1. Drama—Dictionaries.   I. Title.
PN1625.V3   809.2   78-4298
ISBN 0-8044-2937-5
ISBN 0-8044-6946-6 pbk.

To Gerald and Sandra

Acknowledgments

The bulk of the research and writing of this handbook was accomplished under the tenure of a grant from the National Endowment for the Humanities. The author is grateful not only to the Endowment and its program of Summer Seminars for College Teachers but also to Thomas G. Rosenmeyer, Professor of Classics at the University of California, Berkeley, for his advice and encouragement.

Preface

This handbook is intended both as a reference tool for the student of the drama and as a general source of information for the lay reader who wishes to increase his knowledge of dramatic literature, theory, and criticism. The major part of the book is an alphabetical listing of articles defining and discussing approximately 500 words and phrases commonly found in writings on the drama, from Aristotle to the present. The list does not claim to be exhaustive, and the discussions are by no means complete, but each article will give the reader a general idea of how the term has been used most frequently in the history of criticism and, in some cases, an indication of where the term originated.

An appendix, "A Chronology of Dramatic Theory and Criticism," offers a chronological listing of the major works in the field from the *Poetics* of Aristotle through the twentieth century, briefly annotated. When there are correspondences between these critical works and the dictionary articles, they have been so noted.

A final section, "Suggestions for Further Reading," will guide the interested reader to far more thorough treatments of the subject or subjects in which he is chiefly interested.

It is hoped that the user of this handbook will find in it a ready reference tool and a helpful supplement to his study of the drama.

Contents

A Dictionary of Terms and Concepts   1

A Chronology of Dramatic Theory and Criticism   219

Suggestions for Further Reading   235

A Dictionary
of Terms and Concepts

Following are alphabetically arranged articles discussing key words and phrases commonly found in works on dramatic literature, dramatic theory, and the history of the drama. Although many of these terms are used in literary criticism in general, their definitions here have been limited to their specific application to dramatic literature. For example, the article on imagery addresses itself only to the way in which dramatists create images in verse drama, although the subject of literary imagery is far more complex.

These articles are concerned only with the drama as literature, and terms that are relevant primarily to theater history and theatrical production have been excluded. Most of the articles include cross-references to articles on related topics. Occasionally, references are made to sources for further reading.

Cross-references, preceded by a degree sign (°), are used copiously to guide the reader to further information on related topics. Dates of works are given, as are dates of writers, except for those of Shakespeare (1564–1616), the most frequently cited example.

The definitions and discussions of some terms (for example, rhyme and soliloquy) are fairly standard and somewhat brief, but in many cases the variety of meanings a term has acquired over the years (for example, plot and tragedy) has compelled me to set down fairly extensive and often personal interpretations and comments.

It is hoped that these brief articles will prompt the reader to investigate further those areas and topics in which he finds his interest engaged.

ab ovo A Latin term meaning literally "from the egg" and used in dramatic °criticism to refer to an early °point of attack in a °plot. If the playwright begins his plot *ab ovo*, he dramatizes many or all of the early events in the story. This approach to °dramatic structure was typical of Shakespeare and his contemporaries. See °point of attack; also °*in medias res.*

absurdism See °Theater of the Absurd.

academic drama See °school plays.

academies In general, societies of literary, artistic, or scientific persons, organized for the purpose of encouraging cultural activity and learning within various fields. In the drama the influence of such academies began during the Italian Renaissance and continued, in France at least, through the nineteenth century. In sixteenth-century Italy several academies were organized by scholars studying antiquity. Much of the early knowledge of °Greek drama was formulated and preserved by such groups as the Accademia Olimpico of Vicenza, founded in 1555. This organization constructed its own Roman-style theater, which was opened in 1584. This Teatro Olimpico still stands.

Perhaps the most important of all the academies was the literary Académie Française (founded ca. 1629), which established rules and principles governing the writing of drama. The purpose of the Académie Française was "to labor with all care and diligence to give certain rules to our language and to render it pure, eloquent, and capable of treating the arts and sciences" (quoted in William F. Thrall et al., *A Handbook to Literature,* 1960, p. 2). In effect, the Académie Française legislated dramatic composition for at least two hundred years, determining what was fit for public consumption and severely ostracizing those who departed from the accepted forms. The Académie exerted its strongest control in the years immediately following its formation, and its power was confirmed during the great °*"Cid* controversy" of 1636–38. Pierre Corneille's (1606–1684) tragedy *The Cid* (1636) was condemned by the Académie, and heated letters of accusation and defense were exchanged for some time.

Other national academies of note include the Royal Academy of Arts (England), founded in 1768; the Real Academia Española (Spain), 1713; and the American Academy of Arts and Letters, 1904.

See also °neoclassicism.

act   A major section or subdivision of the °action of a drama. The convention of dividing plays into acts has existed for nearly two thousand years, although there is nothing inherent in the nature of °dramatic structure that requires act division. In the ancient °Greek drama plays were written in a standard form in which passages of choral lyrics (°*stasima*) alternated with sections of dramatic °dialogue (°episodes), but the action of the drama was continuous. The ever-present °chorus provided a time continuum during the performance. In about 20 B.C. the Roman critic Horace (65 B.C.–8 B.C.) advocated five-act structure, and the plays of the Roman dramatist Seneca (4 B.C.–A.D. 65) show that by that time the convention was established. Seneca's plays are divided into five separate acts with choral passages between them.

Renaissance dramatists, who at first principally imitated Seneca rather than Greek models, preserved the five-act convention in both their practice and their °criticism, and plays continued to be written in five acts until the late nineteenth century. Henrik Ibsen (1828–1906) was possibly the first major playwright to challenge the convention by writing his dramas in either four or three acts, and other writers of the °modern drama quickly followed suit. The general practice in the twentieth century has been to write either in three acts or in any number of separate °scenes, according to the requirements of the °plot. Even today, however, one finds plays written, like the ancient Greek dramas, as a continuous action, without division into acts. A recent example is Arthur Miller's (1916–   ) *The Price* (1968).

It should be understood that the practice of writing plays in five acts, although rigidly adhered to and defended in the drama and criticism of French °neoclassicism, is fairly arbitrary and essentially meaningless. Shakespeare's plays, though conventionally labeled with acts, are for the most part constructed as a succession of scenes. In *Antony and Cleopatra* (1606–7), for example, there are forty-two separate scenes and the designation of five acts is of little structural meaning. Historically, this is true of most English drama. It was in French °neoclassical tragedy that five-act structure was most meaningful. In the French style each act was conceived of as a continuous and unified succession of scenes, with the conclusion of each act introducing a turn or development in the plot. Lapses in °dramatic time were supposed to fall between the acts (see °*liaison des scènes*).

The German critic Gustav Freytag (1816–1895) attempted to explain five-act structure in terms of an assigned function for each act. Act I is the °introduction; Act II embodies the °rising action; Act III presents the °climax; Act IV contains the °falling action; and Act V is the °catastrophe. Freytag's theory was given much credence in late-nineteenth- and early-twentieth-century criticism, although his analysis of act division is of little value today. (See °Freytag Pyramid.)

In the early twentieth century the form of the °one-act play evolved and earned recognition as a separate °genre. A one-act play may or may not be divided into component scenes.

See also °dramatic structure and °scene.

action   A term applied somewhat loosely in dramatic °criticism, with varying meanings. Action is sometimes used to refer to the physical activity inherent in a drama, such as acts of violence, pageantry, °pantomime, and so on. More precisely, however, action should refer to the motive force of the °plot—the process of change effected during the course of the play. In this sense the action of a drama may not be physical at all, although it may be made manifest partly through physical activity. Thus, the action of Shakespeare's *Hamlet* (1600–1601) is the process by which a son seeks vengeance and meets his death. The action is the sum of the incidents embodying Hamlet's objectives, his failings, and his destruction.

actor   The performer who impersonates, in the theater, the fictional °character in a °drama. Actor and character are not synonymous, although in performance the two merge and are perceived by the spectator as a single living being.

The art of acting began with the °Greek drama and was at that time a highly respected profession. In subsequent ages actors generally have not been highly regarded, and in some societies they have been scorned as purveyors of wickedness. Nevertheless, the profession survives, and acting is today regarded as an art.

See also °protagonist and °Stanislavski System.

actress   The female counterpart of the °actor; a woman who impersonates, in the theater, a °character in a °drama. Female roles have not always been played by women, however. Actresses were unknown on the ancient Greek stage, on the classical Japanese stage (see °Kabuki), and on the English stage before 1660. All of Shakespeare's female characters were originally played by boys. In Spain, Italy, and France professional actresses did not appear until the early seventeenth century.

aesthetic distance   As applied to drama, a kind of detachment on the part of the spectator; a gap between the work of art and its receptor. Through aesthetic distance we are able to view a play not as real life but as an °imitation. Our detachment allows us to enjoy, on a fictional level, stories that, if they occurred in real life, could be unpleasant or even horrifying. "Distance" should not be taken to mean "disinterest." In fact, by divorcing one's personal needs and one's practical self from the work, one is able to appreciate a play with even greater and more vigorous interest, at the level of art.

See also °distancing, °imitation, and °*optique du théâtre.*

afterpiece   A short play performed after a major dramatic work, usually by way of rounding out an evening's entertainment. A comic afterpiece is frequently employed to counteract the sobering effect of a very serious work.

See also °curtain raiser.

agitprop   From "agitation" and "propaganda"; a term coined in 1930 by the Prolet-Bühne, a German-speaking labor group that staged plays in New York City protesting unfavorable working conditions. Agitprop theater became popular throughout America during the 1930s, as a means of dramatizing social protest. Agitprop dramas are usually without much literary or dramatic merit, and their chief value lies in their chronicling of the American labor movement. One exception is the successful *Waiting for Lefty*, written by Clifford Odets (1906–1963) and staged by the Group Theatre in 1935.

The term "agitprop" is still used occasionally to refer to any highly propagandistic drama.

See also °Living Newspaper.

agon   In classical °Greek drama, a dramatized debate or argument between characters, especially one that presents an accusation on one side and a defense or refutation on the other. An excellent example of the *agon* is found in the *Eumenides* (458 B.C.) of Aeschylus (525 B.C.–456 B.C.), in which Orestes is tried for the murder of Clytemnestra before the goddess-judge Athena. The *agon* is an integral part of the structure of Greek °Old Comedy and may be found in almost any play of Aristophanes' (ca. 448 B.C.– ca. 380 B.C).

alarums and excursions   Two devices employed frequently in the °Elizabethan drama to indicate battles and military encounters, both on stage and off. An alarum (modern "alarm") is an offstage sound effect of gunshots, drums, trumpets, and so on. The excursion is an on-stage encounter of a few men, intended to represent full troops in combat.

Alexandrine   A line of verse containing six iambic feet (iambic hexameter). The Alexandrine was the common verse form used by the French in both medieval romances and °neoclassical tragedy. It is thought to have derived its name either from the many romances written about Alexander the Great or from Alexandre Paris, a French poet who commonly used the meter. Though the Alexandrine was well suited to French drama, it never became popular in English, °iambic pentameter being the norm there. Its most conspicuous appearance in English is in the Spenserian stanza, where one Alexandrine follows eight lines of pentameter; but Spenser's use of it was, of course, nondramatic.

The French practice in the seventeenth century of writing °tragedies in rhymed Alexandrines influenced the English writers of °Restoration drama, leading to the vogue of °heroic couplets in tragedy for a few years after 1660.

See also °heroic couplet, °iambic pentameter, and °verse drama.

alienation (German *Verfremdungseffekt*) A central concept in the theory of drama formulated by Bertolt Brecht (1898–1956), the German poet and playwright. Brecht opposed the traditional idea of the theater as a place where a spell is cast over the audience, mesmerizing people into an illusion of reality. He wished his plays to be frankly theatrical and he espoused °presentationalism. To this end he attempted to "alienate" (in the sense of "estrange") the spectator, rather than involve him emotionally. Everything on the stage was to be viewed critically and was to engage the spectator's mind, arousing his intellectual curiosity. Brecht hoped that ultimately an inquiring and critical viewer would relate the stage action to the outside world and work for the improvement of social and economic conditions. Brecht's plays employ °episodic plots with clearly defined °episodes separated by songs, °narration, visual aids, and other techniques of alienation.

See also °epic theater.

allegory A type of literary composition in which objects and characters are equated with meanings and values outside the work itself. Parables and fables are forms of allegory. In the drama, allegory is best represented in the °morality plays of the late Middle Ages, in which characters like Death, Good Deeds, Charity, and Lust obviously represent moral concepts. Allegory belongs to the realm of °didacticism; its purpose is to instruct. As such, it has appeared infrequently in drama since the morality plays. The plays of Bertolt Brecht (1898–1956), however, have sometimes been spoken of as allegorical; he himself identified them as parables. An example is his *The Resistible Rise of Arturo Ui* (1941), in which the rise of a Chicago cauliflower merchant parallels and represents the rise of Hitler in Nazi Germany.

See also °morality play.

alternation A structural technique in early English drama, whereby separate groups of characters are presented alternately,

thus allowing the actors to double in their roles. The practice derived from the early °morality plays, which were performed by troupes so small that it was necessary for an actor to play two or more roles. Christopher Marlowe's (1564–1593) *Doctor Faustus* (ca. 1588) employs the technique of alternation, thus allowing some thirty roles to be taken by only eleven actors.
See also °compression and °parallelism.

anachronism The inclusion in a play of a person, thing, or event which belongs to a period later than that of the play's °setting. There are often anachronisms in Shakespeare's plays, such as the striking of the clock in *Julius Caesar* (1599–1600).

anagnorisis See °recognition.

analytical criticism The type of °criticism that views the work of art as an autonomous whole and seeks its meaning and significance through analysis of form—nature and number of parts, organization, structure, and so on. In literary criticism in general, the New Critics belong to the analytical school; in criticism of the drama, the *Poetics* (ca. 335 B.C.) of Aristotle (384 B.C.–322 B.C.) is perhaps the prototype of analytical criticism.
See °Aristotelian criticism; also °formal criticism, °historical criticism, °mythic criticism, and °textual criticism.

antagonist In a drama of °conflict, the principal character who opposes the °protagonist; the rival or opponent of the chief character. An example is Iago in Shakespeare's *Othello* (1604–5).
See °protagonist.

antecedent action The portion of a dramatic story that is presumed to have occurred before the °action of the drama itself begins.
See °exposition.

anticlimax At the close of a drama, a drop, either intentional or accidental, in the tension or excitement generated by the °climax. If the anticlimax is not intended by the playwright, it represents a serious flaw in the structure of the play, for the attention and interest of the audience will flag and the final effect of the work will be unsatisfying. On the other hand, a skillful dramatist can employ anticlimax to good effect, if the subdued closing is a part of the total plan. A good example of the artistic use of anticlimax is found in Henrik Ibsen's (1828–1906) *A Doll's House* (1879). At the climax Nora announces to her husband that she is going to abandon him and their children to make a life of her own. The anticlimax occurs when the two of them sit down and discuss the emptiness of their marriage and her reasons for leaving. The content of the anticlimax is central to the thought behind the drama, and the play would be incomplete without it.

See also °climax.

antilabe A Latin term describing the poetic technique, in °verse drama, of dividing a single poetic line between alternate speakers. The device originated in °classical tragedy as a means of heightening dramatic tension and was frequently utilized by Renaissance dramatists. The following example of *antilabe* is from the *Medea* (translated by Ella Isabel Harris) of Seneca (ca. 4 B.C.–A.D. 65):

> *Medea.*   I claim a king
>   For father.
> *Nurse.*   Hast thou then no fear of arms?
> *Medea.* I, who saw warriors spring from earth?
> *Nurse.*   Thou'lt die!
> *Medea.* I wish it.
> *Nurse.*   Flee!
> *Medea.*   Nay, I repent of flight.
> *Nurse.* Thou art a mother.
> *Medea.*   And thou seest by whom.
> *Nurse.* Wilt thou not fly?
> *Medea.*   I fly, but first revenge.

See also °stichomythia.

antimasque A portion of the °Jacobean or °Caroline court °masque, intended to contrast with the material of the masque proper by introducing grotesque or humorous elements into the otherwise beautiful and rather serious performance. Whereas the regular performers of the masque were primarily courtiers (and as such, amateurs), the performers of the antimasque were apt to be professional entertainers.

The development of the antimasque has been attributed largely to Ben Jonson (1572–1637). Act III, Scene 3, of Shakespeare's *The Tempest* (1611—12) contains elements of an antimasque, preceding the masque of Act IV, Scene 1.
See °masque; also Enid Welsford, *The Court Masque* (1962).

anti-play   A term coined by the Romanian-French playwright Eugène Ionesco (1912–   ) to describe his play *The Bald Soprano* (1949) and subsequently applied to other dramas that represented a rebellion against conventional °dramaturgy. *The Bald Soprano* was, by Ionesco's admission, largely a joke employing nonsensical language, but the boldness of its conception served to encourage other dramatists to free themselves from preconceived notions about what dramatic form should be.
See also °Theater of the Absurd.

antistrophe   In the choral °ode of °Greek drama, a stanza duplicating the music and structure of the °strophe.
See °strophe.

apocrypha   In drama, plays attributed to a playwright that cannot be authenticated; doubtful works. An example from the Shakespeare apocrypha is *The Two Noble Kinsmen* (1612–13), which some scholars believe was co-authored by Shakespeare and John Fletcher (1579–1625).
See also °canon.

Apollonian-Dionysiac duality   A concept advanced by Friedrich Nietzsche (1844–1900) in *The Birth of Tragedy* (1871) as the basis for the continuing evolution of art, from °Greek drama to modern times. Nietzsche saw in Greek °tragedy an appeal to two basic temperaments in man, as embodied anthropomorphically in two gods. Dionysus represents rapture, intoxication, and the barbaric instincts of man, while Apollo stands for the rational, the ordered, and the lucid. According to Nietzsche, the integration of the two opposing impulses inspires art, and both are essential to human life. To Nietzsche, "tragedy is an Apollonian embodiment of Dionysiac insights and powers."

archetype   A critical term based on the depth psychology of Carl Jung (1875–1961) and formalized in literary °criticism largely by Northrop Frye (1912–   ) ("The Archetypes of Literature," *Kenyon Review*, Winter, 1951). The theory of archetypes is based on the belief that behind each person's conscious mind lies the "collective unconscious" of the human race. This unconscious racial memory allows poets to draw upon "primordial images" shaped by the repeated experience of our ancestors and expressed in °myth and °ritual, religion, dreams, and so on. Thus, an "archetypal image" in the drama evokes strong emotions in the reader or spectator because it speaks to a primordial image in his unconscious memory. Frye defines the archetype as a "symbol, usually an image, which recurs often enough in literature to be recognizable as an element of one's literary experience as a whole."

See °mythic criticism; also Maud Bodkin, *Archetypal Patterns in Poetry* (1963).

argument   A brief prose description of the story of a drama, usually intended to guide the reader or spectator by giving him some idea of what to expect from the play. Arguments are frequently included in printed theatrical programs for this purpose.

The argument in Aristotelian parlance is a statement of the "universal form" of a °plot. In the *Poetics* (ca. 335 B.C.), Chapter XVII, Aristotle (384 B.C.–322 B.C.) suggests that the dramatist should initially conceive of his plot in a universal form—a story outline or argument—before proceeding to particularize by adding characters' names and other details. In this way he will portray universal truths rather than particulars and idiosyncrasies.

See also °scenario and °universality.

Aristophanic comedy   The style of °comedy, also known as °Old Comedy, written by the ancient Athenian poet Aristophanes (ca. 448 B.C.–ca. 380 B.C.).

See °Old Comedy.

Aristotelian criticism   In general, any critical work or system which follows the approach of Aristotle (384 B.C.–322 B.C.) in considering a literary work from a formal and structural standpoint, disregarding historical, moral, or practical implications which the work might possess. In this sense, Aristotelian criticism is the opposite of °Platonic criticism, which identifies extrinsic values in the work and attempts to define its utilitarian worth.

Specifically regarding the drama, Aristotelian criticism is embodied in the *Poetics* (ca. 335 B.C.), perhaps the single most important work in the history of dramatic °criticism. The *Poetics* is an attempt to define °tragedy in its formal manifestation, to identify the constituent parts of the form, and to account for its affective power and the pleasure it affords the reader or spectator. Unfortunately, the *Poetics* presents difficulties in translation and interpretation, for it was probably never intended for publication. It represents, perhaps, an outline, or series of lecture notes on the subject. Still, there is much to be gained from a study of the work, and all dramatic theorists and critics from antiquity on have referred to Aristotle's work, if only, in some cases, to refute it.

In Chapter VI of the *Poetics,* Aristotle offers a capsule definition of tragedy, which is then elaborated in the remainder of the work. The definition reads:

> Tragedy is, then, an imitation of a noble and complete action, having the proper magnitude; it employs language that has been artistically enhanced by each of the kinds of linguistic adornment, applied separately in the various parts of the play; it is presented in dramatic, not narrative form, and achieves, through the representation of pitiable and fearful incidents, the catharsis of such pitiable and fearful incidents.
> (Leon Golden translation)

Proceeding from this introductory definition, Aristotle identifies six qualitative parts of tragedy: °plot, which is the "arrangement of the incidents" and the "soul of tragedy"; °character, which includes the dispositions or characteristics assigned by the poet to the agents of the °action; °thought (*dianoia*); °diction, or the language chosen for the expression of thought and character; °music, an essential part, since the texts of °Greek drama were sung and chanted to the accompaniment of instruments; and °spectacle, which encompasses the visual or presentational aspect of the work.

Possibly the most difficult portion of Aristotle's discussion of tragedy is the concept of °catharsis and its relationship to °pity and fear. Catharsis has been variously interpreted throughout history, but whatever the interpretation, it is clear that Aristotle believed that tragedy possessed an affective power—the capability of profoundly moving its audiences—and that this power produced a pleasurable effect upon the reader or viewer. This pleasure, he asserted, was derived from some sort of learning—not the learning of useful moral or ethical lessons, but a kind of learning common to all the arts.

Aristotle's theory of tragedy has been translated and interpreted by critic after critic, beginning in the mid-sixteenth century. Unfortunately, the Renaissance critics did not understand much of what Aristotle had written and began to impose their own ideas on his work, emerging with new rules and regulations for the drama, which may be subsumed under the general heading of °neoclassicism. Some of these ideas, which were totally foreign to Aristotle's thought, are the prohibition of humorous material from tragedy, the theory of the °Three Unities, the concept of °decorum.

The influence of Aristotle, as filtered through the neoclassical strictures, was strong throughout the seventeenth and eighteenth centuries, and it appears in criticism even today. For example, when Arthur Miller's (1916–   ) *Death of a Salesman* was first staged in 1949, there was much critical debate over Willy Loman's qualifications as a tragic figure in the Aristotelian sense. Undoubtedly, the *Poetics* of Aristotle will continue to exert a considerable influence on the criticism of drama for ages to come.

See also separate entries for the terms cross-referenced above.

ars metrica   The ancient theory of poetry that dominated Greek and Latin literary production in antiquity. The *ars metrica* dictated that there was a proper metric form for each type of writing. The measure of a writer's success was how skillfully he could render his subject within the confines of the prescribed meter or verse form. Iambs were designated for dramatic poetry, hexameters for the epic, and so on.

Aristotle's (384 B.C.–322 B.C.) theory of poetry (*Poetics,* ca. 335 B.C.) served to refute the *ars metrica*. Aristotle maintained that a poet ("creative writer" in general) was a poet not by virtue of the metric form in which he wrote but by his working in °imitation. That is, a poet creates artistic literature, whereas a historian renders facts. To Aristotle, a laundry list written in rhymed verse would nevertheless remain a laundry list, not a work of art, and a drama in prose (although he knew of none) would be no less artistic for its having forsaken verse. Aristotle went a long way toward defining what we today mean by "literary art" and, through the rejection of the *ars metrica,* toward a tentative formulation of aesthetic theory.

See also °Aristotelian criticism.

artificial comedy   A term used in nineteenth-century °criticism to refer to the type of °comedy that ridicules the artificiality of society, such as the °comedy of manners. Charles Lamb defined the type in his essay "On the Artificial Comedy of the Last Century" (1822).

See °comedy of manners.

aside   A °dramatic convention in which a remark or speech of one character is presumed not to have been heard by the other character(s) on the stage. The aside is a comment for the benefit of the audience only and may be spoken either directly to them or in an offhand manner. Asides are quite common in nonrealistic plays. Eighteenth-century °comedy is filled with asides that frankly acknowledge the presence of the spectators. In more realistic drama, however, the asides (if there are any) will be in the nature of a brief remark, perhaps spoken ironically and not necessarily in recognition of the audience.

See also °soliloquy.

astrophon   In the °*stasimon* of Greek °tragedy, that portion of choral singing outside the structure of °strophe and °antistrophe.

See °ode.

Atellan farce   A form of ancient Italic popular °comedy, in the nature of rustic °farces, performed in song and dance by masked actors portraying °stock characters. Atellan farce developed among the Italic peoples well before the influx of Greek dramatic traditions. It owed its popularity not to literary values but to °slapstick action, simple °plots, indecencies, and the predominance of song and dance. Some of its stock characters, who later influenced the °*commedia dell'arte* of the Renaissance, are Maccus (a stupid clown), Bucco (a glutton and braggart), Pappus (the foolish old man), and Dossennus (the cunning swindler).

See °Roman drama.

Attic drama   The °Greek drama of the fifth century B.C. The term derives from the ancient Greek state of Attica, in which the city of Athens was located. The height of Attic culture is referred to as the Age of Pericles (461 B.C.–429 B.C.).

See °Greek drama.

autos sacramentales   Brief religious dramatic performances presented in Spain in connection with the Feast of Corpus Christi, beginning in the thirteenth century. The *autos sacramentales* were similar to the English °Corpus Christi plays in that they were essentially processional street dramas. They often included comic and farcical elements, as did their English counterparts, but they remained fairly simple and did not pass into the mainstream of Spanish drama, as the °miracle plays of England did into that nation's drama. The *autos sacramentales* were discontinued during the eighteenth century.

See also °Corpus Christi plays and the section on Spain under °Renaissance drama.

auxesis   A rhetorical device, used occasionally in °verse drama (especially °Elizabethan drama), in which a statement or idea is intensified through repetition. The meaning of the idea increases as it is expressed in varying forms. An example of auxesis is the following passage from Act II, Scene 1, of Shakespeare's *Richard II* (1595–96):

> His rash fierce blaze of riot cannot last,
> For violent fires soon burn out themselves;
> Small showers last long, but sudden storms are short.
> He tires betimes that spurs too fast betimes;
> With eager feeding food doth choke the feeder.
> Light vanity, insatiate cormorant,
> Consuming means, soon preys upon itself.

ballad-opera In general, an °opera whose music is derived from popular songs and lyrics; specifically, the type of musical °burlesque that became popular on the English stage after the highly successful *The Beggar's Opera* (1728) by John Gay (1685–1732). The ballad-opera drew upon well-known ballads and street songs, combining them with some narrative line for comic effect. One purpose of ballad-opera was to burlesque Italian opera of the day.

See also °burlesque and °opera.

baroque drama In general, any dramatic literature of the period in which the baroque style flourished (late-sixteenth through early-eighteenth centuries). Although the term "baroque" is regularly applied to the art and architecture of the period, the term more commonly used in reference to literature is "neoclassical."

See °neoclassical tragedy and °neoclassicism.

"below-stairs" scene (also **"feather-dusting" scene**) A conventional scene in nineteenth-century drama, the purpose of which is to expedite the task of conveying the play's °exposition. The "below-stairs" scene is usually the opening scene of the play, and it depicts two servants (who work "below stairs," or on the ground floor of a townhouse) dusting the furniture, discussing the background of their employers' lives to date, and setting the scene—all in a highly artificial fashion. The intent was simply to get the necessary exposition over as quickly as possible so that the play could proceed. The "below-stairs" scene had the added advantage of delaying the grand entrance of the star players, so that latecomers would not be deprived of this theatrical moment and the entrance applause would be more substantial. Needless to say, the "below-stairs" scene is difficult to justify on artistic grounds.

See also °exposition.

bienséances, les   The French term for the principles or rules of °decorum in literary composition.

See °academies, °neoclassicism, and °"reason and good sense."

black comedy   A style of °comedy peculiar to the contemporary theater, which finds humor in subjects and situations conventionally treated with the utmost seriousness. Black comedy exploits fears, forbidden subjects, and repressed hostilities to effect its jokes, which are often labeled "sick." An example of the type is Arthur Kopit's (1938–   ) *Oh, Dad, Poor Dad, Mama's Hung You in the Closet and I'm Feeling So Sad* (1960), in which a woman lives with the stuffed corpse of her late husband and jokes are made over Venus flytraps, piranha fish, nymphomania, and castration anxiety.

black drama   In general, any play dealing principally with Negro life and characters. Early examples in the American drama are Dion Boucicault's (1822–1890) *The Octoroon* (1859) and Edward Sheldon's (1886–1946) *The Nigger* (1909). More specifically, the black theater movement is a contemporary manifestation, dating roughly from the early 1960s. Its purpose is to create a body of drama and a theatrical tradition that deal seriously and honestly with issues confronting black people living in America. Its playwrights view the black experience as a valid source of material for artistic production, and their works refuse to compromise with white ideals and sensibilities. The poet and dramatist Imamu Baraka (LeRoi Jones) (1934–   ) was one of the early founders of the black theater movement. Other important contributors have been Ed Bullins (1935–   ), Douglas Turner Ward (1930–   ), Lonne Elder III (1931–   ), and Charles Gordone (1926–   ), whose *No Place to Be Somebody* won the Pulitzer Prize for drama in 1969.

blank verse   Technically, any form of unrhymed verse with a regular metric pattern, although the term is used more specifically to refer to unrhymed °iambic pentameter, the almost exclusive verse form in English °verse drama. Blank verse has the advantage of reproducing most closely the normal rhythms of English speech, but its effective use in drama demands great poetic skill and mastery of the language.

Early English dramatists, in writing °miracle plays and °morali-ties, experimented with a variety of verse forms, but with the first English °tragedy, *Gorboduc* (ca. 1562) by Thomas Sackville (1536–1608) and Thomas Norton (1532–1584), blank verse be-came recognized as the most effective medium for poetic drama. Still, it was not until the plays of Chistopher Marlowe (1564–1593) that the dramatic power of blank verse was fully realized, and Shakespeare followed Marlowe's lead, writing the finest blank verse in all English drama. Blank verse has continued as the nor-mal verse form both for English drama and for much lyric and narrative poetry. Modern verse dramatists, such as T. S. Eliot (1888–1965) and Maxwell Anderson (1888–1959), have frequently used blank verse.

Although the use of blank verse disencumbered the Eliza-bethans from the rigid effects of °rhyme and permitted them greater power of expression, English drama returned briefly to rhymed verse in the °heroic tragedies of the °Restoration period. The practice of writing in rhymed °heroic couplets was quickly abandoned, however, having lasted no more than about fifteen years (1660–ca. 1675).

See also °iambic pentameter and °verse drama.

bombast Excessively extravagant, exaggerated language. The term is derived from the sartorial term for cotton stuffing, and the image is appropriate. Early Elizabethan dramatists especially, in imitating the overblown rhetorical style of °Senecan tragedy, wrote their dialogue in a bombastic style. Almost any passage in Thomas Kyd's (1558–1594) *The Spanish Tragedy* (ca. 1587) will il-lustrate this point. By Shakespeare's time the excesses of bombast were so clearly recognized that he was able to achieve comic ef-fects by having some of his characters (for example, Armado in *Love's Labor's Lost* [1594–95] and Pistol in 2 *Henry IV* [1597–98]) speak little else.

Bombastic dialogue is also frequently found in the °heroic trag-edy of the °Restoration and early eighteenth century. This variety of bombast was delightfully satirized in Henry Fielding's (1707–1754) °mock-heroic, *Tom Thumb; or, The Tragedy of Tragedies* (1730). Frequently used synonyms for bombast are °rant (refer-ring especially to the Senecan style) and °fustian (or Dutch fus-tian).

Boulevard dramatist   A term applied, somewhat derogatorily, to a writer of °melodramas or light °comedies, especially °farces. The term derives from the Parisian Boulevard du Temple, along which a number of popular theaters were established after 1760. In the nineteenth century especially, these Boulevard theaters offered serious competition to the established classical houses such as the Comédie Française, drawing large audiences to their melodramas and farces. Even today Parisian companies catering to popular audiences are referred to as Boulevard theaters.

See also °melodrama.

bourgeois drama   A general term for any type of drama, either comic or serious, that is concerned not with elevated personages such as kings and princes but with common, ordinary characters, especially insofar as they are involved in everyday, middle-class activities and domestic issues. Two principal historical types of bourgeois drama are °realistic comedy, exemplified by Thomas Dekker's (ca. 1572–ca. 1632) *The Shoemakers' Holiday* (1599), and °domestic tragedy, the classic example of which is George Lillo's (1693–1739) *The London Merchant* (1731).

bowdlerize   A term coined from the name of Thomas Bowdler (1754–1825), who in 1818 published an edition of Shakespeare's plays from which he had removed all possibly offensive language and "improper" references. Hence, to "bowdlerize" is to censor or expurgate, with little regard for the integrity of the original work. Dr. Bowdler's *The Family Shakespeare,* which anticipated Victorian sensibilities, makes for amusing reading today.

braggart soldier (or **warrior**)   See °*miles gloriosus.*

breeches part   Either a male role acted by a woman, or a female role in which the character is at some point disguised as a male. The breeches part was quite popular in the English °Restoration theater, since it allowed actresses to appear in men's attire, displaying their legs to good advantage. This particular incentive was not present, of course, in the earlier English theater, where the female role was always acted by a boy. Two notable breeches parts in Restoration comedy are Fidelia in *The Plain-Dealer* (1676) and Margery Pinchwife in *The Country Wife* (1675), both by William

Wycherley (1640–1715). Among the best examples in Shakespeare's plays are Rosalind in *As You Like It* (1599–1600) and Viola in *Twelfth Night* (1599–1600).

Perhaps the outstanding example of the fame which an actress could earn in a breeches part was the success *Mazeppa* (1840), by the Polish dramatist Juliusz Słowacki (1809–1849). In the leading male role the American actress Adah Isaacs Menken donned a pair of tights and rode across the stages of America, strapped to the back of a horse, throughout the 1860s.

Brunetière's Law A theory of the drama advanced by the French critic Ferdinand Brunetière (1849–1906) in 1894. In an attempt to identify the one indispensable element of dramatic °action which distinguishes the drama from all other literary °genres, Brunetière posited that drama is the "spectacle of a *will* striving towards a goal, and conscious of the means which it employs." This definition underlies much of the modern °criticism that cites °conflict as the core of the drama. Brunetière further theorized that the four principal kinds of drama can be distinguished by the nature of the obstacle against which the will is pitted. In °tragedy the obstacle is unsurmountable and the will is defeated or destroyed. In °melodrama the °hero exerts sufficient will to conquer and has a "chance of victory." °Comedy exhibits the struggle of two opposing wills, and in °farce the obstacle against which the will struggles lies in the realm of the "irony of fortune, or in the ridiculous aspect of prejudice, or again in the disproportion between the means and the end."

Although struggle and conflict are frequently components of dramatic action, Brunetière's definition is so broad and his reasoning so shallow as to render his "Law" of little substantive value. His argument, which is based exclusively on content, ignores totally the nature of °dramatic structure. Much contemporary drama lacks conflict in his sense. Still, the conflict theory has had considerable attention in twentieth-century dramatic criticism.

See also °conflict.

Bunraku The classical °puppet theater of Japan, which dates from the late sixteenth century. The development of Bunraku is closely associated with that of the °Kabuki theater, with the same plays being performed in both styles. The greatest of Japanese dramatists, Chikamatsu Monzaemon (1653–1724), wrote extensively for the Bunraku, and the best-known of his plays in the Western world is *Chushingura.*

The texts of the Bunraku plays, known as *joruri,* are delivered entirely by a singer-narrator, seated at the side of the stage. Each of the dolls (approximately three to four feet tall) is manipulated by a master operator and two assistants, all of whom remain visible but mute. The *joruri* are composed of both dialogue and narrative passages, focusing almost invariably on historical tales of both violence and melancholy. These plays are perhaps the closest approximation in classical Japanese drama to Western °tragedy.

For further reading, see Donald Keene, *Bunraku: The Art of the Japanese Puppet Theatre* (1965). See also °Kabuki drama and °Noh drama.

burla   An extended piece of °stage business incorporated into the action of a °*commedia dell'arte* performance; an improvisation.

See°*commedia dell'arte.*

burlesque   In general, a dramatic composition that makes fun of, or satirizes, some other specific work or general form of theater. Satirical burlesque gained popularity in the English theater in the 1730s, where it took the form of musical spoofs of popular plays and contemporary events and personages. An outstanding early example is Henry Fielding's (1707–1754) *Tom Thumb; or, The Tragedy of Tragedies* (1730); Richard Brinsley Sheridan's (1751–1816) *The Critic* (1781) represents a later development of the form. The burlesque flourished also in the nineteenth century, especially between 1850 and 1870, when again it parodied well-known plays and performers. Travesties of Shakespearean plays were popular during this period.

Toward the end of the nineteenth century in America burlesque acquired a new character with the incorporation of female pulchritude and, eventually, sexual humor. This tradition may be said to have originated with *The Black Crook* (1866), an extravagant musical that featured a troupe of scantily clad ballet dancers. This form of burlesque continued into the twentieth century, with increasing emphasis on sexual material, including the striptease act, and a decline in the satiric elements. Modern °vaudeville grew partly from this form of burlesque.

See also °extravaganza and °vaudeville.

burletta A general term in late-eighteenth-century criticism for a variety of different forms of musical drama, such as °ballad-opera, °extravaganza, and °pantomime. One early definition of the burletta is a "drama in rhyme, entirely musical—a short comick piece consisting of *recitative* and *singing,* wholly accompanied, more or less, by the orchestra" (quoted in William F. Thrall et al., *A Handbook to Literature,* 1960, p. 67).

See also °ballad-opera, °extravaganza, and °pantomime.

business See °stage business.

buskin (also *cothurnus*) The thick-soled, elevated boot that, until very recently, was thought to have been worn by tragic actors on the ancient Greek stage. The buskin was said to have increased the height of the actor, making for a more imposing and heroic figure in the large Greek amphitheater. Recent research, however, has shown that use of the buskin cannot be proven with any certainty. The term is significant nevertheless in that critics have occasionally used buskin to refer to °tragedy. John Milton (1608–1674), for example, wrote of the "buskin'd stage."

caesura   A pause or break in the rhythm of a line of verse, dictated by the sense of the passage. In English °verse drama, the best playwrights, Shakespeare included, used the caesura to avoid the monotony inherent in °iambic pentameter and to endow poetic dialogue with rhythms more nearly approximating normal speech. In the following passage, the opening speech of Shakespeare's *Twelfth Night* (1599–1600), the caesuras are marked with a slash.

> If music be the food of love, / play on,
> Give me excess of it; / that, surfeiting,
> The appetite may sicken, / and so die.
> That strain again; / it had a dying fall.
> Oh, it came o'er my ear, / like the sweet sound
> That breathes upon a bank of violets,
> Stealing, and giving odor. / Enough, no more.
> 'Tis not so sweet now, / as it was before.

See also °end-stopped line, °iambic pentameter, and °run-on line.

cameo role   A very small but important role in a play, especially one that serves to provide a brief and impressive appearance for a well-known actor. The term is used most often in motion pictures and television but can apply also to some roles in the theatrical repertory: for example, the Gravedigger in Shakespeare's *Hamlet* (1600–1601).

canon   The undisputed works of an author. Thus, the Shakespeare canon consists of the thirty-seven plays that almost all scholars agree were written by him, although some may have been °collaborations.

See also °apocrypha.

capa y espada Literally, "cape and sword"; a type of Spanish Renaissance play concerned with the Spanish gentry, from whose costume the name derives. One master of the *capa y espada* play was Lope de Vega (1562–1635) whose *The Gardener's Dog* (ca. 1615) and *Madrid Steel* (1603) serve as examples of the type.

See also °*comedia* and °*Siglo de Oro*.

caricature As in cartooning, caricature in the drama is the drawing of °character so as to exaggerate the distinguishing features for immediate recognition by the reader or audience. As such, caricature is related to the writing of °type characters and the term is generally used in a pejorative sense, suggesting lack of skill or subtlety on the part of the dramatist in handling °characterization.

See °stock character and °type character.

Caroline drama (also **Carolean**) The English drama written during the reign of Charles I (1625–49). Caroline drama, definitely inferior to that of the earlier °Elizabethan and °Jacobean periods, displays a certain °decadence in moral and ethical values. The best-known dramatists of the period are John Ford (1586–ca. 1639), a tragedian of considerable merit, and James Shirley (1596–1666), the leading comic writer. The influence of the Puritans, who were violently opposed to the theater, increased steadily during Charles's reign, effecting finally a total closing of the public theatres in 1642. It was also during this period that religious and political struggles were rampant and that the Puritan migration to America was heaviest. It is not surprising then that the Caroline period failed to produce either first-rate playwrights or dramas of lasting merit. It may be considered the end of the English °Renaissance.

See also °Dark Period, °decadence, and °Jacobean drama.

catastrophe The closing portion of a drama; the last of the four parts into which the Ancients divided a play. The events of the catastrophe result from the °crisis of the °plot and effect a tying up of loose ends in the final stages of the °resolution. According to the °Freytag Pyramid, the catastrophe is the fifth and final part of a plot, but Freytag uses the term in exactly the same sense as did the Ancients.

In °tragedy the catastrophe is usually the part of the play in which most of the deaths and other bloody incidents occur; hence, the use of the term today to denote some disastrous occurrence in real life. In the strict critical sense, however, the catastrophe can be a part of both tragedy and °comedy, and it is proper to speak of the "comic catastrophe."

See also °*dénouement* and °resolution.

catharsis   A difficult and widely misunderstood concept in dramatic criticism. The term appears originally in Chapter VI of Aristotle's (384 B.C.–322 B.C.) *Poetics* (ca. 335 B.C.) where it is associated with °pity and fear and is clearly related to the effect or end purpose of °tragedy—to tragedy's affective power. The difficulty in interpretation is due in part to the problem of translation, and at least three theories of catharsis are possible, each based upon a particular translation of a key passage of ten Greek words in the original. The possibilities of translation are:

1. ". . . through pity and fear affecting the proper purgation of these emotions."

   —*S. H. Butcher,* 1895

2. ". . . with incidents arousing pity and fear, wherewith to accomplish its catharsis of such emotions."

   —*Ingram Bywater,* 1909

3. ". . . and achieves, through the representation of pitiable and fearful incidents, the catharsis of such pitiable and fearful incidents.

   —*Leon Golden,* 1968

The problem lies in an accurate rendering of catharsis, for the term was used variously by the Greeks to mean "purgation," "purification," and "clarification." Each of the three translations is based upon a different understanding of the word.

The "purgation" theory of catharsis, substantiated in the Butcher translation, has dominated modern criticism until very recently. This theory suggests that tragedy arouses emotions of pity and fear in the spectator and then purges or eliminates these emotions—a sort of emotional enema, as it were. Such an interpretation is quite in keeping with a critical approach that considers the impact or effect of a drama upon the reader as paramount. Unfortunately, such extrinsic considerations are inconsistent with Aristotle's methods. At no other point in the *Poetics* is he concerned with audience psychology or the emotions of the spectator.

The Bywater translation leads one to a "purification" theory of catharsis, in which tragedy arouses the emotions of pity and fear in order to purify *"such* emotions." Emotion in general is the topic here, and the idea is that the exercising of them in the controlled fiction of tragedy helps us learn to control emotions in real life, thus bettering us and contributing to our emotional health. Again, the spectator-oriented approach is foreign to Aristotle, and a "purification" theory leads to the acceptance of °didacticism in drama, as much Renaissance criticism based upon "purification" has proved.

Golden's translation encourages an interpretation of catharsis as "clarification," a concept which has little to do with audience response. This is not to deny the emotional power of tragedy but to restore catharsis to the realm of Aristotelian methodology. The catharsis (clarification) in tragedy works not upon the spectator but upon the incidents of the plot itself. In other words, through the selecting and ordering processes of art, the incidents of the play are "made clear" in terms of °probability and necessity, and this clarity of action is the source of tragic pleasure. This interpretation, which appears in the O. B. Hardison commentary on Golden's translation and which has been embraced by many recent commentators, is grounded in a thorough knowledge of Aristotelian methodology and is quite illuminating. It is also consistent with much modern aesthetic theory.

For a full discussion of this interpretation of catharsis, see Leon Golden and O. B. Hardison, *Aristotle's Poetics* (1968). See also °pity and fear.

character (Greek *ēthē*) One of the six qualitative parts of °tragedy, according to Aristotle (384 B.C.–322 B.C.) in Chapter VI of the *Poetics* (ca. 335 B.C.), the others being °plot, °thought, °diction, °music, and °spectacle. By character Aristotle meant the dispositions, traits, or behavior patterns which the dramatist assigns to the agents of the °action. He did not refer to the creation of psychologically recognizable °characterizations as we view them today. Thus, character in the Aristotelian sense is closely related to the modern concept of °type characters.

Aristotle identified four requirements for character. It must be "good" (meaning also substantial or functional), "appropriate" (the actions conforming to basic type), "like" (probably, true-to-life), and "consistent." He was not overly concerned with character, for he felt that it would automatically manifest itself if the plot were well constructed. Character, then, was the material that was formalized in plot.

See also °characterization.

character foil   See °foil.

characterization   The rendering by a playwright of actions, incidents, and °dialogue in such a fashion as to cause the reader or spectator to perceive the dramatic °characters as realistic portraits of living human beings. When a dramatist is skillful in characterizing, we tend to refer to his characters as if they had lives of their own, outside the play. Hamlet, for example, has been endlessly "analyzed." It is important for the critic always to realize, however, that dramatic characters are not real people—that they have no life beyond the actions they perform in the drama.

Effective characterization is achieved through various techniques. The °diction the playwright utilizes in the speeches of a character will cause us to assume certain ideas about him. If he consistently curses or mouths obscenities, we will tend to make inferences about his moral tone, based upon our knowledge of real people. Much also can be achieved in the way of characterization through °exposition. In Molière's (1622–1673) *Tartuffe* (1664), the title character does not appear until the third act, but by that point we have heard so much about his past actions that we have already a vivid portrait of the pious hypocrite. Still another method of characterizing involves the ways in which a character affects other characters. If they fear him and express trepidation at his approach, the effect on us is far different than if they express eagerness. Finally, the actions the character himself commits can be most telling. The consistent impulsiveness and rashness in the actions of Oedipus, both narrated and played before us, add up to a powerful characterization of Sophocles' fictional king.

See also °character.

Chinese drama   See °Peking Opera.

chorus   In °Greek drama, portions of the dramatic text composed of lyrical °odes, assigned not to the °actors but to a group of men who danced to musical accompaniment while singing; also, the group or collective °character that performs those portions of the text. Ancient drama evolved mainly from choral worship of gods and mythological heroes, and the chorus remained an extremely important part of early °tragedy. During the fifth century B.C., however, the role of the chorus gradually declined as the importance of the °episodes, or acted portions, increased. The chorus in early tragedy was composed of fifty men, but its size was reduced to twelve or fifteen in the time of Aeschylus (525 B.C.–456 B.C.). The chorus in °comedy numbered twenty-four. Spoken portions of a play text assigned to the chorus were probably delivered by the °*coryphaeus,* or chorus leader, rather than by the full chorus.

The role of the chorus varied, depending on the poet's use of it. Aeschylus, who relied heavily upon his choruses, used them for °exposition, for establishing mood and atmosphere, and for occasional exchanges with the actors. The choruses of Aeschylus contain some of the most beautiful lyric poetry of antiquity. Sophocles (ca. 496 B.C.–406 B.C.) reduced the importance of the chorus and used it for fairly separate lyrical interludes between the episodes. His choruses, often serving as commentary on the action, perform as a sort of °ideal spectator, echoing the opinions the audience might be expected to have regarding the unfolding of the action. In Euripides' (ca. 480 B.C.–ca. 406 B.C.) plays the chorus becomes even less an integral part of the action of the tragedy. His choral odes are often highly philosophical and relate only loosely to the immediate predicaments of the characters.

The chorus was almost exclusively a product of the Greek theater. °Roman drama did not utilize it at all, except in the °closet dramas of Seneca (4 B.C.–A.D. 65). In the °Renaissance, dramatists imitating the classical style occasionally felt compelled to write choruses, but choral passages never became a major element in Renaissance drama. A good example of the vestigial use of the chorus in English drama is found in Shakespeare's *Henry V* (1598–99).

The chorus was a valuable device for allowing the playwright to make direct commentary to the audience without asking his characters to step out of the action. This function is necessary in any kind of drama, and modern playwrights have used various techniques in place of a chorus. One is the °narrator who directly addresses the audience, as in Thornton Wilder's (1897–1976) *Our Town* (1938). Another is the °*raisonneur* (often called the chorus character), who speaks for the author while remaining a part of the action. The Fool in Shakespeare's *King Lear* (1605–6) illustrates this technique. Some modern dramatists have tried to restore the convention of the chorus, for example, T. S. Eliot (1888–1965) in *The Family Reunion* (1939) and Bertolt Brecht (1898–1956) in *The Caucasian Chalk Circle* (1944–45). Nevertheless, the chorus, as it was known to the Greeks, is not an integral feature of the °modern drama, and its purposes have been accomplished largely through other techniques of °dramaturgy.

See also °Greek drama.

chorus character   See °*raisonneur.*

chronicle play   A type of drama based upon English monarchical history, which flourished in the latter years of the reign of Elizabeth I (1558–1603). The chronicle play owed its popularity to the growing national pride resulting from the defeat of the Spanish Armada in 1588 and to the eagerness of the average Englishman to learn, in the theater, of his national heritage.

The first chronicle plays were loosely constructed and episodic, relying mainly upon spectacle and pageantry; the earliest of these is probably *The Famous Victories of Henry V* (ca. 1586). It was Christopher Marlowe (1564–1593) who in *Edward II* (1592) turned the chronicle play into viable drama by carefully selecting historical incidents from his source (Holinshed's *Chronicles*), arranging them into an effective °plot and creating a unified dramatic portrait of the central figure. Shakespeare followed Marlowe's lead by writing the finest of the type, the nine great plays chronicling the history of England from Richard II to Henry VIII. Some of these plays, such as *Richard II* (1595–96), *Richard III* (1592–93), and *Henry V* (1598–99), go beyond mere reporting of history and are fully developed dramas, independent of other plays in the cycle. The first two are often considered °tragedies.

Other Shakespeare plays deal with historical subjects but are not generally regarded as chronicle plays. *Cymbeline* (1609–10) is classified as a romance, *King Lear* (1605–6) and *Macbeth* (1605–6) are listed among the tragedies, and the several Roman plays, of course, are not concerned with English history.

"*Cid* controversy"   A critical battle that took place in France from 1636 to 1638, the subject of which was *The Cid* (1636), a play by Pierre Corneille (1606–1684). The controversy is important as a focal point for the arguments for and against French °neoclassicism. Corneille's °tragedy was immensely successful when it was first produced, even though it did not adhere to the neoclassical rules as determined by the Académie Française (see °academies). *The Cid* is a °tragicomedy that only loosely conforms to the requirements of the °Three Unities, violates °decorum by its mixing of the comic and the serious, and defies °verisimilitude, a controlling doctrine of neoclassicism. Because of its popular success, Corneille was attacked first by the critic Georges de Scudéry (1601–1667) in *Observations on "The Cid"* (1637) and finally by the full force of the Académie in a harsh reprimand penned by Jean Chapelain (1595–1674), *The Opinions of the Académie Française* (1638). The indictment was written at the urging of Cardinal Richelieu, France's literary and theatrical dictator at the time. The controversy over *The Cid,* culminating in Chapelain's essay, confirmed the power of the Académie to determine the principles of literary art in seventeenth-century France. Corneille abandoned writing for a time and, when he resumed, obeyed the dictates of the Académie.

See also °neoclassicism.

classic simile   See °epic simile.

classical tragedy   A term used in reference to at least three types of plays:

1. The °tragedy of ancient Greece and Rome, as exemplified by the plays of Aeschylus (525 B.C.–456 B.C.), Sophocles (ca. 496 B.C.–

406 B.C.) and Euripides (ca. 480 B.C.–ca. 406 B.C.), and the °closet dramas of Seneca (4 B.C.– A.D. 65). (See °Greek drama and °Senecan influence.)

2. Any tragedy based upon subjects taken from antiquity, such as the Roman plays of Shakespeare.

3. Modern tragedy patterned on ancient Greek and Roman models or consciously conforming to the critical doctrines of °classicism. The first English tragedy, *Gorboduc* (1562), exemplifies this third type, since it represents a conscious effort by its authors, Thomas Sackville (1536–1608) and Thomas Norton (1532–1584), to imitate Senecan style.

In the seventeenth century both English and French dramatists created classical tragedies, not only by drawing upon classic themes and plots but also by emulating the style and structure of the Ancients. Jean Racine's (1639–1699) *Andromache* (1667) and *Phaedra* (1677) best illustrate the French style, and notable English examples are John Dryden's (1631–1700) *All for Love* (1677) and, in the following century, Joseph Addison's (1672–1719) *Cato* (1713).

See also °classicism and °neoclassical tragedy.

classicism   In drama, the critical doctrine that advocates the admiration and emulation of ancient °Greek and °Roman drama; a body of critical theory that is, historically, opposed to both °romanticism and °realism. Classicism began to dominate literary thought in general and the drama in particular during the °Renaissance in Italy. Its influence was strongest in France during the seventeenth century. In England one early critical exponent of classicism was Sir Philip Sidney (1554–1586) in *The Defense of Poesy* (1583; published 1595); and the dramatist Ben Jonson (1572–1637) advocated and to an extent practiced the classical style. See, for example, his tragedy *Sejanus* (1603).

Classicism espouses the major characteristics of Greek and Roman plays, including: (1) °plots restricted in scope (time and place); (2) restraint and refinement in language and expression; (3) the dominance of reason as a motive force; (4) careful attention to form and °unity of design; and (5) °decorum in °characterization and °diction.

The spirit of classicism dominated dramatic theory and practice throughout France and England well into the nineteenth century, until romanticism gradually assumed the dominant position. Even today, however, the spirit of classicism finds champions in a poet-playwright like T. S. Eliot (1888–1965), whose *The Family Reunion* (1939) could be considered an example of modern classicism.

See also °classical tragedy and °neoclassicism.

climax   A term that appears frequently in dramatic °criticism with at least two distinct meanings: (1) the high point of emotional excitation in a drama; and (2) the turning point of the °plot—the °crisis. Used in the first sense, climax could refer to a moment such as the closing scene of Shakespeare's *Hamlet* (1600–1601), in which a number of deaths, including that of the °protagonist, occur on stage. Here, clearly, the reader or spectator experiences a maximum of emotional involvement in the action of the drama. In the second sense, the climax of *Hamlet* would be the "mouse-trap" scene (Act III, Scene 2), the point at which the °conflict between Hamlet and Claudius reaches its pinnacle. It is during this °play-within-a-play that the drama's °rising action ends and the °falling action begins. In this case, climax refers to the °dramatic structure of the work and means the "crisis of the plot." In any drama this may or may not coincide with the moment of greatest emotional involvement.

It is important, in considering any discussion of the climax of a play, to determine in exactly which sense the term has been used, and to distinguish between its use as a structural term and its application as a measure of audience involvement.

See also °crisis and °dramatic structure.

cloak-and-sword play (also **cape-and-sword**)   See °*capa y espada*.

closet drama   A play written for a reading public only, without the intention of stage presentation. Since dramas have almost invariably been written for the theater, the number of closet dramas written throughout history is extremely small. Perhaps the most notable author of such works was the Roman writer Seneca (4 B.C.–A.D. 65), whose nine extant Latin °tragedies served as models for many °Renaissance dramatists. Seneca probably never intended his plays for production. They are characterized by features that render them nearly impossible to stage—bloody and gory deeds, long narrative passages, improbabilities in time and place, and so on.

In the English drama, John Milton's (1608–1674) *Samson Agonistes* (1671) is an example of closet drama, as are a number of plays written by major literary figures of the nineteenth century. Possibly because of their disillusionment with the state of the English theater and its trivial entertainments, writers like Percy Bysshe Shelley (1792–1822) in *The Cenci* (1819) and Robert Browning (1812–1889) in *Pippa Passes* (1841) preferred to write "for the closet" rather than for the stage.

Some plays are relegated to the status of closet drama merely by their epic scope or excessive length, which can make stage production nearly impossible. Thomas Hardy's (1840–1928) three-part Napoleonic epic, *The Dynasts* (1904–8), is an example of this type, as is Victor Hugo's (1802–1885) *Cromwell* (1827), which has been termed unactable because of its length.

clown   A °type character found in much drama, especially the °Elizabethan drama. The clown is a humorous and often ignorant boy or man, occasionally a rustic. He achieves his comic effect not by °wit or design but through his simplicity and earthy comments. Shakespeare wrote several clown roles for his °comedies, notably Bottom (*A Midsummer Night's Dream* [1595–96]), Dogberry (*Much Ado about Nothing* [1598–99]), and the nameless "Clown" of *The Winter's Tale* (1610–11). He also wrote smaller clown roles into some of his °tragedies (*Othello* [1604–5], *Hamlet* [1600–1601], *Antony and Cleopatra* [1606–7]) for scenes of °comic relief.

See also °fool.

collaboration   The working together of two or more dramatists to produce a play or a number of plays; also, a play written in such a fashion. The practice of collaboration was especially strong in the °Elizabethan drama and may be traced back at least to the first English tragedy, *Gorboduc* (ca. 1562), written by Thomas Sackville (1536–1608) and Thomas Norton (1532–1584). Perhaps the most famous collaboration in English drama was that of John Fletcher (1579–1625) and Francis Beaumont (1584–1616), who together produced at least fourteen plays between 1606 and 1615. In addition, Fletcher collaborated with several other writers, including, it is believed, Shakespeare.

Collaboration is fairly common in the modern theater as well. It is a standard practice in °musical comedy (for example, Richard

Rodgers [1902–   ] and Oscar Hammerstein II [1895–1960],
Alan Jay Lerner [1918–   ] and Frederick Loewe [1904–   ]),
for which music, book, and lyrics will often be penned by separate
writers. The fine American comic dramatist, George S.
Kaufman (1889–1961), wrote almost all of his many successes in collaboration, notably with Marc Connelly (1890–   ), Edna Ferber
(1887–1968), and Moss Hart (1904–1961).

comedia   In Spanish drama, the generic term for a play of the
°Baroque era; for example, any of the plays of Lope de Vega
(1562–1635). The Spanish made little distinction between °com-
edy and °tragedy, and the dramas of Spain's Golden Age exhibit mixtures of comic and serious material within a single play.
See °Renaissance drama and °*Siglo de Oro.*

comédie larmoyante   The French equivalent of English °weepy
comedy, extremely popular on the French stage from about 1730
to 1750. An example is Pierre Claude Nivelle de La Chaussée's
(1692–1754) *False Antipathy* (1733). The *comédie larmoyante* was an
exaggeration of the sentiment first introduced into French °com-
edy by Pierre Marivaux (1688–1763) and a precursor of the
°*drame.*
See °weepy comedy.

comedy   A major form of drama, which aims at the criticism and
correction, through °ridicule, of unacceptable and potentially
harmful modes of behavior, and whose effect is to provoke laughter through the exposure of human folly. All literate peoples have
produced comedy, and the comedy of any society reflects the accepted modes of behavior and ethical standards of the social
group. Thus, the appreciation of comedy is often limited to the
society that produces it, although there are many great comedies
that, because of their °universality, have transcended time and
place.
  The earliest extant comedies, in ancient °Greek drama, were
written by Aristophanes (ca. 448 B.C.–ca. 380 B.C.). Although they
are far removed structurally and topically from modern comedy,
they illustrate the essential characteristics of comedy as a dramatic
form. Aristophanes satirized the social and political concerns of

fifth-century Athens, criticizing and ridiculing well-known public figures of his time and generally trespassing upon hallowed ground. (See °Old Comedy.)

Nearly all great comic writers since Aristophanes have followed his example, at least as far as utilizing the power of comedy to criticize and ridicule human folly. The great English comic writer Ben Jonson (1572–1637) was a master of satiric comedy, and he mercilessly exposed the minor vices of °Elizabethan and °Jacobean society in a form called °comedy of humours. After Jonson, the English °Restoration dramatists carried on the tradition through the °comedy of manners, and in France, Molière (1622–1673) wrote great comedies satirizing greed, hypocrisy, pretentiousness, and other human failings.

The history of comedy also shows another, different approach to the °genre, based not upon the criticism of human folly but upon the celebration of human happiness and virtue. Plays belonging to this type are often classed as either °romantic comedy or °sentimental comedy. Shakespeare was a master of the former type, in which romantic love is always paramount and happy endings resolve temporary confusion and misunderstandings. *As You Like It* (1599–1600) is a model of the type. Sentimental comedy, on the other hand, aims at putting before us a picture of human distress ultimately relieved by virtue's triumph. It is unique among comic forms in that its principal purpose is not necessarily to provoke laughter. Also called °"weepy comedy," it flourished in eighteenth-century France and England. Sir Richard Steele (1672–1729) was one practitioner of the form, and his *The Conscious Lovers* (1722) best exemplifies the type. (See °*comédie larmoyante* and °sentimental comedy.)

In the history of °criticism, comedy has traditionally been counterposed to °tragedy. The neoclassical critics insisted upon a distinction between the two, stipulating that comedy always pictured middle- and lower-class personages, employed the language of the everyday, and necessarily ended happily for the major figures. Although these comic rules have some validity in an historical sense, they offer only a superficial definition of the true nature of comedy as a dramatic genre, and the problem of defining comedy has intrigued critics down to the present time.

See also °comic theory.

comedy of humours A type of English °realistic comedy that developed in Shakespeare's time and which was brought to perfection principally by Ben Jonson (1572–1637). Humours comedy attempted to create strong, clearly identifiable character types by assigning to each figure some dominant trait or disposition that would determine his behavior in any dramatic situation. As Jonson himself explained, in the °Induction to *Every Man Out of His Humour* (1599):

> Some one peculiar quality
> Doth so possess a man, that it doth draw
> All his affects, his spirits, and his powers,
> In their confluctions, all to run one way.

Thus, a character disposed to merriment will see the best in every trying stituation and laugh in the face of certain disasters; a glutton will see every occasion as an opportunity to eat; a man suspicious of his wife's fidelity will be obsessed by jealousy; and so on.

The humours concept was based on an older medical theory of human health as a proper balance between four "elements" or "humours" in the anatomy: black bile, yellow bile, blood, and phlegm. When these elements became unbalanced, one dominating over the others, a person became ill and thus disposed toward some peculiar sort of behavior. In spite of this medical basis, and the elaborate system of °type characters which grew from it, humours comedy is basically an English way of justifying the character types made popular in the ancient Roman comedies of Plautus (ca. 254 B.C.–184 B.C.) and Terence (ca. 190 B.C.–159 B.C.), and it was from these earlier comedies that Jonson and his contemporaries drew their plots and characters.

The comedy of humours, as it is made manifest in °Elizabethan comedy, is almost always satiric in intent, subjecting to extreme °ridicule the follies it exposes. Situations are almost always based upon intrigues and tricks played by clever schemers upon unsuspecting gulls. Characters are usually assigned °tag names, indicating their obsessive dispositions. In Shakespeare's major humours comedy, *Twelfth Night* (1599–1600), the figures of Sir Toby Belch, Sir Andrew Aguecheek, and Malvolio bear names that label them according to the "elements" that account for their amusing behavior.

The comedy of humours remained popular after the °Restoration, its chief practitioner in that period being Thomas Shadwell (1642–1692).

comedy of intrigue See °intrigue plot.

comedy of manners In general, a style of °comedy in any period aiming at the °ridicule of the artificialities and superficial manners of a given social group.

More specifically, in English drama, the comedy of manners flourished during the °Restoration period (1660–ca. 1700) as the favorite entertainment of the court and the London leisure class. Although it has its roots in °Elizabethan and °Jacobean comedy, the Restoration comedy of manners was strongly influenced by the theatrical tastes of the French court, brought back to England by Charles II upon his restoration to the English throne. It satirizes the heartlessness and licentiousness of Charles's social milieu, and its plots always reveal the two major concerns of its audiences: sex and society. The figures in the plays are basically °type characters, such as the °fop, the °jilt, and the °wittol, and the °setting is almost invariably contemporary London. Rakish young gentlemen seduce and deceive amoral ladies of fashion; coteries of gossips ruin the reputations of their "friends"; would-be wits are exposed and ridiculed for their pretentiousness; marriage is scorned as the ultimate disgrace; and aging is the transgression that can never be pardoned. Elegant prose style is paramount in these comedies, with careful plotting being given only secondary consideration.

Chief practitioners of the Restoration comedy of manners were Sir George Etherege (ca. 1633–1691), whose *The Man of Mode* (1676) set the tone for much that was to follow; William Wycherley (1640–1715), the most bitingly satiric and cynical of the major writers; and William Congreve (1670–1729), author of *The Way of the World* (1700), said to be the most perfect comedy of manners in all English drama.

The tone of English comedy changed considerably around 1700, with the licentiousness of the Restoration giving way to a new trend toward °sentimental comedy. Manners comedy was revived, however, in the late-eighteenth century, largely by Oliver Goldsmith (1728–1774) and by Richard Brinsley Sheridan (1751–1816), whose *The School for Scandal* (1777) recaptures the satiric thrust of the earlier period without its coarseness and sexual license. In more recent times notable comedies of manners have included *The Importance of Being Earnest* (1895) by Oscar Wilde (1856–1900), *Private Lives* (1930) by Noel Coward (1899–1973), and *The Philadelphia Story* (1939) by America's Philip Barry (1896–1949).

comedy of situation See °situation comedy.

comic opera A type of °lyric theater combining songs, music, dance, and scenic spectacle with spoken dialogue, to dramatize a comic story. Comic opera, which has its roots in the °intermezzo of the Italian °Renaissance theater, has played a major role in the evolution of European °opera from the beginnings to the present. An early example of the type is Giovanni Pergolesi's (1710–1736) *The Servant the Mistress* (1733), the first Italian comic opera to achieve widespread fame. Known in Germany as *Singspiel* and in France as *opéra comique,* the comic opera was so popular by the late-eighteenth century that many Continental cities had separate companies for comic and serious operas.

In England comic opera, together with its cousin the °ballad-opera, achieved enormous popularity in the late-eighteenth century. Isaac Bickerstaffe's (1735–1812) *The Maid of the Mill* (1765), Richard Brinsley Sheridan's (1751–1816) *The Duenna* (1775), and John O'Keeffe's (1747–1833) *The Poor Soldier* (1783) are typical of the genre. English comic opera remained popular throughout the nineteenth century, reaching a zenith in the works of W. S. Gilbert (1836–1911) and Sir Arthur Sullivan (1842–1900) in the 1870s and 1880s (for example, *The Mikado,* 1885). The American °musical comedy may be said to have evolved partly from English comic opera.

See also °ballad-opera and °operetta.

comic relief A humorous scene or incident within an essentially serious or even tragic drama, placed there by the dramatist for the purpose of evoking laughter as a release from the accumulating tension of the serious action. Scenes of comic relief, when employed by a master playwright, always function in support of the main action, rather than detracting from it. They often serve to reinforce the serious material through contrast—for example, the Porter scene in Shakespeare's *Macbeth* (1605–6) or the Grave-diggers' scene in *Hamlet.* (1600–1601). Scenes of comic relief are a phenomenon peculiar to the English drama and are not found in French °neoclassical tragedy, because critical dogma forbade the mixing of comic and serious material. The ancient °Greek drama occasionally exhibits such a mixture—for example, the comic Guard's scene in Sophocles' (ca. 496 B.C.–406 B.C.) *Antigone* (ca. 441 B.C.) or the gently humorous speech of Orestes' Nurse in *The Libation Bearers* (458 B.C.) of Aeschylus (525 B.C.–456 B.C.).

comic theory Any work or system of °criticism that attempts to explain the nature and function of °comedy. Theories of comedy have been especially prevalent in modern times, but the subject is largely absent from both classical and Renaissance criticism, where °tragedy was always the major object of attention. Unlike tragedy, which was thoroughly considered in the *Poetics* (ca. 335 B.C.) of Aristotle (384 B.C.–322 B.C.), comedy can boast of no major classical inquiry to serve as a foundation for subsequent theories. Aristotle is thought to have written a treatise on comic form as a second part of the *Poetics,* but it has not survived, and the earliest extant work on comedy is an anonymous tract (fourth to second centuries B.C.) known as the *Tractatus Coislinianus.* Drawing upon this work, Lane Cooper reconstructed an Aristotelian theory of comedy in 1969. It is an intriguing work but is, of course, only conjectural.

The common approach to comedy in Renaissance and neoclassical criticism was to view it as simply the opposite of tragedy. Thus, the requirements for comedy were: middle- to lower-class characters, ludicrous incidents, colloquial diction, and happy endings—not much of real substance so far as comic theory goes. In the modern period, however, many important writers have given serious attention to the subject and have advanced various theories of what exactly constitutes the form and spirit of comedy. Only a few of these can be mentioned here.

An essay by Oliver Goldsmith (1728–1774), "A Comparison between Laughing and Sentimental Comedy" (1772), explored the difference between comedy as an exposure of human folly and comedy as an affirmation of human success and happiness, and it paved the way for subsequent theories of comedy as a social corrective. The many theories citing incongruity as the basic element of the °ludicrous are best represented by passages in Arthur Schopenhauer's (1788–1860) *The World as Will and Idea* (1836–54). Among the English, George Meredith (1828–1909) is a noteworthy comic theorist, and his Prelude to *The Egoist* (1879) and "An Essay on Comedy" (1877) are enlightening. Perhaps the most comprehensive work on comedy and the nature of the ludicrous is French philosopher Henri Bergson's (1859–1941) *Laughter* (1900), a thorough and engaging discussion, which identifies human rigidity and unsociability as the core of comic character. Sigmund Freud (1856–1939), in *Jokes and Their Relation to the Unconscious* (1905), discusses feelings of aggression and superiority in relation to the human need to laugh; and Susanne K. Langer (1895–   ) sees comedy as a restorer of vital feelings through its distinctive rhythm, in *Feeling and Form* (1953).

These represent but a sampling of modern comic theory and the interested reader would do well to turn to Paul Lauter's *Theories of Comedy* (1964) for other viewpoints.

See also °comedy.

commedia dell'arte   The popular °comedy of Italy which flourished in the °Renaissance and influenced Continental comedy well into the eighteenth century. The *commedia* was primarily a performer's art, with minimal literary value. Performances were based not on fully realized texts but on a °scenario of the action, with much of the °dialogue and °stage business developed through improvisation by highly trained and skilled actors playing familiar °stock characters types. The major figures were masked, and their costumes and °masks instantly conveyed their identity to the audience, for the types were well known: Pulcinello, Arlecchino, Pantalone, Brighella, Truffaldino, and so on.

The troupes of professional comedians performing the *commedia dell'arte* eventually toured outside Italy and greatly influenced the course of French comedy. Molière (1622–1673) was especially indebted to the tradition for some of his characters and for his sense of broad comedy. Many of the Italian characters developed French equivalents, such as Harlequin, Pierrot, Columbine, and Sganarelle.

In the eighteenth century the *commedia* tradition centered around Venice and influenced the comedies of playwrights like Carlo Gozzi (1720–1806) and Carlo Goldoni (1707–1793). Even today, playwrights occasionally draw upon the tradition. See, for example, Edna St. Vincent Millay's (1892–1950) *Aria da Capo* (1920).

commedia erudita   The Italian °Renaissance term for classically inspired, written drama, as opposed to the °improvisational theater known as °*commedia dell'arte,* which see.

Commonwealth drama   The drama of England produced during the Commonwealth period (1649–60). See °Dark Period.

complex plot   According to Aristotle (384 B.C.–322 B.C.) in Chapter X of the *Poetics* (ca. 335 B.C.), a tragic °plot that includes incidents of °recognition and °reversal and is therefore superior to the °simple plot, which lacks these incidents. The best example of the complex plot is that of Sophocles' (ca. 496 B.C.–406 B.C.) *Oedipus* (ca. 430 B.C.), in which the recognition by Oedipus that he is himself the murderer he has been seeking is the source of the reversal of fortune—the destruction of the prosperous and just king.
    See °recognition and °reversal.

complication   In °dramatic structure, that portion of a play from the beginning of the °action to the point of °crisis, after which the °resolution begins; also called the °rising action of the °plot. The complication of a drama usually includes the bulk of the °exposition, the °exciting force, and the sequence of incidents whereby a °conflict is established or the entanglements inherent in the action are made manifest. It has been likened to the "tying of a knot." In the *Oedipus* (ca. 430 B.C.) of Sophocles (ca. 496 B.C.–406 B.C.) the complication includes all of the action to the point at which Oedipus learns that he himself is the murderer he has been seeking. That point is the °crisis, after which the °resolution is effected and the "knot" is untied.
    See °dramatic structure.

compression   One of the structural techniques of early English drama, whereby long periods of °dramatic time and a multiplicity of °locales could be reduced to but the "two hours' traffic of our stage." The principle of compression was directly counterposed to the doctrine of the °Three Unities, which severely limited both the time and the place of a dramatic °action. For the English, any number of years could pass during the action (sixteen, for example, in Shakespeare's *The Winter's Tale* [1610–11]), and the stage could represent whatever locale it was said to be. For a full discussion of compression, see David Bevington, *From "Mankind" to Marlowe* (1962).

See also °alternation and °parallelism.

confidant (feminine, **confidante**) A conventional °type character in plays of various periods. The confidant is the friend or companion of the °protagonist, and his function is to serve as a sounding-board for the thoughts and feelings of the central figure. The confidant is the dramatist's way of allowing his °hero to talk aloud without resorting to the °soliloquy. In addition, the confidant can question and argue, providing even greater opportunities for the main character to express himself. In ancient °Greek drama the function of the confidant was often assumed by the °chorus. A good example of the type in English drama is the character of Horatio in Shakespeare's *Hamlet* (1600–1601).

conflict The element of struggle in a dramatic °action resulting from the interplay between opposing forces in the °plot. Much modern dramatic °criticism has concerned itself with conflict as the essential element in drama, ever since the French critic Ferdinand Brunetière (1849–1906) advanced the idea in 1894. Dramatic conflict may occur between the °protagonist and the forces of nature, as it does in Shakespeare's *King Lear* (1605–6); it may be made manifest in a struggle of wills between the protagonist and another character, as between Antigone and Creon in Sophocles' (ca. 496 B.C.–406 B.C.) *Antigone* (ca. 441 B.C.); it may appear in the protagonist's struggle against social forces, as in Henrik Ibsen's (1828–1906) *Ghosts* (1881); or it may be internalized, represented as a struggle between two opposing forces within the character, as in John Dryden's (1631–1700) *All for Love* (1677). Whatever the nature of the conflict, it is, according to some critics, essential to the drama.

See °Brunetière's Law.

contaminatio In ancient °Roman drama the practice by comic writers of combining material from two Greek originals to produce one Latin comedy. The technique is particularly evident in the plotting of the comedies of Terence (ca. 190 B.C.–159 B.C.), such as *The Brothers* and *The Eunuch.*

See °Roman drama.

conventions see °dramatic conventions.

Corpus Christi plays English medieval religious plays derived from the liturgy of the church, based upon events taken from the Bible. In towns like York, Chester, and Coventry the plays were mounted on individual wagons or °pageants and performed in street processions on Corpus Christi Day throughout the fourteenth and fifteenth centuries.

See °miracle play.

coryphaeus In °Greek drama, the leader of the °chorus. The exact role of the *coryphaeus* is not known for certain, but in all probability he spoke those portions of choral material that were neither chanted nor sung by the full chorus.

See also °chorus and °Greek drama.

costume piece A general term for any drama set in an historical period and requiring fairly elaborate or impressive costuming.

See also °period piece.

cothurnus See °buskin.

counterplayer The term used by German critic Gustav Freytag (1816–1895) to describe the character (or characters) in a drama who stands in opposition to, or is dramatically pitted against, the main character or °protagonist. In Shakespeare's *Hamlet* (1600–1601), for example, virtually all of the characters are counterplayers since Hamlet stands alone against almost the entire court of Denmark. In Shakespeare's *Othello* (1604–5) there is a single dominant counterplayer (Iago), known as the °antagonist. Here, the °hero-player is pitted against a °villain-counterplayer. Freytag's concept of counterplayers applies specifically to °romantic tragedy and may not be meaningful in other types of drama.

coup de théâtre An unexpected, surprising, or startling incident in the °action of a drama, especially one near the end that alters the course of the °plot. The term is often used derogatorily to describe any fairly arbitrary or poorly motivated bit of claptrap.

See also °*deus ex machina*.

couplet In °verse drama, a pair of poetic lines with end °rhyme, usually expressing a complete thought. The rhymed couplet was a common feature of the °Elizabethan drama, particularly at the end of a °scene. Such closing couplets are almost invariably in °iambic pentameter, as is this example from the opening scene of Shakespeare's *Twelfth Night* (1599–1600):

> Away before me to sweet beds of flowers.
> Love-thoughts lie rich when canopied with bowers.

See also °heroic couplet, °iambic pentameter, and °rhyme.

court comedy A type of English °comedy written expressly for performance at court, especially from 1558 to 1625, during the reigns of Elizabeth I and James I. The leading writer of the genre was John Lyly (ca. 1554–1606), who developed the elegant style of prose known as °euphuism and wrote several comedies for the court of Elizabeth. Most of these plays were written for boy actors, notably the boys of St. Paul's choir school. Lyly was not the only writer of court comedy; Shakespeare's *Love's Labor's Lost* (1594–95) is also an excellent example of the type.

English court comedy differed from the comedy of the public theaters in its refinement, its elegance of expression, and its references to classical learning. The plays often had classical and mythological subjects, as in the case of Lyly's *Endimion* (ca. 1588), *Gallathea* (1587), and *Love's Metamorphosis* (ca. 1590). It has been suggested that some of the references to classical figures in Lyly's comedies were thinly veiled allusions to persons in Elizabeth's court. The °action of such plays was more verbal than visual, although they were staged with a fair amount of spectacle, including music and dance. Essentially, emphasis was placed on the language—°puns, wordplay, °wit, and neatly structured sentiments. This was entertainment for the erudite, and its performance by small boys must have been a precious treat for Elizabeth and her courtiers.

Court comedy of the Elizabethan and Jacobean years had little effect upon later English comedy, although its utilization and development of dramatic prose may be said to have influenced the better comic writers of the °Restoration period, such as William Congreve (1670–1729).

See also °euphuism.

courtly love convention A literary convention, predominant during the °Renaissance, that influenced the ways in which love was dramatized in much °romantic comedy. The characteristics of the courtly love convention were best realized in lyric poetry, especially the °sonnet, as written by literary gentlemen in honor of their lady-loves. This convention dates at least from the Italian poets Dante (1265–1321) and Petrarch (1304–1374), and Shakespeare and his contemporaries continued the tradition in England.

According to the convention, a lover experiences great emotional disturbances, including even physical pain. His symptoms include pallor, trembling, loss of appetite, sleeplessness, sighing and weeping. His distress is often described in terms associated with burning: flames, furnaces, sparks, and fires. Ideally, his love is not consummated. In some cases the lady in question is not even aware of his passion. She is enshrined in the poet's verse, worshiped and idolized. Love issues from her eyes and enters his, for the eyes are the windows of the soul.

When this convention of courtly love is incorporated into the drama, we find lovers like Shakespeare's Romeo in *Romeo and Juliet* (1594–95) spouting sonnets to his Rosaline, Duke Orsino in *Twelfth Night* (1599–1600) pining away for love of Olivia, and whole quartets of suitors in *Love's Labor's Lost* (1594–95) sending gifts of poetry to their chaste ladies. In short, the Renaissance poetic convention of courtly love underlies nearly all examples of romantic love in °Elizabethan drama. For further discussion, see C. S. Lewis, *The Allegory of Love* (1936).

See also °romantic comedy and °sonnet.

crisis In °dramatic structure, the point in a °plot at which the °complication reaches its highest level and the °resolution begins.

Often the crisis is a turning point at which the fortunes of the °protagonist are reversed. For example, the crisis in Sophocles' (ca. 496 B.C.–406 B.C.) *Oedipus* (ca. 430 B.C.) occurs at the moment when the king learns that he himself is the murderer he has been seeking. In °romantic tragedy the crisis is often a scene of confrontation between the protagonist and the °antagonist, such as the "mousetrap" scene (Act III, Scene 2) of Shakespeare's *Hamlet* (1600–1601).

The term "crisis" has also been used in reference to the general nature of a dramatic °action, insofar as it represents a critical moment in the lives of the characters. In this sense, crisis denotes the urgency or immediacy of the dramtic event. This idea is advanced in William Archer's *Play-Making* (1912).

See also °climax and °dramatic structure.

critical comedy   °Comedy that aims at the criticism, through °ridicule, of human folly. Most comedy is critical in that it asks us to laugh at its characters when they behave foolishly. Thus, familiar comic character types are frequently based upon behavior that, in real life, is not at all comic but, rather, unpleasant or even harmful: greed, lechery, hypocrisy, drunkenness, and so on. The opposite of critical comedy would be that which does not ridicule but sympathizes with its characters, as is the case with °sentimental comedy.

See also °comedy and °comic theory.

criticism   The systematic study of a work of art or an art form in order to describe, justify, analyze, or judge it. In literature, and in the drama especially, critics throughout the ages have employed a variety of approaches in attempting to understand the essential nature of certain individual plays and of the form of drama in general. Though these various critical strategies sometimes overlap and may even be utilized simultaneously in varying combinations, it is possible to identify basic critical approaches and to classify them.

Works of dramatic criticism may be classed as either °Aristotelian or °Platonic. The Aristotelian critic attempts to understand the work as a whole according to its form, its constituent parts, and its organization. Little attention, if any, is given to its historical, moral, social, or political values. In Platonic criticism

the opposite is true. The work is related to extrinsic considerations and judged by how well it serves to perform a predetermined function: to relate historical events, to illustrate moral or
ethical precepts, to serve the body politic, and so on.

Criticism may be classified also according to whether it is *relativistic* or *absolutist*, meaning either that the critic draws upon any
available system of values to which the work may be meaningfully
related or that he holds the work up to certain "absolute" and
predetermined standards for that type of work. Another way of
saying this is that relativistic criticism is primarily *descriptive* while
absolutist is *prescriptive*, relying upon rules and standards. In dramatic criticism Aristotle's (384 B.C.–322 B.C.) *Poetics* (ca. 335 B.C.) is
descriptive, while most neoclassical French criticism is decidedly
prescriptive.

Historically, dramatic theorists and critics have utilized criticism
to serve various purposes:

1. To justify oneself, in which case the dramatist explains his
   work and the principles according to which he operates, for
   example, Victor Hugo's (1802–1885) °Preface to *Cromwell*
   (1827).
2. To justify the drama in general to a society that looks scep-
   tically on it, such as Sir Philip Sidney's (1554–1586) *The Defense of Poesy* (1583; published 1595).
3. To prescribe rules for playwrights and to regulate public
   taste (the opinions of the Académie Française in the °"*Cid*
   controversy," as set down by Jean Chapelain [1595–1674] in
   1638).
4. To open the way for new approaches to drama by attempting to repudiate formerly accepted opinions, for example,
   Lope de Vega's (1562–1635) *The New Art of Writing Plays*
   (1609).
5. To speak out against decadence and abuses of the public
   trust by dramatists insensitive to the temper of their times,
   such as the Reverend Jeremy Collier's (1650–1726) *A Short
   View of the Immorality and Profaneness of the English Stage*
   (1698).
6. To attempt, through careful analysis, to arrive at the fundamental principles of the art (Aristotle's *Poetics*).

Criticism may also be classified according to basic approaches:

1. °*Historical,* which examines and evaluates a work in terms of the historical context in which it was produced.
2. °*Textual,* which concerns itself with the printed text or texts of a work, by way of determining the author's exact intention.
3. °*Formal,* which examines a work in relation to the characteristics of the type or °genre to which it belongs.
4. °*Analytical,* which views the work as an autonomous whole and seeks its meaning through analysis of form.
5. °*Mythic,* which explores the °archetypes and possible patterns of °ritual in the work.

See also separate entries for the various kinds of criticism listed above.

cruelty   See °Theater of Cruelty.

cup-and-saucer drama   The name given to a type of play popular in the nineteenth century, which featured realistic, domestic actions and situations set in upper-class drawing rooms. Also known as drawing-room dramas, such plays earned the "cup-and-saucer" label from the mundane, realistic °stage business indicated in the scripts, such as the serving of tea. The British dramatist Thomas William Robertson (1829–1871) was a leading writer of cup-and-saucer dramas, such as *Society* (1865) and *Caste* (1867).

curtain   (1) A drapery, employed in various periods of theater history, to conceal the stage from the spectators; (2) a moment or situation, at the end of a scene or act, just before the curtain falls. Thus, a scene may be said to have a "strong curtain" if the action is particularly tense or laden with °suspense.
      For this latter sense, see also °tag line.

curtain raiser   A short play performed before a major dramatic work, usually either to fill out an evening's entertainment or to "warm up" the audience.
      See also °afterpiece.

cycle play   See °miracle play.

cyclical plot   A dramatic °plot that is organized and unified not by a °linear sequence of events in a cause-and-effect relationship but by a pattern of repetition or recurrence of events. Any dramatic °action whose final situation suggests or reproduces its opening situation may be said to be cyclical. Anton Chekhov's (1860–1904) *The Cherry Orchard* (1904), for example, comes full circle by ending with a leave-taking that strongly echoes, in reverse, the homecoming of the first act. In this way, the plot suggests a completed action. Samuel Beckett's (1906–   ) *Waiting for Godot* (1953) is even more clearly cyclical in structure. Act II is almost an exact structural repetition of Act I, and when the play ends Vladimir and Estragon are in precisely the same situation as when it began. The plot has come full circle. The cyclical plot is a modern development in °dramatic structure.

See also °episodic plot and °linear plot.

Dadaism A brief but extreme revolt against °realism in the arts that erupted between 1916 and 1920, partly as a manifestation of the horror and frustration caused by World War I. Dadaism was essentially anti-art in that it rejected all order and meaning. Although the movement produced many programs of lectures, readings, and short plays, no major drama emerged from the movement. Its chief historical importance is as a precursor of °surrealism.

See °surrealism.

dance One nonliterary art form which has always been associated with the theater and which is frequently incorporated into the °drama itself. In the ancient °Greek drama, dance comprised a significant part of the dramatic effect, for the °chorus danced while chanting or singing its °odes. Greek and Roman °mimes and °pantomimes, as well as English °masques and °operas, all utilized dance. The French dramatist Molière (1622–1673) wrote ballet sequences into his °comedies, and dance has a prominent role in modern °musical comedy.

Dark Period In England, the years from 1642 to 1660, during which the public theaters of London were closed and virtually all professional dramatic activity ceased. The closing of the theaters was due to pressure from the Puritans, who were shortly to wrest power from the monarchy and initiate the Commonwealth period (1649–60).

There was some "bootleg" theatrical activity during the Dark Period, but the continuity of English theatrical tradition was largely interrupted. When the theaters reopened in 1660 under the royal patronage of Charles II, English drama took a decidedly new course. °Restoration drama bore little resemblance to the great Golden Age of °Elizabethan drama.

See also °Caroline drama, °decadence, and °Restoration drama.

decadence   Used in dramatic °criticism to describe the gradual decline of quality in °Jacobean and °Caroline drama from the excellence of the Elizabethan period. This decline was marked by a relaxation of critical standards, a confusion of °genres resulting in °tragicomedy, an emphasis upon sensationalism, a decline in the moral tone as evidenced by a preoccupation with explicitly sexual content, and an inferior handling of dramatic verse.

In the late-nineteenth century literature in general experienced another period referred to as "decadence," attributable mainly to French poets like Paul Verlaine (1844–1896), Arthur Rimbaud (1854–1891), and Charles Baudelaire (1821–1867). These writers and others of their kind were known as the decadents, and among their ranks was the English playwright Oscar Wilde (1856–1900). Still, the influence of the decadents on the drama was minimal.

See also °Caroline drama and °Jacobean drama.

decorum   The concern in °criticism with that which is proper or fitting in °character, °action, or °diction. Decorum has been called the controlling doctrine of °neoclassicism; its impact upon seventeenth- and eighteenth-century drama was considerable. According to the French neoclassicists, the °unity and harmony of a dramatic work would be enhanced if the poet observed propriety. This meant that the style of the language or dialogue should be appropriate to the speaker and the situation, according to well-defined ideas of character types. A king necessarily spoke in a "high" style, an old man in a "dignified" style, lower-class characters in prose, rustics in pastoral language, and so on.

The influence of decorum upon English drama can be seen in Shakespeare's practice of generally assigning prose dialogue to clowns and rustics and reserving verse for more elevated personages. In the °heroic tragedy of the Restoration years (1660–1700), decorum was a powerful determinant of style. John Dryden (1631–1700) was careful to justify, in his °Preface to *All for Love* (1677), the scene in which Octavia and Cleopatra quarrel, acknowledging that the French (strict observers of decorum) "would not . . . have suffer'd Cleopatra and Octavia to have met, or, if they had met, there must only have pass'd betwixt them some cold civilities, but no eagerness of repartée, for fear of offending against the greatness of their characters and the modesty of their sex."

See also °neoclassicism.

delight and instruction The dual function of drama, according to the *Art of Poetry* (24 B.C.–20 B.C.) of Horace (65 B.C.–8 B.C.). Horace stated that the drama should provide more than simple entertainment for the reader or spectator—that it should as well provide moral or ethical instruction. Thus, °tragedy might serve a useful purpose by illustrating good and bad in human conduct.

Horace's assertion about delight and instruction paved the way for subsequent theories of the drama as an instrument for °didacticism, and that is precisely what the neoclassical critics, following his suggestion, propounded. Throughout the sixteenth, seventeenth, and eighteenth centuries tragedy was uniformly accepted as a useful kind of literature, valuable in the teaching of morality.

See also °Horatian criticism and °neoclassicism.

dénouement The French term for the final unravelling of a °plot, in which the mystery is solved, misunderstandings are set aright, and all questions are answered; the °catastrophe. *Dénouement* is used principally for lighter kinds of plays, with the more technical term "catastrophe" being reserved for °tragedy, though they are essentially the same. A good example of comic *dénouement* is the final scene of Shakespeare's *As You Like It* (1599–1600), in which a banished duke is restored to his throne, the °villain is miraculously converted, the two disguised girls are unmasked, and four couples are happily united in wedlock.

See also °catastrophe.

descriptive criticism Any work or system of °criticism primarily concerned with describing and analyzing a work of art in terms of its own form and content, as opposed to evaluating it in terms of a predetermined system of rules or requirements for its °genre. Aristotle's (384 B.C–322 B.C.) *Poetics* (ca. 335 B.C.) is the outstanding example of descriptive criticism.

See °criticism.

deus ex machina Literally, "god from the machine"; a cranelike device used in the ancient Greek theater to lower actors portraying gods onto the stage from the roof of the *skene* or stage house. Euripides (ca. 480 B.C.–ca. 406 B.C.) used this device frequently for the divine appearances that end almost all of his plays. Since these Euripidean divinities frequently tie up the °plot or release the chief characters from some difficulty, the term has come to be used for any dramatic device used at the last minute to effect a miraculous solution to the play's entanglements. Thus, *deus ex machina* is used pejoratively to imply that the playwright lacks the skill to end his play logically, through °probability and necessity, and must rely on a last-minute turn of events—an unmotivated change of heart by the °villain, a telegram announcing that the impoverished °hero has won the Irish Sweepstakes, or some similarly incredible contrivance.

It is true that the use of a *deus ex machina* in °tragedy testifies to the inferior skill of the playwright, but in °comedy and in °melodrama the *deus ex machina* is perfectly acceptable and, in fact, often accounts for the delight which we experience from these forms of drama. The history of comedy is filled with such surprising endings, and the °suspense of melodrama is heightened when we can see no escape for the unfortunate hero. The last-minute rescue delights us, as when the cavalry comes riding over the hill at the finale of a Western film.

See also °probability and necessity.

deuteragonist   In the °Greek drama, the secondary °actor. The use of two actors rather than one was introduced by Aeschylus (525 B.C.–456 B.C.). The deuteragonist played all the secondary roles, while the °protagonist, or chief actor, played the central role.

See also °protagonist and °tritagonist.

dialect   A style of speech deviating from the accepted standards of usage and pronunciation in any given language. Dialects play an important role in certain plays, especially in modern or realistic drama. In some cases, the playwright almost totally ignores the problem of dialects, leaving it to the actor to make the distinction in speaking the lines. This is the case in many of the plays of Tennessee Williams (1912–   ), where it is assumed that the actors will provide the necessary Southern drawl. At the other extreme is the playwright who attempts to incorporate dialect into the lines, writing his speeches with phonetic spellings, as a guide to the actor. Examples of this technique may be found in the lines of the Welshman Fluellen in Shakespeare's *Henry V* (1598–99) and in George Bernard Shaw's (1856–1950) *Candida* (1895), in the role of the Cockney father, Burgess. In some dramas, the appropriate dialect dictates the structure and rhythms of the lines, as in the Irish plays of John Millington Synge (1871–1909). In his *The Playboy of the Western World* (1907), for example, the vocabulary and rhythms of the Mayo dialect are essential to the language of the work and account, in large measure, for the lyrical beauty of the play.

In °comedy the use of dialects is a traditional device for generating laughter. Any character who speaks a substandard version of the language spoken properly by the other characters is easily mocked and ridiculed.

dialogue In general, the portions of a dramatic text intended to be spoken by the actors, as opposed to °stage directions. More specifically, a dialogue is an interchange of speech between two characters; thus it is distinguished from the °soliloquy, the °chorus, and °narration. Dialogue is, of course, the essential language of drama, and its construction is often considered to be the crucial test of a skillful dramatist. It is principally through dialogue—the words assigned to the speakers—that °characterization is achieved. This may be accomplished in a fairly realistic fashion, as in modern °naturalism, or it may be totally conventional, as in Shakespeare's plays in which the dialogue of kings is °blank verse, or in the Restoration °comedy of manners, in which witty style is paramount. In any case, the dialogue must seem to be appropriate to the character speaking.

diction One of the six qualitative parts of °tragedy, according to Aristotle (384 B.C.–322 B.C.) in Chapter VI of the *Poetics* (ca. 335 B.C.), the others being °plot, °character, °thought, °music, and °spectacle. Diction consists of the actual words the dramatist chooses for his °dialogue. Of course, Aristotle was writing of °verse drama, in which the construction of the verses would be most important, but even in °prose drama, the words are the chief medium of dramatic realization. It is well known that many of the greatest playwrights have repeatedly revised their plays before allowing them to be produced, giving special attention to the precise words that would best convey their meanings. Diction is the medium through which a dramatist's ideas are expressed, as well as through which °characterization is most effectively achieved.

didacticism   Instructiveness in a dramatic work; the use of a drama to teach a moral lesson or to set forth a position, usually social or political, with the intention of convincing the audience of its validity. It is generally acknowledged that a play whose primary purpose is didactic is inferior as a work of art, although there have been exceptions in the history of the drama. In fact, it is often difficult for critics to agree on what constitutes pure didacticism, as opposed to plays which legitimately dramatize ideas. The °problem plays of Henrik Ibsen (1828–1906) are a case in point.

The concept of utilitarian value in drama stems from °Horatian criticism, and it dominated dramatic theory in the °Renaissance and throughout the seventeenth century. It was believed that the purpose of °tragedy was to teach. Perhaps the best English example of a purely didactic drama is George Lillo's (1693–1739) *The London Merchant* (1731), a °domestic tragedy that suffers greatly from its preachy tone and pious moralizing.

See also °delight and instruction.

dilemma   See °tragic dilemma.

direct address   The device of having a dramatic character speak directly to the audience, as in a °soliloquy or an °aside.

See °aside, °presentationalism, and °soliloquy.

discovery   See °recognition.

disguising   An early form of English court entertainment that evolved into the elaborate °masque typical of the court of James I (reigned 1603–25). In a disguising the courtiers would don °masks and fancy dress, appearing before the monarch with gifts, to celebrate some holiday. Half play and half party, the disguising included music, dancing, eating, and drinking. One early disguising is known to have occurred at the court of Richard II in 1377.

See also °masque.

distancing The technique in drama of discouraging deep emotional involvement on the part of the spectator and promoting a detached contemplation of the action. Many nonrealistic devices of theater—the °chorus, the °narrator, songs, °masks, and so on—contribute to the distancing effect, but in illusionistic, °representational theater, °empathy is encouraged and distancing is not desired. Essentially, distancing techniques ask us to contemplate a dramatic action in the same way that we perceive other art forms. In viewing a painting of flowers, for example, we are constantly aware of it as a representation and not as real flowers.

See also °aesthetic distance, °imitation, °*optique du théâtre,* and °presentationalism.

distichomythia A variation of °stichomythia in which two consecutive lines of verse dialogue are assigned to each speaker.

See °stichomythia.

dithyramb A form of lyric poetry characterized by excited and passionate language, originally written in ancient Greece for ceremonies in honor of the god Dionysus. It is from the dithyramb that °tragedy is thought to have evolved, and from the goatskin-clad °chorus of dithyramb singers that the term *tragoedia* (goat-song) originated. This chorus of satyrs became the foundation for the chorus of tragedy, and the god Dionysus continued as the chief diety of the great tragic festivals.

See °Greek drama.

doctrine of tragic waste See °tragic waste.

documentary drama A type of drama that originated in West Germany in the 1960s in which actual events are dramatized by way of exploring questions of morality, guilt, and responsibility in public affairs. Rolf Hochhuth (1931–), Peter Weiss (1916–), and Heinar Kipphardt (1922–) are representative writers of documentary drama (also called Theater of Fact). Hochhuth's *The Deputy,* which suggests Pope Pius XII's complicity in the Nazis' extermination of German Jews, earned major attention in 1963. This German movement has given rise to documentary writing in American drama, as exemplified by Daniel Berrigan's (1921–) *The Trial of the Catonsville Nine* (1970) and

Eric Bentley's (1916–   ) *Are You Now, or Have You Ever Been?* (1975).

domestic tragedy   The type of °tragedy that is concerned not with the heroic actions of elevated personages, such as kings and princes, but with the domestic tribulations of recognizable, middle-class figures. Though the °neoclassical critics insisted that tragedy was the exclusive province of the high and the mighty, based upon their observations of °Greek drama, tragedy has sometimes been domesticated, even in classic times. The *Electra* (ca. 413 B.C.) of Euripides (ca. 480 B.C.–ca. 406 B.C.) in many ways resembles domestic tragedy, with its mythological heroine reduced to little more than a neurotic scullion. Some °Elizabethan tragedies also qualify as domestic, such as the anonymous *Arden of Feversham* (ca. 1590) and Thomas Heywood's (1574?–1641) *A Woman Killed with Kindness* (1603).

Domestic tragedy flourished during the eighteenth century in England, and the form vied successfully for public attention with °classical tragedy. Most successful was George Lillo's (1693–1739) *The London Merchant* (1731), a prose tragedy extolling the virtues of mercantilism and warning of the perils that beset middle-class Londoners if they stray from the path of virtue.

In our own time, tragedy is almost exclusively of the domestic variety. The plays of Eugene O'Neill (1888–1953), Arthur Miller (1916–   ), and Tennessee Williams (1912–   ) entirely shun elevated personages, opting instead for prostitutes, derelicts, salesmen, and other common types. Perhaps the greatest of all modern domestic tragedies is Miller's *Death of a Salesman* (1949).

The objections usually leveled against domestic tragedy are: it is essentially °melodrama; it tends toward °didacticism; it lacks °universality; and it contravenes Aristotle's (384 B.C.–322 B.C.) definition considered as violations of the °unity of a tragic action (see °Three Unities). A °plot with a double action was variously defined the greatest twentieth-century playwrights have proven.

See also °tragedy.

double action (also **double issue**)   A term used in much neoclassical °criticism to describe a variety of flaws in dramatic construction considered as violations of the °unity of a tragic action (see

°Three Unities). A °plot with a double action was variously defined as:

1. One in which the emphasis is divided between two central figures. Thus, a clearly identifiable °hero is lacking, and the work is said to be flawed. An example would be the *Antigone* (ca. 441 B.C.) of Sophocles (ca. 496 B.C.–406 B.C.), in which Creon and Antigone share focus and both end in misfortune.

2. One involving a fall from happiness to misery for the central character, with an accompanying rise to good fortune by another character. An example might be Shakespeare's *Richard II* (1595–96), in which Bolingbroke's rise to power as Henry IV could be considered to detract from the tragic impact of Richard's fall from the throne.

3. One in which a secondary intrigue is added to the plot after the first one has been resolved. This is frequently the technique of °melodrama, in which unexpected salvation comes in the final act, after all had seemed lost. John Dryden (1631–1700), in *An Essay of Dramatic Poesy* (1668), objected to this type of double action, citing Ben Jonson's (1572–1637) *Volpone* (1606) as an example. Although *Volpone* is a °comedy, and thus partially exempt from the rules of °neoclassicism, it does serve to illustrate the technique of initiating a new intrigue in the fifth act. Another example might be Victor Hugo's (1802–1885) *Hernani* (1830), a melodrama that seems to end happily after four acts, only to plunge into a trio of deaths in the fifth.

Of these three distinct types of the double action, the first two pose no real threat to structural unity, as many great tragedies illustrate, but the third type may be reasonably objected to, at least in high tragedy.

See also °dramatic structure and °unity.

double plot   See °subplot.

drama   A major literary form, dating from the fifth century B.C., in which the text is comprised mainly of °dialogue to be spoken by °actors, who impersonate the °characters of the story. The word derives from the Greek *dran,* "to do." Drama is also used to refer to a play of a serious, rather than comic, nature; and "the drama" implies the whole body of work written for the theater.

Throughout history, most drama has been written to be performed in the theater, though there is a type intended for reading only, called °closet drama. The four principal types of drama are °tragedy, °comedy, °melodrama, and °farce, although some plays defy easy classification. The writer of a drama is called a dramatist or a playwright (not "playwrite"), and the art of playwriting is called °dramaturgy. Because of its alliance with the theater, the drama is the most immediate and vital of literary forms. As opposed to the novel or lyric poetry, it can literally "come alive" in performance.

See also °dramatic structure.

drama of discussion   A type of play in which the characters discuss their problems and their situations, thereby engaging the audience's attention in ideas rather than in emotions. George Bernard Shaw (1856–1950) used the term in analyzing the technical novelty of the plays of Henrik Ibsen (1828–1906), and Shaw himself wrote dramas of discussion (see Shaw's *The Quintessence of Ibsenism*, 1913). Essentially, Shaw was opposed to the slick sensationalism of the °well-made play, with its intrigues, surprises, and artificial °suspense. He advocated a type of drama which would engage the audience intellectually—which would ask them to listen and consider the playwright's ideas. Two outstanding examples of the drama of discussion are Ibsen's *A Doll's House* (1879) and Shaw's *Man and Superman* (1901–3).

See also °problem play.

drama of ideas   See °problem play.

drama of stasis   See °static drama.

dramatic conventions   Certain techniques of °dramaturgy or theatrical artifice which serve as substitutes for reality and which the reader or spectator is asked to accept as real. Every period of dramatic literature has its particular conventions, which depend upon the audience's participation in making a theatricalized reality. In the ancient °Greek drama actors wore °masks and the °chorus sang and danced their role. These were conventions of that theater. Shakespeare's stage, too, had its conventions—the °soliloquy, the °aside, and the nonscenic stage, which was assumed to represent any number of °locales. The mistaking of identities when actors donned disguises also was accepted conventionally, even in cases where a person of one sex was to be mistaken for one of the opposite. In the modern realistic theater the convention of the °fourth wall dominates. In any period, the theatrical conventions we accept so readily remind us that the theater is not an exact copy of reality but an artistic representation of life.

See also °dramatic illusion.

dramatic illusion That special reality created in the theater, which encourages the spectator to accept, for the moment, an admitted fiction as a sort of truth. The theater deals in fiction. Its actors are not the characters they represent; its stone walls are painted canvas; its deaths are make-believe. The spectator knows all this, but he is willing, as Samuel Taylor Coleridge (1772–1834) maintained, to suspend for the moment his disbelief and accept the stage action *as if* it were real. He does not believe it *to be* real; he accepts the dramatic illusion.

In his *Poetics* (ca. 335 B.C.) Aristotle (384 B.C.–322 B.C.) recognized the nature of dramatic illusion by pointing out that "there are some things that distress us when we see them in reality, but the most accurate representations of these same things we view with pleasure." Thus, it is the very assurance that the stage action is *not* real that allows us to accept it and to believe in it—as a dramatic illusion. We do not doubt, question, or object to the falseness of the presentation; to do so would be to complain, for example, that Hamlet does not speak Danish. Dramatic illusion reconciles truth and artifice.

See also °*optique du théâtre,* °presentationalism, °representationalism, and °"willing suspension of disbelief."

dramatic irony A technique of the drama in which the audience is provided with knowledge which is not available to the characters of the play. Thus, the spectator feels himself in some sense superior to the characters and can see implications in the action of which the dramatic figures are unaware.

Dramatic irony can be employed in both °comedy and °tragedy. In comedy it is valuable for creating situations of misunderstanding, mistaken identity, and general confusion. In tragedy, irony can render even more terrible the unhappy events which unfold on the stage. In the *Oedipus* (ca. 430 B.C.) of Sophocles (ca. 496 B.C.–406 B.C.) King Oedipus relentlessly seeks the slayer of the former King Laius, unaware that he himself is the culprit. We, the audience, know the truth. Thus, virtually every statement he makes regarding his search is laden with irony and takes on meanings unknown to the speaker. His vow of vengeance becomes, for us, a vow of self-destruction.

Apart from dramatic irony, playwrights frequently employ another device—verbal irony—in the °dialogue of their dramas. In verbal irony, a character makes a statement that is different from his intended meaning. His words may be sarcastic or tongue-in-cheek, as when Shakespeare's Antony in *Julius Caesar* (1599–1600), over the corpse of the slaughtered Caesar, repeatedly claims that "Brutus is an honorable man."

dramatic monologue   See °monologue.

dramatic poetry   A term used somewhat imprecisely to refer to any kind of poetry exhibiting dramatic elements. In a more precise application, the term should exclude °verse drama (plays clearly intended for stage presentation) and °closet drama (plays intended for reading only). The °monologue is an example of dramatic poetry, as is any other work essentially lyric in nature but employing °dialogue, °characterization, °conflict, or other elements commonly associated with the drama.

See also °closet drama, °monologue, and °verse drama.

dramatic structure   The system of organization and arrangement of elements that is unique to the drama as a literary °genre. There are certain structural features common to all dramatic works, regardless of period, °style, or national origin. Thus, it is possible to speak of the "structure of drama" in a generic sense, while phrases like the "structure of the novel" or the "structure of lyric poetry" are virtually meaningless.

Plays are written, as Aristotle (384 B.C.–322 B.C.) noted in the *Poetics* (ca. 335 B.C.), in the dramatic manner, meaning that they consist entirely of the °dialogue spoken by the agents of the °action—the °characters. This has two important implications. First, since the language of the work is the speech of the characters, a drama is cast in the present tense. Narrative works (novels, short stories, and so on) are almost always written in the past tense. Thus, even without presentation on the stage, the drama has great immediacy and affective power in creating images of ongoing action. Second, because the words are conveyed only by the agents themselves, the playwright's point of view cannot be presented directly, as can the novelist's. The dramatist cannot tell us what he feels about a character's behavior, his motivations, or his thoughts. Even in a °soliloquy, the character must speak for himself in his own voice. Moreover, the playwright cannot tell us about actions that may be taking place simultaneously in some location other than on the stage, nor can he change his scene with a new paragraph. Thus, dramatic form is, paradoxically, both powerful and limiting. This limitation means that the dramatist must observe certain structural principles.

One such principle of dramatic composition is that of °magnitude. Because it is intended to be performed before an audience, a play is circumscribed as to length. It usually lasts from two to four hours and can be read at a single sitting, whereas a novel may take days to read. This means that a drama gains its effect through concentration and intensity, rather than from elaboration of details or digressive °episodes. It must, in a brief space of time, present a tightly unified and complex action. Its magnitude is limited, chiefly through the way in which its component elements (language, character, episodes) are arranged.

The action of a drama illustrates a process of change. The circumstances at the outcome of a play are different from what they were at the beginning. This change is accomplished through a structural pattern—the °complication leads to a °crisis, which effects a °resolution. This is not a prescriptive rule of the drama; it is inherent in the nature of dramatic form.

The complication, often referred to as the °rising action, is composed of all action that develops from the beginning of the play to the point at which the crisis occurs. It includes the °exposition—the background material necessary for the understanding of the characters, their relationships and past actions—the °setting, and so on. The complication presents incidents and actions that are cumulative and are related to one another through causality and dramatic °probability. Event A leads to event B, B leads to C, and so on. In simple terms, "the plot thickens."

The crisis of the drama is that moment or incident in which the potential for action in the complication becomes realized. It is also sometimes referred to as the °climax, and it represents a turning point, after which the action no longer grows more complex but begins to become simplified, showing the results of all that has gone before.

The resolution, or °falling action (French °*dénouement*), includes all of the play following the crisis and is, perhaps, the most significant part of the action. In the resolution we learn the meaning of all that has gone before. We see the results and grasp the implications of the total change. The resolution must always appear to be a probable and necessary outcome, not an arbitrary event contrived merely to bring the drama to a close. It has often been called the supreme test of the playwright's skill.

In °classical and °neoclassical tragedy, as well as °modern drama, the crisis generally occurs quite near the end of the play, while in the drama of °romanticism (Shakespeare, for example) the crisis will more often be near the middle, with almost as much time devoted to the resolution as to the complication. In *Hamlet* (1600–1601) the crisis is the "mousetrap" scene (the °play-within-a-play, Act III, Scene 2), in which the °conflict between Hamlet and Claudius reaches a turning point through a mutual °recognition. Hamlet knows that Claudius is guilty, and Claudius knows that Hamlet knows. From that point on, the results of that recognition are played out, although the resolution is by no means dull. Much of the excitement and all of the deaths in *Hamlet* occur in the resolution.

Another element affecting dramatic structure is the °point of attack, the moment in the story at which the playwright chooses to begin his dramatic action. If he chooses an early point of attack (called °*ab ovo*), as the romantic playwrights tended to do, he proceeds to dramatize, episode by episode, the entire story, developing his action over a long period of °dramatic time. A late point of attack (called °*in medias res*) means that the first scene is apt to be set quite near the critical moment, with much of the antecedent action and exposition related or narrated by the characters (or perhaps a °chorus), rather than enacted. This was the method of the ancient °Greek dramatists. The °tragedy of Sophocles' (ca. 496 B.C.–406 B.C.) *Oedipus* (ca. 430 B.C.), for example, begins, in dramatic time, only an hour or so before Oedipus learns that he himself is the murderer he seeks. The entire earlier history of the Oedipus legend is worked into the exposition.

A drama may be constructed as a single, uninterrupted action, as in most Greek drama, or as a series of distinct and separate °acts or °scenes, as in the plays of Shakespeare. Whatever the playwright's choice in this respect, the basic principles of dramatic structure, as outlined above, apply. The pattern of *complication→crisis→resolution* does not change.

See also °Freytag Pyramid and °plot, as well as separate entries for the terms cross-referenced above.

dramatic time The fictional time that is presumed to have passed during the stage °action of a given drama. For example, if the opening scene is set at sunrise and the final scene at sunset of the same day, the dramatic time would be one day, or approximately twelve hours. Dramatic time should be distinguished from °stage time, which is the real time of the duration of a play— usually two to four hours. Dramatic time may vary greatly from play to play, depending upon the dramatist's °point of attack. In Sophocles' (ca. 496 B.C–406 B.C.) *Oedipus* (ca. 430 B.C.), for example, dramatic time coincides exactly with stage time. The action is continuous and all background incidents are presented through °exposition. In Shakespeare's *Antony and Cleopatra* (1606–7), on the other hand, the dramatic time encompasses years, as the playwright shows us events early in the affair between the two lovers and takes us up to their deaths—at least several years later.

See also °point of attack.

dramatis personae The Latin term for "characters of the drama." The printed version of a play almost always includes a listing of the characters at the front of the text. From the Renaissance until roughly the mid-nineteenth century, the term *"dramatis personae"* headed such lists, regardless of the language in which the play itself was written. In modern times the Latin has been abandoned in favor of "characters," "cast," or some such simpler term. In the printing of many seventeenth- and eighteenth-century plays, the *dramatis personae* also included the names of the original actors, as is the case with many modern plays.

dramaturgy   The craft or technique of writing drama; the particular methods and individual °style of a dramatist's work, as in "Shakespeare's dramaturgy."

drame (or *drame bourgeois*)   A form of French drama which originated in the eighteenth century and which attempted to blend comic and serious material into a kind of domestic °melodrama. The *drame* was defended by the French critic and encyclopedist Denis Diderot (1713–1784) as a compromise between °comedy and °tragedy, and his own *The Illegitimate Son* (1757) serves as an example of the type. The *drame* never gained widespread popularity in a France dominated by the spirit of °neoclassicism; in the nineteenth century it was absorbed into melodrama.

drawing-room drama   See cup-and-saucer drama.

droll   A short, farcical entertainment (also known as "drollery" or "droll humour") of the English Commonwealth stage, performed in lieu of the conventional drama banned by the Puritans from 1642 to 1660. The droll was little more than a °scene, or an excerpt from a longer play, performed in conjunction with a dance.
See also °Dark Period and °jig.

dumb show   A scene performed in °pantomime, incorporated into the action of a play. The dumb show was especially important in the °Elizabethan drama, usually in °tragedies marked by the °Senecan influence. It was probably always accompanied by music, and it served a variety of functions. It could foreshadow coming events, illustrate some incident assumed to be happening in another °locale, serve as a °prologue or °entr'acte, or make commentary, in the nature of a °chorus. In any case, the dumb show provided the opportunity for music and spectacle. There are at least fifty examples of its use in Elizabethan plays.
    Possibly the earliest examples of the dumb show are found in the first English °tragedy, *Gorboduc* (ca. 1562), by Thomas Sackville (1536–1608) and Thomas Norton (1532–1584). Other notable examples appear in John Marston's (1576–1634) *The Malcontent* (1604), John Webster's (ca. 1580–ca. 1630) *The Duchess of Malfi*

(1613–14), Thomas Middleton's (1580–1627) *The Changeling* (1622), and Shakespeare's *Hamlet* (1600–1601), in which, uncharacteristically, it serves as a silent preenactment of the succeeding °play-within-a-play.

Einfühlung   See °empathy.

Elizabethan drama   The drama written in England during the reign (1558–1603) of Elizabeth I, although the term is sometimes understood to include also plays written during the subsequent reign (1603–25) of James I and even of Charles I (1625–49), until the closing of the public theaters in 1642 (see °Dark Period). During the Elizabethan period, and in the later years of Elizabeth's reign especially, the English drama developed from tentative beginnings in °morality plays, °interludes, °school plays, and °liturgical drama, to culminate in the "Golden Age" of Shakespeare and his contemporaries at the turn of the century.

Elizabethan plays are of several fairly distinct forms, including: (1) °court comedy, practiced principally by John Lyly (ca. 1554–1606); (2) °revenge tragedy, made popular by Thomas Kyd's (1558–1594) *The Spanish Tragedy* (ca. 1587) and brought to full development in Shakespeare's *Hamlet* (1600–1601); (3) °romantic comedy, as exemplified by Robert Greene's (1558–1592) *Friar Bacon and Friar Bungay* (ca. 1589) and Thomas Dekker's (1562?–1632?) *The Shoemakers' Holiday* (1599); (4) the °chronicle play, brought to its finest form in the great Shakespearean cycles concerning the houses of York and Lancaster; (5) the °comedy of humours, practiced chiefly by Ben Jonson (1572–1637); (6) °classical tragedy; and (7) °masques. Richness and variety characterized the Elizabethan drama.

The playwrights of this period were influenced by a variety of traditions. Much of their inspiration was derived from native English dramatic activity: the °miracle plays of the late Middle Ages; the °morality plays, which paved the way for professional acting companies; and the °interludes, which had already established the roots of English °comedy. A second influence was that of °classicism, which spawned Elizabethan °tragedies rich in the °Senecan tradition and comedies based on plots from the Roman comedies of Plautus (ca. 254 B.C.–ca. 184 B.C.) and Terence (ca. 190 B.C.–159 B.C.) (See °Roman drama.) Still another source of plots was the Renaissance literature of Italy and Spain, so well suited to the °intrigue plot. The Italian *novelle,* such as those comprising the *Decameron* (1353) of Giovanni Boccaccio (1313–1375), were especially useful to Shakespeare and his contemporaries.

The age of Elizabethan drama may be said to have begun its decline in the reign of James I, as the social and political unity achieved under Elizabeth gave way to the divisiveness of the growing Puritan influence and the factionalism of the Catholic-Protestant struggle. The Puritans succeeded in closing the public theaters in 1642, bringing to an end the Golden Age of English drama.

See also °Caroline drama and °Jacobean drama.

empathy (German *Einfühlung*) In the drama the act of the reader or spectator identifying himself with a character and participating in his emotional responses. Empathy is an "involuntary projection of ourselves" into another person so that we share his experiences. The concept of empathy is a modern one, and critics disagree on the extent of its importance in the theater. The German dramatist Bertolt Brecht (1898–1956), for one, did not want his audience to empathize with his characters but to view them objectively and analytically.

See also, by contrast, °alienation and °distancing.

end-stopped line A line of verse whose sense and structure indicate a pause at the end of the line; the opposite of a °run-on line. End-stopped lines occur frequently in English °verse drama, especially in the earlier plays of the °Elizabethan period and in the °heroic tragedy of the °Restoration years.

The repeated use of end-stopped lines, especially when they are also rhymed, creates a halting, stilted effect ill-suited to stage delivery. A passage from John Dryden's (1631–1700) *The Indian Emperor* (1667) will illustrate this awkwardness:

> *Cortez:* In what a strange condition am I left!
> More than I wish, I have! Of all I wish bereft!
> In wishing nothing we enjoy still most;
> For e'en our wish is, in possession, lost.

Restless we wander to a new desire,
And burn our selves by blowing up the fire.
We toss and turn about, our feav'rish will,
When all our ease must come by lying still.
For all the happiness mankind can gain
Is not in pleasure, but in rest from pain.

—*Act III, Scene 1*

See also °blank verse, °heroic couplet, and °run-on line.

entr'acte Literally, "between the acts"; a musical selection, dance, °pantomime, or other entertainment presented between the °acts of a play. Entr'actes were quite popular in the English theater during the °Restoration and eighteenth century and they ranged from simple songs to elaborate variety acts. In modern °musical comedy, the entr'acte is usually an orchestral selection preceding the second act, following the intermission.

See also °intermezzo.

environmental determinism A controlling doctrine in the drama of °naturalism, which views man as essentially a product (and victim) of the social and economic forces in his environment. Thus, characters in naturalistic plays tend to represent the downtrodden—prostitutes, thieves, beggars, and so on—and they are dramatized as incapable of rising above their immediate circumstances. The concept of environmental determinism evolved in the late nineteenth century as a part of the intellectual revolution that modern science was then effecting. Especially important was Charles Darwin's (1809–1882) work on evolution, which seemed to reduce man from the status of the godlike to the level of the jungle animal struggling for survival. Also significant in the development of environmental determinism were Karl Marx's (1818–1883) interpretations of history as a battleground of vast economic and social forces, and Sigmund Freud's (1856–1939) explorations into the realm of the subconscious mind.

See °naturalism.

environmental theater A mode of theatrical production that evolved in the 1960s, the aim of which was to fuse performer and spectator in a single environment and eliminate the traditional separation of stage and auditorium. Influenced by the °happenings of the 1950s, environmental theater minimized the importance of a dramatic text and placed major emphasis upon interaction between audience and performers, utilization of the total environment of the theater as performance space, and production elements that include the audience as a part of the scene. Frequently such productions are staged in "found" spaces rather than in theater buildings.

Some American groups which achieved success with environmental theater were the Open Theater, the Living Theater, and the Performance Group, founded in 1968 by Richard Schechner, a leading proponent of the style.

epic simile (also **classic simile**) An extended comparison, stated in terms of the formula: "As ⸺ is to ⸺, so ⸺ is to ⸺." The epic simile was used frequently in °Elizabethan drama and °heroic tragedy, in imitation of the style of Homer and Virgil, principally as a proof of erudition on the part of playwrights attempting to imitate the classic style. It differs from a conventional simile in that it is more elaborate, the second half being developed as an image in its own right, independent of the first half. This passage from the opening scene of George Chapman's (1559?–1634) *Bussy D'Ambois* (ca. 1604) will serve to illustrate the technique:

> And as great seamen, using all their powers
> And skills in Neptune's deep invisible paths,
> In tall ships richly built and ribbed with brass,
> To put a girdle round about the world,
> When they have done it, coming near their haven,
> Are glad to give a warning-piece, and call
> A poor staid fisherman, that never passed
> His country's sight, to waft and guide them in;
> So when we wander furthest through the waves
> Of glassy Glory and the gulfs of State,
> Topt with all titles, spreading all our reaches,
> As if each private arm would sphere the world,
> We must to Virtue for her guide resort,
> Or we shall shipwrack in our safest port.

epic theater   A style of playwriting and theatrical production emphasizing the drama as a means of story-telling and stressing the narrative or "epic" elements of the action through a variety of °distancing techniques. Epic theater was first developed by the German director Erwin Piscator (1893–1966) in the late 1920s, but it quickly became associated with the name of Bertolt Brecht (1898–1956), the German poet and dramatist who incorporated epic techniques into most of his major plays.

Essentially, epic theater attempts to make the audience accept the drama as frankly theatrical story-telling with definite social and political implications—a sort of dramatic parable. To this end, the dramatist utilizes songs, °narration, °episodic plotting, and a number of other techniques to keep the spectator from becoming emotionally involved in the characters' fates. In staging, epic theater, as pioneered by Piscator, employs theatrical devices such as exposed lighting instruments, changes of scenery in view of the audience, musicians seated on the stage, films and slides to reinforce the dramatic text, and signboards and legends to inform the audience of what is to follow—all by way of eliminating the traditional spectator involvement and accumulation of °suspense.

Epic theater has had a profound effect on twentieth-century theater, particularly in the realm of stage production. Epic techniques, startlingly revolutionary in the 1920s, have passed into the standard repertory of theatrical craft. While the philosophy of °alienation that dominated Brecht's thinking has had only minimal effect upon subsequent playwrights, Brecht's plays remain popular and are frequently revived in both realistic and epic style. A few representative Brecht plays are *The Threepenny Opera* (with music by Kurt Weill, 1928), *Mother Courage* (1937), *Galileo* (1938–39), *The Good Woman of Setzuan* (1938–40), and *The Caucasian Chalk Circle* (1944–45).

See also °alienation and °distancing.

epilogue   A closing speech, following the action of a drama, delivered by one of the actors directly to the audience. Epilogues first appeared in °Renaissance plays, and in the °Restoration years and the eighteenth century they were considered an indispensable closing to both °comedies and °tragedies. Frequently, important literary figures wrote epilogues for one another's plays. Characteristically, an epilogue seeks the audience's approval and asks for applause. In the Restoration years it was not uncommon for the poet to insult the spectators in his epilogue, implying that if they did not care for the play, it was because of their lack of taste.

See also °prologue.

episode In general, an incident or °scene in the course of the °action of a drama; specifically, in °Greek drama, that portion of the play performed by the °actors, as opposed to the °odes of the °chorus. In Greek °tragedy the odes alternated with the episodes, each of which was a more or less complete scene between the °characters. An episode could be a single speech by one character, a °dialogue between two characters, or a section of dialogue between a character and the chorus (probably spoken singly by the °*coryphaeus,* or chorus leader). The episodes in Greek drama may be said to be the forerunners of the °acts into which dramas were divided in subsequent periods.

See also °act and °scene.

episodic plot A dramatic °plot constructed in such a way that its individual °episodes do not follow one another in the usual pattern of logical causality but appear as a randomly organized series of separate incidents. The term "episodic structure" is usually applied pejoratively to indicate a plot that is poorly constructed, but episodic plots can be handled with artistry, as they frequently are in the plays of Bertolt Brecht (1898–1956). At its best, the episodic plot contains incidents which are inextricably interwoven by their relationship to some unifying principle—a philosophical outlook, a °theme, an historical event, or some such factor.

See also °cyclical plot, °dramatic structure, and °linear plot.

epistle dedicatory The introductory letter affixed to the printed version of a play, dedicating the work to the author's patron. Such epistles were standard in the printing of most late-seventeenth- and eighteenth-century plays. The typical dedication praises the many virtues of the patron, begs his forgiveness for the author's temerity in dedicating such an "unworthy" work to him, and hints at the need for continued support. Many of these letters, in the °Restoration period especially, strike the modern reader as blatant flattery and are, indeed, little more than that.

See also °preface.

epithalamium (Greek *epithalamion*)   A song or poem written in celebration of a wedding; a bridal song, occasionally incorporated into the action of some °Elizabethan dramas. The epithalamium dates from the ancient world, where its chief practitioners were Pindar, Sappho, Catullus, and others, but perhaps the finest example in English is Edmund Spenser's (1552–1599) *Epithalamion* (1595). It contains the basic features of the type: an invocation of the Muses, the bedecking and praise of the bride, the welcoming of the night, and so on. One fine example of the use of the epithalamium in drama is found in Shakespeare's *Romeo and Juliet* (1594–95). With her speech beginning "Gallop apace, you fiery-footed steeds" (Act III, Scene 2) Juliet calls upon the night to descend in preparation for the approach of her groom (Romeo) and anticipates the consummation of their marriage vows.

epode   In °Greek drama, a portion of a choral °ode or °*stasimon* which follows a °strophe and °antistrophe but which belongs structurally to neither. Not all *stasima* include an epode.
   See °ode.

euphuism   A style of English prose, named from John Lyly's (ca. 1554–1606)*Euphues* (1578), which influenced Elizabethan and Jacobean °court comedy. Euphuism stresses the structural elements of English prose and elegance of expression, causing critics today generally to consider it affected and precious. The standard euphuistic devices are: (1) balanced and antithetical clauses, usually combined with much alliteration; (2) excessive use of the rhetorical question; and (3) abundance of similes and examples, drawn from classical material.
   Euphuistic style was not Lyly's alone. It was popular among most of the court poets in the 1580s, appealing particularly to the ladies. It may be seen as a natural result of the desire to establish a modern English prose style. Unfortunately, it was not well suited to being spoken on the stage, as a reading of Lyly's major comedy, *Endimion* (ca. 1588), will show. The following passage, from the opening scene of that comedy, illustrates the euphuistic device of metaphorical antithesis:

> Flowers in their buds are nothing worth till they be blown, nor blossom accounted till they be ripe fruit; and shall we

then say they be changeable for that they grow from seeds to leaves, from leaves to buds, from buds to their perfection? Then, why be not twigs that become trees, children that become men, and mornings that grow to evenings, termed wavering, for that they continue not at one stay?

See also °court comedy.

exciting force   A term coined by the German critic Gustav Freytag (1816–1895) in 1863 to refer to that early point in a drama at which the °rising action is set in motion. It is also referred to as the "inciting action." It may take the form of some idea, commitment, or resolution on the part of the °hero, or it may occur through some external force imposed upon him. For example, the exciting force in Shakespeare's *Hamlet* (1600–1601) occurs when the Ghost tells the young prince how his father was murdered (Act I, Scene 5) and Hamlet vows revenge. In Shakespeare's *Othello* (1604–5) on the other hand, the exciting force is Iago's vow to destroy the hero. According to Freytag, the exciting force may be a single moment or an entire scene, but it should occur as early as possible in the play, since it serves as the transition from the °introduction to the rising action. Freytag also cautions against the playwright's placing too much emphasis upon the incident, lest it detract from the audience's interest in what is to follow.

See °Freytag Pyramid.

existentialist drama   A variety of twentieth-century drama illustrating or embodying the precepts of philosophical existentialism; closely associated with the °Theater of the Absurd. The chief spokesman for contemporary existentialism is Jean-Paul Sartre (1905–   ), whose plays such as *The Flies* (1943) and *No Exit* (1944) best represent dramatic existentialism. Briefly, the existentialist conceives of man as existing without essence or meaning. Existence is the only fact, and from this existence each individual is free to create for himself his own essential identity or meaning. Existentialist plays frequently dramatize characters faced with the meaninglessness or "absurdity" of their universe, struggling toward some commitment or course of action, which is the only salvation in such a world.

See also °Theater of the Absurd.

exodos In °Greek drama, the general term for the concluding portion of a °tragedy; the final °episode. Usually, the *exodos* is sung at least in part by the °chorus and provides an exit for them. See °Greek drama.

exposition The story material or narrative background which is antecedent to the °action of a drama and which must be made known to an audience for their complete understanding of the play. The manner in which this information is conveyed is often a crucial test of the skill of the dramatist. In general, the exposition may be accomplished in one of two ways. It may be concentrated in the earlier portion of the play and gotten out of the way as quickly as possible, or it may be apportioned throughout the drama, providing only that information necessary at any given moment for the understanding of the play to that point. The second method is generally acknowledged as the superior one.

When the audience is confronted in the first act by excessive exposition, interest wanes and the drama becomes little more than illustrated story-telling. Still, this is the technique of much romantic drama and of the °well-made play. It was accepted in nineteenth-century criticism that the first act of any play would of necessity be dominated by the exposition. Such material was often conveyed through the °"below-stairs" scene. In early English drama a good example of this approach to exposition is the second scene of Shakespeare's *The Tempest* (1611–12).

With the renewed interest in °dramaturgy that occurred late in the nineteenth century, a better method of handling exposition was recognized, innovated largely by Henrik Ibsen (1828–1906). In Ibsen's best plays the exposition is woven so skillfully into the total fabric of the °plot that the spectator is hardly aware that he is being given background material. The telling of past events is motivated by, and in turn determines, present action. A good example is *Rosmersholm* (1886), in which the very important past history of Rebecca West is not fully presented until the final moments of the play.

expressionism A movement in the °modern drama that developed at the turn of the century as a reaction against °realism, and whose practitioners attempted to dramatize not the objective reality of events but a subjective picture of them as seen usually through the mind of one central consciousness. Dramatic expressionism opposed realism on the grounds that surface reality does not represent truth as it is known by the subconscious mind. "Truth" to the expressionist is subjective. Although the movement was predominantly German, it had its roots in the expressionistic plays of the Swedish dramatist August Strindberg (1849–1912), such as *The Dream Play* (1902) and *The Ghost Sonata* (1907). *The Dream Play* is perhaps the finest example of dramatic expressionism, presenting events as perceived in a dream. All objective reality is distorted. Characters change identities, combining and fragmenting. One scene melts into another, and objects and persons take on symbolic meanings. There is no attempt at psychological °characterization, and the dialogue is repetitious and often mechanical.

The most representative of the German expressionist dramas are Georg Kaiser's (1878–1945) *From Morn to Midnight* (1916), *The Coral* (1917), *Gas I* (1918), and *Gas II* (1920). The Germans emphasized distortion and mechanization in their expressionistic plays. The characters become automatons, dialogue is jingoistic and telegraphic, and the °settings are frequently structural, employing steps and platforms. The frankly didactic message of such plays usually concerns the victimization of the individual in a mechanistic and materialistic society.

Although dramatic expressionism in its pure form had begun to decline by the 1920s, a number of American playwrights of that period were influenced by the style. Eugene O'Neill (1888–1953) experimented with expressionistic techniques in plays like *The Hairy Ape* (1922) and *The Great God Brown* (1926), and Elmer Rice (1892–1967) cast *The Adding Machine* (1923) in an almost purely expressionistic style.

Expressionistic techniques have continued to influence the contemporary theater. Arthur Miller's (1916–   ) *Death of a Salesman* (1949), for example, owes its structural organization to expressionism, with its shifting of present into past, its °flashbacks, and its filtering of events through the mind of its °protagonist, Willy Loman. Expressionism has also influenced film techniques to a great extent.

extravaganza   A nineteenth-century English form of elaborate musical presentation, usually based on a fairy tale, featuring music and dance. The extravaganza was developed by J. R. Planché (1796–1880) between 1830 and 1870; he himself wrote about 175 of them. The extravaganza has been seen as a forerunner of the modern °musical comedy, and its influence upon the °comic operas of W. S. Gilbert (1836–1911) and Sir Arthur Sullivan (1842–1900) was considerable.

See also °burlesque, °burletta, and °pantomime.

fable Sometimes offered as a translation of the Greek word *"mythos"* as used in Aristotle's (384 B.C.–322 B.C.) *Poetics* (ca. 335 B.C.); more commonly translated as °plot, which see.

fabula The Latin term for "fable" or "story"; used in combination with various adjectives to describe types of °Roman drama, such as °*fabula Atellana,* °*fabula palliata,* °*fabula praetexta,* and °*fabula togata.*
See °Roman drama.

fabula Atellana See °Atellan farce.

fabula palliata "Comedy in Greek dress"; the Latin term for ancient Roman °comedy adapted from Greek °New Comedy. The only extant examples are the comedies of Plautus (ca. 254 B.C.–184 B.C.) and Terence (ca. 190 B.C.–159 B.C.).
See °New Comedy and °Roman drama.

fabula praetexta A type of °Roman drama dating roughly from the third century B.C. whose subject matter was taken from Roman history. The name derives from *toga praetexta,* the costume of magistrates.
See °Roman drama.

fabula togata "Comedy in native dress"; a form of ancient Roman °comedy that followed the Golden Age of Plautus and Terence (roughly, early second century B.C.) and was popular from approximately 150 B.C. to 50 B.C. There are no complete extant works representing this style, but we know that the °themes and °plots of *fabula togata* followed the lives of ordinary people of the lower, rural classes. The plays were lively, often indecent, and quite farcical.
See °Roman drama.

falling action   In the system of °dramatic structure according to
the °Freytag Pyramid, the fourth major section of the five-part
°plot. The falling action immediately follows the °climax and pre-
cedes the °catastrophe; in it the °hero's fortunes decline and the
°counterplayers begin their ascendency over him. Falling action is
also used as a general term for the °resolution of the plot, inclu-
sive of all °action from the °crisis to the end.
    See °Freytag Pyramid.

farce   A form of °comedy that relies principally on artificial contrivances of °plot and the exploitation of comic situations, rather
than on °characterization, °wit, or other more intellectual elements. Farce is a popular comic form with broad appeal, for it
makes us laugh while asking a minimum expenditure of cerebral
effort. Farce dates at least from the *fabula Atellana* of ancient
Rome (see °Atellan farce). It was the dominant theatrical form
throughout the Middle Ages, manifesting itself in the °*sotties* of
France, the °Shrovetide plays of Germany, the English °in-
terludes, and others.
    Typically farce operates at a low level of credibility. We accept
willingly the absurd central premise of the plot, because we know
that the many situations that may result from it will delight us. A
classic English example, cited by some as the finest farce ever written, is *Charley's Aunt* (1892) by Brandon Thomas (1849–1914), in
which an Oxford scholar dons female clothing and is subsequently
mistaken for a woman throughout three acts of unrelenting nonsense. Several hilarious scenes are wrung from the one central
gimmick until the imposter is exposed at the finale.
    Farce often incorporates a great deal of physical and visual
humor, called °slapstick, as well as certain standard plot devices:
confused or mistaken identity, misunderstandings, overhearings,
accidental discoveries through letters misdelivered, chance meet-
ings, reunions of long-separated relatives, coincidences, and sud-
den reversals. In farce solution of the plot through the °*deus ex
machina* is not only acceptable but desirable. The surprise ending
in farce adds to our delight.

fear   See °pity and fear.

"feather-dusting" scene   See °"below-stairs" scene.

flashback The technique of showing, or dramatizing, °antecedent action in a drama, as opposed to narrating it as a part of the °exposition. Flashback is a common technique in motion pictures, but it has rarely been incorporated into the drama until modern times. One excellent example of the use of flashback is found in Arthur Miller's (1916–   ) *Death of a Salesman* (1949), in which Willy Loman relives experiences from his past. As past characters come on the stage, Willy steps out of the present action and participates in the flashback scenes.

foil (also **character foil**) A dramatic character whose principal function is to serve as a contrast to the central figure, or °protagonist, thereby adding to the effectiveness of the latter's °characterization. The character foil was used as far back as the °Greek drama and is exemplified there by the submissive sister of Antigone, Ismene, in Sophocles' (ca. 496 B.C.–406 B.C.) *Antigone* (ca. 441 B.C.). A more modern example is Laertes in Shakespeare's *Hamlet* (1600–1601), whose strength and decisiveness are in contrast with the hesitancy of the play's title figure.

folio (Latin for *leaf*) The size and format of one type of book in early printing, in which a single sheet of "foolscap" (size 17″ x 13½″) was printed on both sides as four pages, folded in half, and bound with other sheets similarly treated. The most famous such book is the First Folio of Shakespeare's plays, printed in 1623. In it all of his dramas, some of which had never before been printed, appeared together in a single volume for the first time.

See also °quarto.

folk drama In general, any dramatic activity which emerges from the lore and folk themes of a given people and is expressed in unsophisticated forms devoted mainly to festivals and religious observances. More specifically, folk drama refers to the tradition of such plays in the Middle Ages, especially in England. The medieval English folk drama ranged from such extra-literary activities as the sword dance to the more formal St. George plays, Robin Hood plays, °mummers' plays, and °disguisings. These forms were responsible for keeping alive a theatrical tradition during the Middle Ages until the °liturgical drama evolved, and they influenced later forms such as °romantic comedy and °pastoral drama.

For further reading, see Sir Edmund K. Chambers, *The English Folk-Play* (1933). See also °medieval drama.

fool   An important °type character in °Elizabethan drama. The fool, his name notwithstanding, is an intelligent and witty character, and the type is best represented in the plays of Shakespeare. He is usually a retainer or a jester in the service of some noble person, and he almost invariably serves as a commentator or °*raisonneur* with his witty observations on the other characters. Feste in *Twelfth Night* (1599–1600) is the finest example of the jester type, with Touchstone from *As You Like It* (1599–1600) a close second. In the Fool of *King Lear* (1605–6), Shakespeare brought the type to its highest degree of artistry. Lear's Fool becomes almost an alter ego of the king himself, providing the voice of reason in counterpoint to Lear's descent into madness.
   See also °clown.

fop   An extremely popular °type character in the Restoration °comedy of manners and one unique to English drama. The fop is a gentleman who carries to excess all that is considered fashionable. He is always overdressed, excessively vain, and either a failure or a cad when it comes to lovemaking. His attempts at °wit always fall short of the mark, and he earns the general contempt of the other characters and the derisive laughter of the audience. The fop has his origins in the °Elizabethan drama, but he achieved full form in George Etherege's (ca. 1633–1691) *The Man of Mode; or, Sir Fopling Flutter* (1676). Other delightful examples of the type are Sir Novelty Fashion in Colley Cibber's (1671–1757) *Love's Last Shift* (1696) and Mr. Witwould in William Congreve's (1670–1729) *The Way of the World* (1700).

foreshadowing   In playwriting, the technique of dramatic preparation, whereby the reader or audience is led to expect some event or occurrence, thereby rendering it more dramatically credible when it actually happens. Foreshadowing can be simple and direct, as when a character is said to be expected to arrive shortly and then does just that, or it can be handled in less obvious and more suggestive ways. In Henrik Ibsen's (1828–1906) *The Master Builder* (1892), for example, much is made throughout the play of Solness's fear of heights and his reluctance to climb to the top of his latest architectural creation. This serves as foreshadowing, for at the final curtain, having been persuaded by Hilda to climb the tower, he falls to his death.

formal criticism The type of °criticism that examines a work in relation to the characteristics of the type or °genre to which it belongs. Thus, a formal critic, writing of a play that is serious in nature and ends with the death or destruction of its °protagonist, would attempt to evaluate the work in terms of the characteristics of °tragedy and make judgments based on the work's success as a tragic drama.

See also °analytical criticism, °historical criticism, °mythic criticism, and °textual criticism.

fourteener A line of verse consisting of fourteen syllables (or seven feet) occurring in a passage of °iambic pentameter. Fourteeners were occasionally incorporated into the dialogue of °Elizabethan drama, in contrast to the regular °blank verse (ten syllables to the line), as a means of achieving variety. Thomas Kyd's (1558–1594) *The Spanish Tragedy* (ca. 1587) includes several fourteeners, such as the final line in this closing °couplet to Act III, Scene 2:

> I'll trust myself, myself shall be my friend;
> For die they shall. Slaves are ordainéd to no other end.

See also °blank verse.

fourth wall Technically, the proscenium wall of a theater, separating the stage from the audience; by extension, a °dramatic convention of the realistic stage. "Fourth wall" was used by the late-nineteenth-century playwrights of °naturalism to refer to the invisible wall of the stage room that was to be imagined as actually existing and closing off the dramatic action from the audience. Thus, the actors would perform naturally and the audience would feel that it was eavesdropping on a real-life situation.

The leading practitioner of fourth wall staging was André Antoine (1858–1943), founder of the Théâtre Libre in Paris in 1887. Antoine, in his quest for naturalism, went so far as to place furniture against the fourth wall, facing away from the audience. He then directed his actors to ignore the audience and play with their backs to the front if they felt like it. Needless to say, pure fourth-wall technique quickly died. Even the naturalists came to realize that the audience is always an integral part of any theatrical situation.

See also °naturalism and °slice-of-life.

Freytag Pyramid   An illustration of the nature of °dramatic structure devised by Gustav Freytag (1816–1895), a German critic and playwright whose book *The Technique of the Drama* (1863) became an influential manual on playwriting for several decades. In attempting to analyze the form of drama, Freytag posited a pyramidal structure to illustrate the progress of the °action of a play:

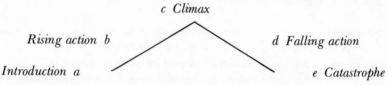

c Climax

Rising action b   *d Falling action*

Introduction a   *e Catastrophe*

The pyramid is based on five-act structure and assigns a specific dramatic function to each °act. This function determines the shape of a play as it builds tension and °suspense and then resolves its entanglements. The first act, or part, is the °introduction. In it the playwright establishes such necessary facts as time and place, nationality of the °characters, character relationships, mood or tone, and other elements of °setting and °exposition. Part two is the °rising action. This consists of scenes that build °complication and excitement, leading to the third, or central, part, the °climax. The climax brings all the threads of the story to a high pitch of excitement, after which the action begins to decline. This is the fourth part, the °falling action, in which the °hero begins his descent toward an unhappy fate. Last is the °catastrophe, in which the destruction of the hero is completed and any loose ends are quickly tied up.

Freytag's pyramid is not greatly credited today as a satisfactory explanation of dramatic structure. While it may be valid in analyzing much °romantic tragedy, such as Shakespeare's, it is virtually useless in a study of the forms and structural principles of most modern plays.

See also °dramatic structure.

fustian (also **Dutch fustian**) Pompous, turgid language, especially as used in the °dialogue of much °Elizabethan drama. The term is derived from the name of a thick, coarse cloth.

See °bombast.

futurism A minor theatrical movement in Europe from about 1910 to the 1930s, representing a revolt against conventional forms and a championing of the machine age. In Russia the major playwright of the movement was Vladimir Mayakovski (1894–1930), an associate of Vsevelod Meyerhold (1874–1940). In Italy Filippo Tommaso Marinetti (1876–1944) led the movement. The principal value of the futurists lay in their experiments with modern technology, paving the way for the multimedia performances so popular in the contemporary theater, and in their attempts to intermingle performers and spectators.

genre Literally, "type" or "kind." The term is used in literary °criticism to refer to the major forms, such as the drama, the novel, the lyric, the epic, and so on. In dramatic criticism it refers to the major types of drama—°tragedy, °comedy, °melodrama, and °farce. Use of the term is nonrestrictive, and virtually any identifiable form may be referred to as a genre—for example, °comedy of manners, °revenge tragedy, and °Gothic melodrama. In the history of dramatic criticism the greatest emphasis upon distinction between genres is found in the writings of the °Renaissance and °neoclassical critics, who insisted upon the strict separation of tragedy and comedy.

genteel comedy A term used by Joseph Addison (1672–1719) and Sir Richard Steele (1672–1729) (for example, *The Spectator*, No. 65) to refer to the early-eighteenth-century °comedy of manners, exemplified by Colley Cibber's (1671–1757) *The Careless Husband* (1704). These plays, evidencing the new trend toward sentiment, preserved some of the witty flavor of °Restoration comedy (1660–ca. 1700) but were lacking in the coarseness and amorality of the earlier period. Their dialogue is typically free from profanity and obscenity, their love intrigues are sentimentalized and nearly devoid of sex, and their characters behave with some degree of moral conscience. Unfortunately, from the modern perspective, genteel comedy lacks the sparkle and °wit of the best Restoration comedies.

See also °comedy of manners and °sentimental comedy.

Golden Age See °*Siglo de Oro.*

Gothic melodrama A special type of °melodrama that gained great popularity in Europe and America at the end of the eighteenth century. Gothic melodrama, like the Gothic novel, utilizes mysterious °settings, usually out of the Middle Ages, and features frightening and supernatural occurrences in ruined castles, abbeys, and the like. The action often includes outcast °heroes, ghosts, long-lost relatives, helpless heroines, and long-concealed crimes. Two early examples of the type are Matthew Gregory ("Monk") Lewis's (1775–1818) *Ambrosio; or, The Monk* (1795) and his *The Castle Spectre* (1797).

See °melodrama.

gracioso The °type character of the simpleton comic servant in the Spanish drama of the °*Siglo de Oro.* Lope de Vega (1562–1635) brought the type to full development in his °*comedias,* a fine example being the character of Tello in *The Knight from Olmedo* (1618–25).

See also °*comedia,* °*Siglo de Oro,* and the section on Spain under °Renaissance drama.

Grand Guignol In general, a theatrical performance featuring sensational portrayals of horror, violence, and blood; named after the Théâtre du Grand Guignol in Paris, which was very popular in the late nineteenth century for its macabre fare.

Greek drama The drama which flourished in Athens in the fifth century B.C. and which is considered to be the foundation for all Western drama; the beginnings of dramatic literature as we know it. Greek drama originated in religious celebrations performed in honor of various gods and mythical °heroes. These poetic songs, originally choral in nature, began by the sixth century to take on characteristics of the dramatic, with °actors being distinguished from the °chorus and portions of °dialogue being interspersed with choral °odes. At its height, during the Age of Pericles (461 B.C.–429 B.C.), Greek drama was partly choral and partly dramatic, based primarily upon °myths about the great families of heroes—the house of Atreus, the house of Cadmus, and so on.

Plays were staged annually in groups, as a part of civic festivals. The major Athenian festival was the City Dionysia (March–April) honoring the god Dionysus, who was considered the patron god of the dramatic events. Although the Greek drama never lost its religious associations, the worshipful aspect became insignificant compared to the dramatic elements. The plays were powerful, exciting, and rich in poetry.

The works that have come down to us—some thirty-three °tragedies and eleven °comedies—represent the work of four dramatists: the tragedians Aeschylus (525 B.C.–456 B.C.), Sophocles (ca. 496 B.C.–406 B.C.), and Euripides (ca. 480 B.C.–ca. 406 B.C.), and the comic poet Aristophanes (ca. 448 B.C.–ca. 380 B.C.). There were, however, many other successful writers whose works are lost. Among the extant plays there is great variety, but the structural pattern of a typical Greek tragedy can be identified.

The play opens with a °prologue, either in dialogue (as often in Sophocles) or a single speech of °exposition (as most frequently in Euripides). This is followed by the entrance of the chorus (originally fifty men, but reduced to twelve or fifteen by the time of Aeschylus), singing the °*parodos* or entry song. Major °characters then appear, and the bulk of the play consists of an alternation of dramatic °scenes or °episodes between the actors and the odes of the chorus, called °*stasima*. The final portion of the play is called the °*exodos* and usually includes the exit of the chorus. Originally, the plays were written in groups of three, each group or °trilogy being followed by a °satyr play—a lighter, often comic, work. In the time of Aeschylus, however, the concept of the unified trilogy was abandoned. The only extant trilogy is the *Oresteia* (458 B.C.) of Aeschylus.

The plays were staged in an outdoor amphitheater in a conventionalized, nonrealistic fashion. Actors wore lavish costumes and °masks; the text was sung and chanted more than spoken; there was no stage scenery; and all the roles in a play were taken by three male actors who doubled in the parts (see °protagonist).

In comedy, the works of Aristophanes are the sole survivors, and the style of his work is known as °Old Comedy. It too utilizes a chorus alternating with character dialogue, but the subject matter is fanciful, satiric in intent, and often bawdy and irreverent. The plays of Aristophanes have been likened to modern °musical comedy.

See also separate entries under the various terms cross-referenced above.

grotesque   The term used by Victor Hugo (1802–1885) in his °Preface to *Cromwell* (1827) to describe elements of the comic and the ugly that he wished to see incorporated into the dramas of °romanticism. Hugo objected to the exclusive dominion of the "beautiful" and the "sublime" in serious drama. He saw it as a violation of nature: "Everything in creation is not *beautiful*. . . . The ugly exists beside the beautiful, the misshapen beside the graceful, the grotesque beside the sublime, evil with good, darkness with light." Thus, he incorporated into his °romantic tragedies, for example, *Hernani* (1830), humor and other elements that violated French neoclassical °decorum.

Hugo's use of the term "grotesque" should not be confused with the movement in °modern drama known as the °Theater of the Grotesque, which is discussed separately.

hamartia   A Greek term, used by Aristotle (384 B.C.–322 B.C.) in the *Poetics* (ca. 335 B.C.) to describe the mistake or error which a tragic character commits and which accounts in part for his misfortunes. In discussing the relationship of °character to °plot, Aristotle asserts that the best sort of character is not one who is "unqualifiedly good" or one who is "extremely evil" but one who falls into misfortune "through some miscalculation [*hamartia*]." Thus, Aristotle rejects the concept of °heroes and °villains and points to the tragic character as one with noble intentions who succumbs through error, such as Oedipus.

Until very recently *hamartia* was traditionally translated as "tragic flaw," a concept incompatible with Greek notions of character behavior. The implication of this rendering of *hamartia* is that tragic characters must be flawed by some innate shortcoming—pride, ambition, rashness, and so on. This concept, though untrue to Aristotelian thought, was very useful to modern critics in approaching °romantic tragedy, such as the tragic plays of Shakespeare. Because of the modern preoccupation with abnormal psychology, the concept of the "tragic flaw" continues to surface in serious criticism. Nevertheless, it is not an Aristotelian concept and *hamartia* should be understood in the sense of "mistake" or "error."

See °Aristotelian criticism.

happening   In contemporary art, an event, usually theatrical in nature, in which improvisation and chance play major roles. Happenings evolved in the late 1950s under the leadership of Allan Kaprow (1927–   ), reviving many of the techniques of °futurism, °Dadaism, and °surrealism. Kaprow's *18 Happenings in 6 Parts* (1959) incorporated simultaneous action in separate areas, projections, music and sound effects, and audience participation. At the heart of such happenings was the attempt to remove art (including theater) from the fixed limitations of the gallery or the stage and to encourage the spectator to participate actively rather than watch passively. Happenings paved the way for much contemporary °improvisational theater and for the staging concepts developed by the practitioners of °environmental theater.

harlequinade   A play written in the tradition of the °*commedia dell'arte* or featuring any of the °stock characters of the *commedia,* especially the Harlequin. A modern example is Edna St. Vincent Millay's (1892–1950) *Aria da Capo* (1920).
See °*commedia dell'arte.*

"heavy"   A slang term for the actor in a dramatic company whose usual assignment is to play the °villain in a °melodrama; also the role itself.
See °villain.

hero (feminine, **heroine**)   In general, the central figure or °character in a drama; the °protagonist. More specifically, hero refers to the larger-than-life protagonist typical of so much °heroic tragedy and °romantic tragedy. The concept of the "tragic hero" has often been attributed to Aristotle's (384 B.C.–322 B.C.) *Poetics* (ca. 335 B.C.), but there is nothing in Aristotle's work which suggests the degree of idealization and perfection in tragic character usually understood in the term "hero." The hero is an invention first of °neoclassicism and then of °romanticism.

The romantic or heroic hero is a figure of superhuman proportions with an infinite capacity for suffering. He embodies all that is good in human conduct, his nobility is beyond question, and he is usually torn between conflicting forces—his passionate love for a lady and his responsibilities to state or family. This "love versus honor" struggle leads inevitably to defeat and usually to death. A typical example in heroic tragedy is Antony in John Dryden's (1631–1700) *All for Love* (1677). In romantic tragedy, the title figure of Victor Hugo's (1802–1885) *Hernani* (1830) illustrates the type.
See also °heroic tragedy and °romantic tragedy.

heroic couplet   In °verse drama, a pair of °end-stopped lines of °iambic pentameter. The heroic couplet was the exclusive form for °dialogue in English °heroic tragedy of the Restoration years, from 1660 to about 1675. The following example is from John Dryden's (1631–1700) *The Indian Emperor* (1667), Act I, Scene 2:

> *Montezuma.* When parents loves are order'd by a son,
> Let streams prescribe their fountains where to run.
> *Odmar.* In all I urge, I keep my duty still,
> Not rule your reason, but instruct your will.
> *Montezuma.* Small use of reason in that Prince is shown,
> Who follows others, and neglects his own.

See also °couplet.

heroic tragedy   The type of serious drama that dominated the English stage for approximately twenty years after the Restoration of Charles II, from 1660 to about 1675. Heroic tragedy was characterized by superhuman °heroes in exotic and faraway settings (Mexico, India, and so on), torn between the call of honor (state and familial obligations) and the temptations of passionate love, embodied in some perfectly beautiful and virtuous heroine. This "love versus honor" struggle usually resulted in his death. There was always a great deal of spectacle—processions, battles, dances—and the language of the dialogue was exaggerated and filled with °bombast, almost always written in °heroic couplets.

Heroic tragedies were so far removed from reality, and so stilted and artificial in their verse form, that they are generally regarded as the nadir of English drama. They owed their brief success to several influences: the renewed interest in theatrical spectacle after the Puritan interregnum, the attempt to imitate French court romances and French °neoclassical tragedy, the native English tradition of sensational and bombastic romance in the pre-Commonwealth years (for example, the plays of Francis Beaumont [1584–1616] and John Fletcher [1579–1625]), and the continuing fascination with the exotic and the ancient world.

Even John Dryden (1631–1700), the chief exponent of heroic tragedy (for example, *The Conquest of Granada*, 1669–70), quickly recognized the shortcomings of the type and by 1677 had abandoned the heroic couplet and other stylistic restrictions in his *All for Love.* As early as 1671 George Villiers (1628–1687), satirized heroic tragedy in *The Rehearsal.* Nevertheless, heroic drama,

though of a less extravagant type, continued into the eighteenth century.
See also °Restoration drama.

high comedy   °Comedy that attains its humorous effect through an appeal to the intellect, arousing thoughtful laughter, as opposed to °low comedy. High comedy exposes the vices and follies inherent in social living and ridicules eccentric behavior patterns, rather than drawing on visual or physical humor. It exhibits a high reliance on clever language and witty dialogue, and it often steps into the realm of °satire. Appeal to the emotions and sentimentality are usually avoided; the source of laughter is always intellectual.

An effective treatment of high comedy may be found in George Meredith's (1828–1909) "An Essay on Comedy" (1877). Meredith states: "One excellent test of the civilization of a country . . . I take to be the flourishing of the Comic idea and Comedy; and the test of true Comedy is that it shall awaken thoughtful laughter." Meredith cites the comedies of Molière (1622–1673) as examples of high comedy.
See also °low comedy, °satire, and °wit and humor.

historical criticism   The type of °criticism that examines a work and evaluates it in terms of the historical context in which it was produced, including the social and political milieu and even the playwright's life and other works. The historical critic aims at reconstructing the meanings and implications the work may have had in its own time. Thus, for example, criticism of °Greek drama that is concerned with the religious and theatrical background of ancient Greece, conjecturing as to what the plays may have meant to fifth-century Athenians, would fall within the realm of historical criticism.
See also °analytical criticism, °formal criticism, °mythic criticism, and °textual criticism.

history play   See °chronicle play.

histrionic sensibility   The term used by Francis Fergusson (1904–   ) in *The Idea of a Theater* (1949) to describe man's natural and innate propensity for imitating the actions of others and learning through that imitative process. This, according to Fergusson, lies at the heart of the theater as a cultural phenomenon and of the creation of dramatic literature as an instrument of the theater. According to Fergusson: "The trained ear perceives and discriminates sounds; the histrionic sensibility (which may also be trained) perceives and discriminates actions." Fergusson likens the histrionic sensibility in humans to the play of kittens, where they perceive one another's actions as they stalk pretended prey, "imitating" the movements of the hunt, and thus learning what hunting is.

The concept of histrionic sensibility is grounded in Aristotle's (384 B.C.–322 B.C.) assertion in Chapter IV of the *Poetics* (ca. 335 B.C.) that the "process of imitation is natural to mankind from childhood on," and that "all men find pleasure in imitations." The pleasure derives from the learning experience involved in perceiving imitations.

See also °imitation.

homiletic drama   Drama whose chief purpose is to preach to the audience, by way of advancing some moral, ethical, or religious lesson. Homiletic drama falls under the general category of °didacticism. It is best exemplified by the medieval °morality plays, such as *Everyman* (ca. 1500), and the English eighteenth-century forms of °sentimental comedy and °domestic tragedy, which see.

See also °didacticism.

Horatian criticism   The theory of poetry as propounded by Horace (Quintus Horatius Flaccus, 65 B.C.–8 B.C.) in his "Epistle to the Pisos," also known as his *Art of Poetry* (24–20 B.C.). This classical work on the art of poetry, second in importance only to the *Poetics* (ca. 335 B.C.) of Aristotle (384 B.C.–322 B.C.), greatly influenced the Italian Renaissance critics and helped to shape neoclassical ideas of the drama. Unlike Aristotle's work, the *Art of Poetry* is a highly prescriptive work which lays down rules and regulations for the writing of plays.

Among the more influential of Horace's precepts are: (1) that °comedy and °tragedy are distinct °genres that must not be mixed, each having its appropriate meter, style, and tone; (2) that characters should be true to the °type from which they are drawn, especially through the language assigned to them; (3) that deeds of violence and other unpleasant incidents should not be shown on the stage but narrated; (4) that a play should be written in five °acts; (5) that no more than three characters should be engaged in conversation at any one time; (6) that the °chorus, which should be as integral to the °plot as the characters, must propound virtuous sentiments; and (7) that drama exists for the dual purpose of °delight and instruction, "instruction" meaning moral usefulness. All of these ideas were incorporated into the canons of Renaissance °criticism and are reflected in the drama of the sixteenth and seventeenth centuries.

See also °Aristotelian criticism.

hubris (also **hybris**) A Greek term denoting a type of behavior occasionally exhibited in the characters of Greek °tragedy, which contributes to their misfortunes. *Hubris* may be rendered as "overreaching" or "self-will." The figure exhibiting *hubris* goes beyond what is wise or prudent in self-assertion, often ignoring warnings and portents, when dealing with opposition. The frequent translation of the term is "pride," but it should be understood that pride in the Christian sense was a concept unknown to the ancient Greeks. An example of a character who exhibits *hubris* is Creon in Sophocles' (ca. 496 B.C.–406 B.C.) *Antigone* (ca. 441 B.C.).

Much has been written of the relationship between *hubris* and the Aristotelian concept of °*hamartia*, but the two are not synonymous. The incidence and significance of *hubris* in Greek tragedy are minimal.

See also °*hamartia*.

humor See °wit and humor.

humour A term used in reference to a variety of characters in early English °comedy, beginning with the Elizabethan period, who exhibit distinctive types of eccentric behavior.

See °comedy of humours.

iambic pentameter   A verse form consisting of ten syllables (five iambic feet) to the line. Iambic pentameter evolved in the sixteenth century as the most appropriate form for English °verse drama and has continued to the present as the most popular of all English meters not only in drama but in lyric and narrative poetry as well. The popularity of iambic pentameter may be attributed to its proximity to the natural rhythms of English speech and to its flexibility. When used skillfully in conjunction with the °caesura, the °run-on line, and other devices aiding the flow of the meter, iambic pentameter is a very effective and pleasing verse form for English dramatic dialogue.

The following lines, from Act IV, Scene 1, of Shakespeare's *The Tempest* (1611–12), illustrate the variety and richness possible through the skillful use of iambic pentameter:

> Our revels now are ended. These our actors,
> As I foretold you, were all spirits, and
> Are melted into air, into thin air,
> And like the baseless fabric of this vision,
> The cloud-capped towers, the gorgeous palaces,
> The solemn temples, the great globe itself,
> Yea, all which it inherit, shall dissolve
> And, like this insubstantial pageant faded,
> Leave not a rack behind. We are such stuff
> As dreams are made on, and our little life
> Is rounded with a sleep.

See also °blank verse, °scansion, and °verse drama.

ideal spectator   A term coined by August Wilhelm von Schlegel (1767–1845) in reference to the function of the °chorus in °Greek drama. According to Schlegel's understanding, the chorus served as a bridge between the action of the play and the audience—

explaining, commenting, and generally expressing the sentiments the spectator could be presumed to be experiencing. The Greek chorus, according to Schlegel, "mitigates the impression of a heart-rending or moving story, while it conveys to the actual spectator a lyrical and musical expression of his own emotions, and elevates him to the region of contemplation" (*A Course of Lectures on Dramatic Art,* 1809).

The concept of the ideal spectator is limited in that it describes only a portion of the duties of the chorus as it functions in the extant tragedies. In fact, the sentiments most often expressed by the choruses in Sophocles (ca. 496 B.C.–406 B.C.) and Euripides (ca. 480 B.C.–ca. 406 B.C.) are in no sense "ideal." They rather represent an untutored, unimaginative approach to the problems besetting the characters. The chorus is characteristically ingenuous and seldom understands the implications of the heroic acts undertaken in °tragedy.

See °chorus.

imagery   In a dramatic work, and especially in °verse drama, appeals to the sensuous experience or memory of the reader or auditor through repeated references to sight, sound, and other reminders of the physical world. A great deal of attention has been focused on the images and patterns of imagery in Shakespeare's plays, since a study of imagery often reveals the deeper meanings or unconscious motivations of the dramatist.

Dominant "image-clusters" often underscore and reinforce the °action of a drama in ways of which the reader may be only marginally aware. For example, in *Romeo and Juliet* (1594–95) one finds repeated imagery concerned with light and darkness, including lightning, sunlight, stars, flashes of light, violent and brief explosions, and so on. All these images cumulatively suggest the direction of the °plot itself. The brief flash of light that is the love between Romeo and Juliet cannot survive in the encompassing darkness of the Montague-Capulet feud. In *King Lear* (1605–6) the dominant imagery is of animals of prey engaged in rapacious acts. Wolves, vipers, foxes, serpents, and others are described as tearing, rending, biting, scratching, and clawing their victims. This imagery clearly underscores the violent and rapacious behavior of the offspring (Goneril, Regan, and Edmund) against their helpless fathers (Lear and Gloucester). Imagery, whether used consciously or instinctively by the dramatist, is a powerful device for embodying the very essence of a dramatic action in the language of the play and of making a strong sensory appeal to the reader or auditor.

The interested reader should consult Caroline Spurgeon, *Shakespeare's Imagery* (1935).

imitation (Greek *mimesis*)   A term central to the understanding of the nature of artistic creation; a concept underlying much dramatic °criticism from ancient to modern times. The term first appears as a fundamental idea in Aristotle's (384 B.C.–322 B.C.) *Poetics* (ca. 335 B.C.), and it was variously interpreted in Renaissance and neoclassical criticism.

Aristotle posited that °tragedy was an "imitation of an action," but he did not mean an exact copy of actions as they occur in real life. To Aristotle, imitation was not mere copying but the creative act whereby an artist draws upon reality to produce an artistic representation transcending the real world. This representation conveys certain universal truths, thus producing pleasure in the perceiver. An art object embodies in a *particular* representation some *universal* truth.

Imitation in this sense is quite different from Plato's (427 B.C.–347 B.C.) use of the term, for Plato saw art as a second-hand product, once removed from the real original, twice removed from the ideal, and, therefore, useless. This Platonic view of imitation as mere copying of the real world led to the doctrine of °verisimilitude, which dominated Renaissance and neoclassical criticism.

For Aristotle, all art was imitation, and each art form drew upon certain *means* (materials) that were applied to certain *objects* in a specific *manner* in order to achieve the appropriate pleasure, pleasure being the raison d'être of art. In tragedy, the means of imitation are linguistic (speech, rhythm, and harmony), and the objects imitated are the actions of "good" men. The means are applied to the objects in the dramatic manner; in other words, the agents of the action perform or act out the story.

See also °Aristotelian criticism.

impressionism   In literature generally, the evocation of a mood or impression to the exclusion of objective reality. In the drama, impressionism is represented by the historical movement known as French °symbolism, which see.

improvisational theater   Any form of dramatic presentation in which the °dialogue and °stage business are made up spontaneously by the actors, usually from a loose °scenario, rather than being written in a script. The best known form of improvisational theater of the past is the °*commedia dell'arte,* dating from the Italian Renaissance. Improvisation is also quite popular in the contemporary theater, as well as being one of the major techniques used in actor training today.

See °*commedia dell'arte.*

in medias res   A latin term meaning "into the middle of things," used in dramatic °criticism to refer to a relatively late °point of attack in the structure of a °plot. The playwright who begins his plot *in medias res* shows only the culminating events in a story and includes °antecedent action through °narration or exposition.

See °point of attack.

inciting action   See °exciting force.

induction   An introductory scene that serves as a framework for a drama and, in effect, prepares the audience by stating frankly that they are about to see a play. The induction is somewhat similar to the °prologue but differs in that a prologue is a single speech, whereas an induction may be written in dialogue. Moreover, the induction is a more self-conscious device, since it sets the audience at one remove from the drama by pointing out that the play which is to follow is just that—a play and not a real occurrence.

The induction was used frequently in °Elizabethan and °Jacobean drama. Shakespeare's *The Taming of the Shrew* (1593–94) opens with an uncommonly lengthy induction in which the drunken tinker Christopher Sly is persuaded that he is a lord, for whose amusement a group of players then perform *The Taming of the Shrew* itself. An even more entertaining example occurs in Francis Beaumont's (1584–1616) *The Knight of the Burning Pestle* (1607). The actors who begin the play are suddenly interrupted by hecklers—a grocer and his wife—who persuade them to enact

a different play altogether and to use their boy Ralph as the leading man.
See also °play-within-a-play and °prologue.

ingenue The role of an inexperienced, innocent, unworldly young woman in a drama; also, in theatrical parlance, the actress assigned to such roles. The term "ingenue" is usually applied only to roles in fairly unsubstantial plays, such as °melodramas and light °comedy. One does not, for example, speak of Desdemona in Shakespeare's *Othello* (1604–5) as an ingenue.

instruction See °delight and instruction.

interlude The term used generally in late-medieval and °Tudor England to refer to a play. The term was used so broadly and in reference to such a variety of dramatic pieces that its precise definition is impossible. Its derivation has been explained in at least two ways: (1) that it denoted a brief comic play performed between (*inter*) two more substantial plays (*ludi*); or (2) that it refers simply to a dialogue (*ludus,* play) between (*inter*) two characters. Neither theory is very enlightening.

Some critics have distinguished the interlude from the °morality play as principally a secular and comic work, the morality being more serious and religious. Others maintain that interlude was understood in Tudor times as a brief play to be presented by professionals in the banqueting halls of great estates. In any case, some Tudor dramas were (and are today) clearly referred to as interludes: for example, Henry Medwall's (flourished 1490–1500) *Fulgens and Lucrece* (ca. 1497), often called the first English secular °comedy; John Rastell's (died 1536) *The Nature of the Four Elements* (ca. 1518); and John Heywood's (ca. 1497–ca.1580) *The Four PP* (ca. 1530).
See also °Tudor drama.

intermezzo A brief entertainment of music, °dance, or °pantomime designed for performance between the °acts of a play; similar to an °entr'acte. The intermezzo developed in Renaissance Italy as a diversion from the heavier fare of °classical tragedy and by the late sixteenth century had evolved into an elaborate theatrical spectacle that quite overshadowed the literary drama with which it was performed. By about 1650 Italian intermezzi as such had disappeared, having been absorbed into the emerging form of °opera.

The convention of performing intermezzi between the acts of both comedies and tragedies passed into the theatrical life of other European countries. It was especially popular in France during the reign of Louis XIV (1643–1715), and it may be said to have inspired, at least in part, the evolution of the court °masque in England. The history of the intermezzo is treated in Enid Welsford's *The Court Masque* (1962).

See also °entr'acte and °masque.

intermission   See °entr'acte and °intermezzo.

intrigue plot   A type of dramatic °plot, either comic or serious, that relies heavily upon clandestine scheming, trickery, and clever machinations by a character or characters against others. In °comedy the intrigue plot is quite common. It was most popular in the °Restoration drama and usually concerned sexual intrigue—illicit love affairs, infidelities, cuckoldry, and so on. One popular practitioner of the comedy of intrigue was Thomas D'Urfey (1653–1723), whose *Madam Fickle* (1676) and *A Fond Husband* (1677) illustrate the type.

The intrigue plot in °tragedy is chiefly a product of the °Elizabethan drama. An outstanding example is Shakespeare's *Othello* (1604–5), in which the °villain Iago schemes and plots the downfall of the title figure.

introduction   The opening °act or °scene of a drama, according to the system of analyzing °dramatic structure devised by Gustav Freytag (1816–1895). According to Freytag, the introduction establishes the °setting, introduces the major °characters, and sets the mood for the °action.

See °Freytag Pyramid.

Irish Literary Theatre   An organization founded in 1899 by William Butler Yeats (1865–1939), Edward Martyn (1859–1923), George Moore (1853–1933), and Lady Augusta Gregory (1852–1932) to promote the writing and performance of plays reflecting the Celtic culture and language. The Irish Literary

Theatre served as the foundation for the °modern drama in Ireland and, after evolving into the Irish National Theatre Society, was responsible for producing such major dramatists as John Millington Synge (1871–1909), Lord Dunsany (1878–1957), and Sean O'Casey (1884–1964).

irony   See °dramatic irony.

Jacobean drama The English drama written during the reign of James I (1603–25). It is often considered together with drama of the reign of Elizabeth I (1558–1603) under the general classification of °Elizabethan drama, and there is clearly a continuity of dramatic tradition from one reign to the next. Shakespeare, for example, was active between 1592 and 1612, spanning both reigns, as were Ben Jonson (1572–1637), Thomas Dekker (ca. 1572–ca. 1632), and other major dramatists.

If the Jacobean drama is to be distinguished from the Elizabethan, one can cite a certain °decadence that characterized many of the plays as the period wore on, beginning in about 1610. °Tragedy began increasingly to draw upon cheap sensationalism, sexual themes, and abnormal character psychology. °Comedy, at the same time, moved away from the gentle °romanticism of Shakespeare's earlier works (for example, *Twelfth Night* and *As You Like It,* both 1599–1600) either toward biting °satire, best exemplified in the °critical comedies of Ben Jonson, or toward coarseness and sexual intrigue.

Some leading Jacobean tragedians, besides Shakespeare, were George Chapman (1559?–1634), Cyril Tourneur (1580–1626), and John Webster (ca. 1580–ca. 1630). In comedy, Jonson led the field, followed by the popular team of Francis Beaumont (1584–1616) and John Fletcher (1579–1625). Other important dramatists of the period were Thomas Heywood (ca. 1574–1641), Thomas Middleton (1580–1627), and Philip Massinger (1583–1640).

See also °Caroline drama, °decadence, and °Elizabethan drama.

Japanese drama See separate entries under °Bunraku, °Kabuki drama, and °Noh drama.

jig A farcical song-and-dance routine, of no literary importance, presented often as an °afterpiece on the °Elizabethan stage. The jig might be considered a forerunner of the °droll, popular during the °Commonwealth period.

jilt A °type character in English Restoration °comedy of manners, especially in the comedy of sexual intrigue. The jilt is a lady who entertains a number of lovers simultaneously but manages to keep each of them unaware of his rivals. This situation is exploited to the full, until the gentlemen become aware of the truth and the plot ends. An example of the type is the title figure of Thomas D'Urfey's (1653–1723) *Madam Fickle* (1676).

Kabuki drama   The popular classical drama of Japan, which originated in the early seventeenth century. As with most forms of classical Asian theater, the emphasis in Kabuki is upon performance, rather than upon literary values. It is one of the most lavish and visually exciting theatrical forms in the world, and the skill of the actor-singer-dancer is at the heart of its appeal.

Although it began as pure °dance, Kabuki has evolved into a highly complex amalgam of dramatic text, instrumental music, singing and chanting, spectacular scenery, and lavish costuming. The action relies heavily upon certain theatrical conventions that must be understood by the spectator for full appreciation. One of the more fascinating of these conventions, for the Westerner, is the *onnagata,* the male actor who plays the female role; in traditional Kabuki, all roles are played by men.

Kabuki dramas fall into three categories: *jidaimono,* or history plays depicting codes of loyalty and morality formulated in the Tokugawa period (1603–1868); *sewamono,* domestic dramas that tell stories of the middle and lower classes in unabashedly sentimental and melodramatic fashion; and *shosagoto,* pure dance pieces based on °Noh dramas. The plays are not thought of as literary works so much as texts for performance. They are by Western standards °episodic, sprawling, and frequently narrative rather than dramatic. In the seventeenth century, a single performance could last for twelve hours, but today only acts selected from favorite plays are performed, reducing the playing time to two or three hours.

The greatest of Kabuki dramatists were Chikamatsu Monzaemon (1653–1724), often referred to as the Japanese Shakespeare, and Takedo Izumo (1691–1756), whose masterpiece *Chushingura* (1748) is the most popular of all Kabuki plays.

For further reading, see Earle Ernst, *The Kabuki Theatre* (1956); see also °Bunraku and °Noh drama.

kommos   In °Greek drama, a musical °dialogue either between two °characters or between a character and the °chorus. The *kommos,* a sort of lyric responsory, frequently expressed lamentation. See °Greek drama.

komos   In Greek °Old Comedy, the final scene of a play, in which usually the characters are reconciled, the °conflict of the °action is resolved, and everyone exits to a feast or celebration. See °Old Comedy.

laughing comedy A term coined by Oliver Goldsmith (1728–1774) in 1772 to describe the type of °comedy that attempts to make its audience laugh by exposing human folly, as opposed to °sentimental comedy, the aim of which is to move its audience through the depiction of human distress. Sentimental comedy dominated the English stage through much of the eighteenth century, and Goldsmith and others attempted, in the 1770s primarily, to turn the tide away from sentiment and to revive the type of witty comedy characteristic of the °Restoration period (1660–ca. 1700). Although they never succeeded in defeating sentiment entirely, Goldsmith and Richard Brinsley Sheridan (1751–1816), in comedies like Goldsmith's *She Stoops to Conquer* (1773) and Sheridan's *The Rivals* (1775) and *The School for Scandal* (1777), did manage to restore laughter to the English theater.

See also °sentimental comedy.

lazzo (plural *lazzi*) A brief piece of °stage business incorporated into a °*commedia dell'arte* performance, improvised by the actor. The °scenario for the performance would indicate that the actor was to execute a "fear" *lazzo* or an "anger" *lazzo,* and the actor would perform some stock piece of comic business at that point.

See also °*burla* and °*commedia dell'arte.*

legitimate theater The term for spoken °drama, as opposed to musical theater, °vaudeville, film, and so on. The term derives from eighteenth-century England, when the licensed theaters presented only spoken drama, and musical entertainment was the fare of unlicensed or "illegitimate" theaters.

liaison des scènes A term describing the practice of French neoclassical dramatists of writing each °act of a drama as a continuous, uninterrupted °action. According to the rules of °neoclassicism, each drama should contain five acts, each act should be composed of from four to seven continuous °scenes, and any necessary lapses in °dramatic time should be supposed to occur in the breaks between the acts. These rules, established by the Académie Française in the 1630s, were set forth repeatedly in the works of the major critics of the time.

See also °neoclassicism and °scene.

libretto The text or "book" of the °dialogue and lyrics for a °musical comedy, °opera, or other work for the °lyric theater. The libretto is distinct from the score, which contains the musical notation. "Libretto" is the diminutive of the Italian *libro* (book).

linear plot A type of dramatic °plot in which the incidents are constructed in a line of direct causality to tell a clear and comprehensible story. This is the conventional method of plotting in °tragedy, as opposed to the °episodic plot, which is characteristic more of °melodrama and °comedy. An example of linear plotting is the *Oedipus* (ca. 430 B.C.) of Sophocles (ca. 496 B.C.–406 B.C.), in which each event, with minor exceptions, is made to spring from the preceding incident and lead logically to the following one.

See also °cyclical plot, °dramatic structure, and °episodic plot.

Little Theater Movement The term given to the development of nonprofessional theater in America in the second decade of the twentieth century. The Little Theater Movement was the American counterpart of the independent theater movement that had sprung up in Europe during the last quarter of the nineteenth century. The attempt of the Movement was to introduce into American theater and drama the artistic principles and experimental techniques of the °modern drama movement abroad. The shallowness and commercialism of the American professional theater were largely responsible for the Little Theater Movement.

Some important early groups in the Movement were the Toy Theatre, opened by Mrs. Lyman Gale in Boston in 1912; the Chicago Little Theatre, under Maurice Brown in 1912; the Neighborhood Playhouse, established by Irene and Alice Lewisohn in New York in 1915; the Washington Square Players of New York in 1915; and the very important Provincetown Players, organized in Provincetown, Massachusetts, in 1915. This latter group was responsible for producing the early plays of Eugene O'Neill (1888–1953), perhaps America's greatest playwright.

The Little Theater Movement, which served as the foundation for the development of so many community theaters, was important for bringing new drama and production methods to American audiences, a contribution that the professional New York theater was at that time unable to make.

See also °modern drama.

liturgical drama Early °medieval drama growing out of religious worship in the cathedrals of England and the Continent. This early dramatic activity evolved from the °*"Quem Quaeritis"* trope of the Easter mass into the great cycles of °miracle plays of the late Middle Ages.

See °miracle play and °*"Quem Quaeritis."*

Living Newspaper A theatrical form of news reporting and commentary, developed in America by the Federal Theatre Project in the late 1930s. Each script of the Living Newspaper dealt with a current socioeconomic problem and drew on a combination of straight news reporting and dramatized vignettes. Representative titles were *Triple-A Plowed Under* (1936), *Power* (1937), and, perhaps the best known, *One-Third of a Nation* (1938), which dramatized the deplorable slum conditions in American cities.

The career of the Living Newspaper was brief; Congress withdrew funds from the Federal Theatre Project in 1939. The form was essentially theatrical rather than literary and its scripts are of interest more to the theater historian than to the student of the drama.

locale The fictional environment within which a dramatic °action is supposed to occur. Locale differs from °setting in that setting denotes the specific location represented on the stage, while the locale can include the offstage environment, such as an entire house, neighborhood, town, and so on.

See also °setting.

low comedy A particular type of comic material that may be present in a number of different forms of °comedy (°comedy of manners, °comedy of humours, °romantic comedy, and so on).

Low comedy is not necessarily a form of comedy in itself, though it is possible to speak of an entire play as being composed of low comedy. The elements of low comedy include physical and visual humor, such as beatings, chases, and pratfalls; boisterous conduct, such as quarreling, drunkenness, and loud singing; jokes and trickery among buffoons and servants. Whatever in comedy is of little intellectual appeal, subtlety, or seriousness is usually referred to as low comedy.

Low comedy has always been a staple of the English drama, beginning with the farcical elements of the °miracle plays and °morality plays. Shakespeare and his contemporaries frequently incorporated scenes of low comedy into more serious works, as a means of pleasing the less sophisticated in their audiences. The Porter scene (Act II, Scene 3) in *Macbeth* (1605–6), the Clown scene (Act III, Scene 1) in *Othello* (1604–5), and the Trinculo-Caliban-Stephano nonsense in *The Tempest* (1611–12) illustrate Shakespeare's use of low comedy.

See also °farce and °slapstick.

ludicrous (the)   That which is laughable and therefore suitable as subject matter for °comedy. The study of what constitutes the ludicrous has always been important in works of °comic theory, one of the more illuminating of which is Henri Bergson's (1859–1941) comprehensive essay *Laughter* (1900).

See °comic theory.

ludus (plural *ludi*)   The general Latin term for a play in the °medieval drama.

See °interlude and °medieval drama.

lyric theater   A general term for any form of drama that includes songs or music as an integral part of the work. The ancient °Greek drama can be classed as lyric theater, as can °opera, °operetta, °ballad-opera, °comic opera, °music-drama, and °musical comedy.

See separate entries under these terms.

Machiavel A popular °type character in °Elizabethan drama, motivated solely by the desire to perform evil; a type of °villain. The Machiavel derives his title from Niccolò Machiavelli (1469–1527), the Italian scholar and author of *The Prince* (1513). This work describes the qualifications necessary for a ruler of the typical Italian city-state, and the emergent portrait is one of a ruthless, "politick" (scheming, crafty) despot. For Machiavelli's prince, the end justifies the means. The work was well known in England, and the concept of a scheming, heartless conniver passed quickly into dramatic tradition. So popular was the type of the villainous Machiavel that he emerged as the °protagonist in several Elizabethan °tragedies.

Major characteristics of the Machiavel are: (1) his devotion to evil for its own sake, with no other °motivation required; (2) the total lack of awareness by other characters of his propensity for evil; (3) his delight in his own evil, expressed in humorous °soliloquies; (4) his utilization of a dupe or gull to assist him; (5) his treachery against those who have aided him; (6) his lust and lechery; and (7) his contempt for religion and conventional morality.

Examples of the Machiavel type are Barabas in Christopher Marlowe's (1564–1593) *The Jew of Malta* (1589–90), Edmund in Shakespeare's *King Lear* (1605–6), Richard III in *Richard III* (1592–93), and perhaps the most famous of all, Iago in *Othello* (1604–5). The Machiavel is discussed extensively in C. V. Boyer's *The Villain as Hero in Elizabethan Tragedy* (1964).

See also °villain.

magnitude The term used by Aristotle (384 B.C.–322 B.C.) in Chapter VII of the *Poetics* (ca. 335 B.C.), for the appropriate length in poetic composition. Aristotle makes the point that the magnitude of °tragedy is necessarily less than that of epic poetry,

for a tragedy is meant to be perceived as one whole (one reading or one performance) while the epic can be perceived as separate °episodes without its °wholeness being destroyed. The proper magnitude for a tragedy is partly determined by the limit of the reader's or spectator's memory and attention, but more importantly it is determined by the narrow scope and compactness of the tragic °action itself. It is almost an organic consideration, for Aristotle says that the proper limit of magnitude for a tragedy is "whatever length is required for a change to occur from bad fortune to good or from good fortune to bad through a series of incidents that are in accordance with °probability and necessity."
   See also °plot.

malapropism   The mistaken use of a word in place of another of similar sound, especially for comic effect. The term derives from the character of Mrs. Malaprop in Richard Brinsley Sheridan's (1751–1816) *The Rivals* (1775), although the technique dates at least from some of Shakespeare's comic creations—for example, Dogberry in *Much Ado about Nothing* (1598–99), and Costard in *Love's Labor's Lost* (1594–95). Among Mrs. Malaprop's more notable blunders are: an "allegory on the banks of Nile"; and a "nice derangement of epitaphs" instead of a "nice arrangement of epigrams."

malcontent   A popular °type character in English drama, beginning with the °Elizabethan period, whose dissatisfaction with the world as he sees it motivates his actions. The best example is the title character of John Marston's (1576–1634) *The Malcontent* (1604). The malcontent is characterized by cynicism and a refusal to accept the superficiality, hypocrisy, and immorality of his fellow human beings. The type is a precursor of the "plain-dealing" °protagonist of °Restoration drama, such as the character of Manly in William Wycherley's (1640–1715) *The Plain-Dealer* (1676).

manner (of imitation)   See °imitation.

manners   The term used frequently in Renaissance and neoclassical criticism as a rendering of the Greek *ēthē* in Aristotle's (384

B.C.–322 B.C.) *Poetics* (ca. 335 B.C.). In modern translations the Greek is almost always rendered as "character," which see.

marionette   See °puppet theater.

mask   Any device used to conceal the face of an actor; an important stage property throughout the history of the theater. The mask was used in ancient °Greek drama, both in °tragedy and in °comedy. In the preliterary theatrical activities of the Italic peoples masks became identified with the °stock characters of °Atellan farce. The °*commedia dell'arte* tradition utilized masks throughout the Renaissance and into the eighteenth century. In modern times, many dramatists have experimented with the use of masks, notably Eugene O'Neill (1888–1953) in *The Great God Brown* (1926) and Bertolt Brecht (1898–1956) in *The Good Woman of Setzuan* (1938–40).

In nonrealistic theater the mask serves as a medium for capturing the essential nature of the dramatic °character and of separating the living face of the actor from the fictional personage of the drama. In effect, the mask neutralizes the actor's facial expressions and forces him to utilize his whole body in representing the character. Moreover, masks suggest primitive °ritual and religious observance. Thus, they remind us of the source of drama and awaken in us responses possibly similar to those of primitive man as he enacted his triumphs and defeats before the communal campfire.

See also °*commedia dell'arte.*

masque   A semi-dramatic form of court entertainment, popular in England at least as far back as the reign of Richard II (ca. 1377) and culminating in the court of James I (reign 1603–25). In its early form, the masque was essentially a °disguising, in which the courtiers would don °masks and costumes, appearing before the monarch with gifts and dancing in celebration of high days and holidays. There was initially little, if any, distinction between participant and observer. Enid Welsford (*The Court Masque,* 1962) makes a distinction between the disguising, in which the masked performers danced only with one another, and the "mask," in which the dancers selected partners from among the ladies of the court.

As the masque evolved, it became more formalized as a pre-pared theatrical performance. Such development was greatly en-couraged by Elizabeth I, whose taste for theatrical events is well known, and by James I, who spent incredible amounts of money for costumes, scenery, musicians, and dancers, all for a single eve-ning's entertainment. The later masques were staged more for court and political celebrations—royal weddings, birthdays, visits of foreign dignitaries, and so on—than for holidays.

At its pinnacle, the masque became a dramatic, literary work to some extent, its chief practitioners being Samuel Daniel (1562–1619), Francis Beaumont (1584–1616), Thomas Middleton (1580–1627), and the great comic dramatist Ben Jonson (1572–1637), who collaborated with the court architect and de-signer Inigo Jones (1573–1652) for some of the more spectacular masques in James's court.

The masque had its impact on other literary forms as well. John Milton's (1608–1674) *Comus* (1634) represents the masque carried to its finest poetic development, and there are masquelike epi-sodes in Edmund Spenser's (1552–1599) epic narrative, *The Faerie Queene* (1590–96). George Peele's (1558?–1597?) °pastoral drama, *The Arraignment of Paris* (ca. 1581–84), is like an extended masque, and Shakespeare himself occasionally incorporated masquelike el-ements into his plays. *Love's Labor's Lost* (1594–95) presents a masque of the early "disguising" type (Act V, Scene 2), *As You Like It* (1599–1600) ends with a mini-masque, and *The Tempest* (1611–12) contains a betrothal masque (Act IV, Scene 1).

The English court masque, a product of the Renaissance delight in elaborate theatrical and scenic spectacle, came to an end with the closing of the public theaters in 1642.

For further reading see Enid Welsford, *The Court Masque* (1962).

See also °antimasque.

means (of imitation) See °imitation.

medieval drama European drama from the sixth century to ap-proximately the beginning of the °Tudor drama (ca. 1500), espe-cially the religious drama and its allied types. Medieval drama took many forms, chief among them the °folk drama of the late Middle Ages; the °morality play, which greatly influenced later

English drama; the °interlude, its lighter counterpart; and the °miracle play, which evolved from the liturgy of the church in the ninth and tenth centuries. It is principally from the miracle play that the °Elizabethan drama evolved.

See separate entries for each of the above forms of medieval drama.

melodrama A form of serious drama that utilizes artificial °plot contrivances, unexpected reversals, and sensational effects to impress and move the audience, rather than striving, as does high °tragedy, for a meaningful commentary on the nature of the human condition; a sort of subspecies of tragedy. The term derives from the eighteenth-century French *melodrame* (music play), a sentimental and emotional genre that employed background mood music to underscore moments of high feeling, thus providing the maximum emotional charge for the spectator.

The structure of melodrama is usually contrived to lead the audience's expectations in one direction, only to result in a different or opposite conclusion, usually through the employment of the °*deus ex machina.* Moral and ethical issues, although raised, are never explored as deeply in melodrama as they are in tragedy, for the characters in melodrama are quite clearly drawn as either good or bad. The tone of such plays is idealistic, and the commonly accepted moral and ethical beliefs of the day are reaffirmed in the play's action. Melodrama is the form for °heroes and °villains, and the case for good is always clearly impressed upon the spectator.

Although the great age of melodrama, in both America and Europe, was the nineteenth century, the type has been present in all periods of dramatic literature. In the ancient °Greek drama some of the plays of Euripides (ca. 480 B.C.–ca. 406 B.C.) can be called melodramas. Plays like his *Helen* (412 B.C.) *Alcestis* (438 B.C.), and *Iphigenia in Tauris* (ca. 413 B.C.) are essentially domestic melodramas, with their playing upon the emotions and their contrived happy endings, usually through the *deus ex machina.* In Shakespeare's age, many of the more sensational tragedies, such as Christopher Marlowe's (1564–1593) *The Jew of Malta* (1589–90), Thomas Heywood's (1574?–1641) *A Woman Killed with Kindness* (1603), and even Shakespeare's *Richard III* (1592–93) are essentially melodramas. And in eighteenth-century England, the form known as °bourgeois tragedy was a kind of domestic melodrama.

In a very informative study, *Melodrama* (1973), James L. Smith identifies three distinct species of the genre, all of which were highly popular in the nineteenth-century theater. The first, the "Melodrama of Defeat," seems closest to tragedy because of its unhappy ending. Its heroes, in spite of their association with the good, meet with unhappy fates, and our tears allow us to purge our frustrations and unhappiness for a few moments over fictional disasters. In the "Melodrama of Triumph" the case is the opposite. Good triumphs and the evil are punished, all in good order according to our moral expectations. This incorporation of °poetic justice shows us the world as we wish it were but know full well it is not. The third form, the "Melodrama of Protest," attempts to arouse our anger or sense of injustice by serving as a polemic for or against some social or political position. Of course, the object of the protest can never be truly controversial; the writer wants either to stir up our admiration for motherhood and the flag or to cause us to curse taxes and injustice. Nothing truly significant is ever at stake in melodrama, although it always is made to seem so.

Melodrama can concern itself with a variety of subjects. In the nineteenth century the °Gothic melodrama was popular, as were military melodramas, temperance melodramas, and melodramas of disaster (fires, volcanoes, and so on). In our own times melodrama, which is still the dominant form of serious drama and the form with mass popular appeal, is evident on the stage, in the cinema, and on television.

Melodrama will always be a major form of serious drama, for it allows us to release our emotions through its emphasis on sentiment, and it idealizes the world, allowing us, if only briefly, to escape the harsh realities of life.

melody (Greek *melopoiia*) See °music.

messenger (Latin *nuntius*) A conventional character in ancient °Greek and °Roman drama, whose function is to narrate off-stage occurrences. In the Greek drama acts of violence were usually avoided on the stage. Murders and maimings were done behind the scenes, and messengers would narrate such incidents in poetic passages of powerful °imagery. An example of such is the Messenger's description of the hanging of Jocasta and the self-blinding of Oedipus in Sophocles' (ca. 496 B.C.–406 B.C.) *Oedipus* (ca. 430 B.C.).

In the tragedies of the Roman dramatist Seneca (ca. 4 B.C.–A.D. 65), which were written as °closet dramas (intended for reading, not performance), acts of blood and violence abound, but Seneca still retains the °dramatic convention of the messenger for purposes of °exposition and °narration. Renaissance dramatists, in imitation of both the Greeks and Seneca, frequently utilized messenger speeches to narrate offstage events. George Chapman (1559?–1634) in *Bussy D'Ambois* (1604), includes a character called Nuntius, who describes an extremely important dueling scene that has just taken place off stage.

Excessive use of the messenger convention can be detrimental to a drama, for the device is more narrative than dramatic.

See also °narration.

Middle Comedy   A transitional form of ancient Athenian °comedy, written from around 400 B.C. to 336 B.C. Middle Comedy represented a decline from the freedom of expression in °Old Comedy, caused in part by the decline of Athenian democracy. Comic poets, as is evidenced in the last plays of Aristophanes (ca. 448 B.C.–ca. 380 B.C.), began to soften the satiric tone of their works and to rely less on frank sexuality. The only extant works that could be considered to display elements of Middle Comedy are two late plays of Aristophanes, *Women in Parliament* (392–391 B.C.) and *Plutus* (388 B.C.), and perhaps the *Iphigenia at Aulis* (405 B.C.?) of Euripides (ca. 480 B.C.–ca. 406 B.C.). The demise of Middle Comedy is usually thought to coincide with the beginning of Alexander's reign in the Attic world (336 B.C.).

See also °New Comedy and °Old Comedy.

miles gloriosus   The comic °stock character of the braggart warrior, dating back to Roman °Atellan farce. The name comes from the *Miles Gloriosus* by Plautus (ca. 254 B.C.–184 B.C), and the type has been a favorite throughout the history of °comedy. The title figure of *Ralph Roister Doister* (ca. 1540), an early English comedy, is descended from this type, as are Captain Bobadil in Ben Jonson's (1572–1637) *Every Man in His Humour* (1598), Don Adriano de Armado in Shakespeare's *Love's Labor's Lost* (1594–95), and

even the great comic creation Sir John Falstaff in Shakespeare's
Henry IV plays (1597–98). The general characteristics of the *miles
gloriosus* are cowardice, parasitism, boastfulness, and gullability.
He is easily victimized by his fellows.

mime   An ancient Greek and Roman form of popular °comedy
which featured °dance, broad gestures, and some °dialogue.
When the Christian church succeeded in driving mime from the
public theaters, it was preserved by wandering entertainers. Thus,
the tradition of semi-dramatic performances continued throughout the Middle Ages and undoubtedly brought some influence to
bear upon later forms such as °miracle plays, °interludes, and
°pantomimes. The mime may be thought of as an ancestor of
°vaudeville.

In contemporary usage, mime is a style of performance that
depends solely upon gesture and eschews speech. Also, one who
performs in such a style is referred to as a mime.

See also °pantomime.

mimesis   See °imitation.

minstrel show   A type of entertainment popular in America in
the mid-nineteenth century, in which white men, made up to impersonate Negroes, presented a variety show or °revue featuring
songs, °skits, dances, and brief jokes. The jokes were often delivered in dialogue by the fictional Mr. Bones and Mr. Tambo, the
"end-men" of the semi-circle in which all the performers were
seated. Though they were popular theatrical events in their time
(roughly 1850–70), nothing of literary value emerged from minstrel shows, and today they are viewed as historical evidence of the
attempt by whites to encourage a condescending and ridiculing attitude toward blacks.

miracle play   A type of °medieval drama derived from the liturgy of the church, depicting events taken either from the Bible
or from the lives of the saints, although the latter type is almost
nonexistent. In 1744 the editor Robert Dodsley (1703–1764) gave
the name of "mystery," from the French plays known as *mystères,*
to the English plays based upon biblical subjects, reserving the
term miracle for the saint's play, but modern criticism favors the

use of "miracle" as an all-inclusive term for any of these medieval liturgial dramas.

The miracle plays evolved from brief dramatizations or °tropes, such as the Easter °"*Quem Quaeritis*," that were inserted into the mass in English and Continental cathedrals during the tenth century. From this tentative beginning a full-blown dramatic tradition emerged, with entire °cycles of plays being presented during great festivals in the fourteenth and fifteenth centuries. In England the miracle plays were presented on movable wagons, called °pageants, in connection with the Corpus Christi celebration. Hence, they came to be known as °Corpus Christi plays. The texts that have come down to us are from the towns of York, Chester, Coventry, and Wakefield (called the "Towneley" cycle), and the many component plays of each cycle deal with events beginning with the Creation, through the old Testament, into the events of the life of Christ, and ending with the Day of Judgment.

By modern standards, most miracle plays are rather crude in composition and of little value for the stage, but they served as a foundation for much that is excellent in later English plays and may be said to represent the beginning of English drama. Those of most likely interest to the modern reader include *The Second Shepherds' Play* (from the Towneley cycle), *Abraham and Isaac* (the Brome MS), *Noah's Flood* (Chester cycle), and *Herod the Great* (Towneley).

See also °pageant and °"*Quem Quaeritis.*"

mise en scène The French term for the total visual aspect of a theatrical production, including settings, costumes, lighting, and the positions and movements of the actors. Critical attention to the *mise en scène* dates from the late nineteenth century, in the writings of theorists like Adolphe Appia (1862–1928) and Edward Gordon Craig (1872–1966). In the °modern drama, which tends to stress environment as a motivating force in dramatic °action (see °environmental determinism), the handling of the *mise en scène* becomes an important adjunct to the drama, often augmenting and reinforcing the intentions of the playwright.

mock heroic (also **mock epic**) In general, a literary work which spoofs the conventions and traditions of epic poetry by rendering some trivial subject in the grand manner. In the drama, mock heroic describes a type of play which is intended as a °burlesque of serious, heroic drama, especially of the °heroic tragedy. An early English example is Francis Beaumont's (1584–1616) delightful *The Knight of the Burning Pestle* (1607), and the best known of the type in later periods are George Villiers's (1628–1687) *The Rehearsal* (1671) and Henry Fielding's (1707–1754) *Tom Thumb; or, The Tragedy of Tragedies* (1730).

See also °burlesque and °heroic tragedy.

modern drama   The major reform movement in drama and theater that took place throughout Europe beginning in the last quarter of the nineteenth century and continuing into the twentieth, motivated principally by the demand for °realism. The movement is often said to have begun with Henrik Ibsen (1828–1906), the Norwegian poet and playwright who attempted to strip the theater of many of the artificial conventions and inanities of typical nineteenth-century °melodrama and restore the drama to the realm of art. Ibsen used the drama as a serious means of communication, often taking contemporary social problems as his subjects. One such °problem play is his *A Doll's House* (1879), which seriously questions Victorian morality, the relationship between the sexes, and the institutions of home and marriage.

Ibsen's realistic prose style at first shocked the public, but he was quickly imitated throughout Europe—by August Strindberg (1849–1912) in Sweden, Anton Chekhov (1860–1904) in Russia, Gerhart Hauptmann (1862–1946) in Germany, George Bernard Shaw (1856–1950) in England, and others.

The realistic revolution led quickly to experimentation and to the development of other forms. °Naturalism carried realism to an extreme, inspired principally by the new emerging scientific thought. Dramatic °expressionism and °symbolism were reactions against realism. In all, the various "-isms" of the modern drama movement gave new life to the drama and established writing styles and production techniques that have determined the course of twentieth-century theater.

See also separate entries under °epic theater, °existentialist drama, °expressionism, °naturalism, °realism, °surrealism, °symbolism, and °Theater of the Absurd.

monodrama A rather unconventional theatrical form advocated by Nikolai Evreinov (1879–1953), in which the audience was to become the alter-ego of the °protagonist and share in the stage action. This was to be accomplished by dramatizing everything as seen through the mind of the protagonist, rather like °expressionism. Evreinov argued that the theater should not become like life but rather that life should imitate the theater—that real life was theatrical and that all men tend toward role-playing. His theories are expressed in his "Apology for Theatricality" (1908), and his principal monodrama is *The Theater of the Soul* (1912). The monodrama did not amount to much, but it exerted an influence on dramatic expressionism and on film techniques.

monologue An extended speech or composition to be spoken by one person only. The term is sometimes used interchangeably with °soliloquy, but a soliloquy should be understood as a part of a drama in which a °character, alone, utters his thoughts, while a monologue may be complete in itself and usually is addressed to someone—either the reader-spectator or an imagined second character.

Some monologues are intended for reading only, while some have been written for the stage. Outstanding examples of the first type, often called "dramatic monologue," are Robert Browning's (1812–1889) "My Last Duchess" and T. S. Eliot's (1888–1965) "The Love Song of J. Alfred Prufrock." The second type is exemplified by Anton Chekhov's (1860–1904) "On the Harmfulness of Tobacco" (1886), Robert Benchley's (1889–1945) "The Treasurer's Report" (1930), and any of the excellent monologues by Dorothy Parker (1893–1967).

See also °soliloquy.

morality play A type of drama written in the style of °allegory for the purpose of illustrating some moral or ethical lesson. The type evolved, both in England and on the Continent, in approximately the late fourteenth century. Although essentially religious, morality plays, unlike °miracle plays, do not depict biblical events or the lives of saints. Rather, they portray an invented °hero faced with some moral problem or temptation that confronts all men in real life. In keeping with the style of allegory, the °characters in morality plays are little more than symbolic representations of abstract concepts, from which they take their names: Death, Perseverance, Charity, Youth, Riot, and so on.

The best-known morality play is *Everyman* (ca. 1500), in which the hero, representing all mankind, is called to make his reckoning with God before being claimed by Death. He seeks company on his journey to the grave but is quickly abandoned by such personages as Fellowship, Cousin and Kindred, and Goods (worldly possessions). Finally, Good Deeds and Knowledge lead him to Confession and Repentance, and he goes to his grave accompanied only by Good Deeds. The lesson, as in all moralities, is direct and uncomplicated.

Everyman is, however, somewhat atypical. The more common pattern for a morality play is to show a central mankind-hero torn between two alternative courses of action, the one quite clearly good in the religious or moral sense and the other distinctly sinful. The tempters representing sin might be Riot, Vanity, Shame, and so on. The forces of good are personified by such figures as Conscience, Piety, and Humility. This soul-struggle is termed °"psychomachia" by Richard Bevington (*From "Mankind" to Marlowe*, 1962).

While morality plays passed out of popularity by the time of Elizabeth I, they had a strong influence upon the development of English drama both before and during her reign (1558–1603). The popular figures of the °Vice and the Devil in later moralities and °interludes passed into English °comedy as common character types. Shakespeare's Falstaff in *Henry IV* (1597–98) has been said to descend from this tradition. Some of the structural principles of the °Elizabethan drama are derived from the morality plays—for example, °parallelism, °compression, and °alternation. Christopher Marlowe's (1564–1593) *Doctor Faustus* (ca. 1588) especially depends upon the morality tradition, with its psychomachia, personified in the Good Angel and the Evil Angel, and its pageant of the Seven Deadly Sins.

See also °allegory.

Moscow Art Theater   The national theater of Russia, founded in 1898 by Vladimir Nemirovich-Danchenko (1858–1943) and Konstantin Stanislavski (1863–1938). The founding of the Moscow Art Theater did much to encourage playwrights throughout Europe by its dedication to stage °realism, especially to realistic acting.

The plays of Anton Chekhov (1860–1904), considered the greatest of Russian dramatists, were first produced there under Stanislavski's direction. The Theater was later responsible for pioneering in styles other than realism, chiefly under the inspiration of Vsevelod Meyerhold (1874–1940), who placed primary emphasis upon the role of the director.
See also °Russian realism and °Stanislavski System.

motivation The reasons and justifications that a playwright provides for the given actions of a dramatic °character. Motivation is one of the tests of an author's skill in °characterization, for if the characters are not sufficiently motivated in performing the acts the °plot requires, the play will seem disunified and illogical—possibly no more than a series of disparate incidents. In such cases, we have no sense of a unified, believable character.

Motivation may be embodied in overt acts, as when a character responds directly to some act committed against him, or it may be primarily psychological, as in much contemporary drama. If the second, the character's actions will seem believable and consistent according to some psychological predisposition that has been well established and made apparent to us.
See also °characterization.

multi-plotting The constructing of a drama to include more than one °linear plot line; the use of one or more °subplots. English drama from the beginning utilized multi-plotting, although the technique is alien to most other Western dramatic traditions.
See °subplot.

mummers' play A simple, quasi-dramatic entertainment, popular in England in the late Middle Ages and early Renaissance. The term is derived from a French word meaning to play in °dumb show, °mask, or disguise. The presenters, or mummers, were usually common folk who would perform in some great house, in celebration of a high day or holiday (Christmas especially). The play usually featured a character killed in combat who was then revived by the doctor. Songs and dances abounded, and the mummers might expect food and other offerings from the master of the house. For further reading, see Enid Welsford, *The Court Masque* (1962).
See also °disguising and °masque.

music (Greek *melopoiia,* also translated **melody**)   One of the six qualitative parts of °tragedy, according to Aristotle (384 B.C.–322 B.C.) in Chapter VI of the *Poetics* (ca. 335 B.C.), the others being °plot, °character, °thought, °diction, and °spectacle. Aristotle summarily dismissed the topic of music in his discussion of tragedy, claiming that its meaning was "completely obvious." This makes sense when we remember that the °Greek drama was a form of °lyric theater, much like °opera today, with most of the text sung to musical accompaniment. That music was integral to the whole is "completely obvious."

   Although Western drama after the ancient Greek period largely does without actual music, it is possible that *melopoiia* can still be considered an integral part of the drama if we extend its meaning to include the music of speech—the entire aural component of a play in performance. This is especially applicable to °verse drama, where the rhythms of speech and even occasional °rhyme contribute to the pleasure of the total effect.

music hall   The British form of °vaudeville, popular from the late nineteenth century through the present. See °vaudeville.

musical comedy   A distinctively twentieth-century form of °lyric theater featuring songs, dance, and a dramatic °plot whose dialogue is usually spoken rather than sung. Although there are historical antecedents for the modern musical comedy, such as °operetta, °ballad-opera, and °comic opera, in twentieth-century America the form has been brought to a high level of artistry. Beginning with Jerome Kern's (1885–1945) and Oscar Hammerstein II's (1895–1960) *Show Boat* (1928), the importance of a coherent and carefully plotted story line in musical comedy was recognized. While music and spectacle have by no means been ignored in the development of the form, it is the emphasis upon dramatic values that makes the American musical comedy special.

   Musical comedy is usually the result of °collaboration, and some of the more successful teams have been Richard Rodgers (1902–   ) and Oscar Hammerstein II (1895–1960) (*Oklahoma* [1943], *Carousel* [1945], *South Pacific* [1949], and others), Alan Jay Lerner (1918–   ) and Frederick Loewe (1904–   ) (*Paint Your Wagon* [1951], *My Fair Lady* [1956], *Camelot* [1960]), and Tom Jones (1928–   ) and Harvey Schmidt (1929–   ) (*The Fantasticks* [1960]).

music-drama A form of °lyric theater advocated and practiced by the German composer-dramatist Richard Wagner (1813–1883), often referred to simply as Wagnerian °opera. Wagner wanted a form of theater which was not tied to °realism and which would draw upon mythology in order to evoke, without the spoken word, "the ideal." He stated that drama should be "dipped in the magic fountain of music" by way of achieving a synthesis of the greatness of both Shakespeare's drama and Beethoven's music. To Wagner, music was the controlling force of the drama, measuring and determining every action on the stage. Contrary to traditional opera, the singer was not to dominate but to serve as only one element—another musical instrument—in the total art work. Wagner also insisted that the author-composer was the only one who could successfully realize the work on the stage, and that he should control all aspects of production. Many of Wagner's ideas are articulated in his essay "The Purpose of the Opera" (1871).

See also Edward L. Burlingame, *Art, Life and Theories of Richard Wagner* (1875).

mystery play A type of °medieval drama, derived from the liturgy of the church, dramatizing events taken from the Bible. The term "mystery" was assigned to this type of play by the editor Robert Dodsley (1703–1764) in 1744, on the analogy of the French *mystère*, to distinguish it from similar plays based on the lives of the saints, referred to as °miracle plays. Before Dodsley, no distinction had been made between the two types, and most modern critics prefer the term "miracle" in reference to all medieval liturgical dramas.

See °miracle play.

myth In general, any story of unknown origin, usually encompassing heroes, gods, and the supernatural, which finds credence among a given group of people. An understanding of myths is important in dramatic °criticism, for the °drama itself evolved from the mythology of ancient Greece. In the broadest sense, a myth is any commonly held belief in a society—hence, the myth of democracy or the myth of success. The ancient °Greek drama found its unifying force, its °themes, and its significance in the commonly accepted myths of great heroes such as Oedipus and

Agamemnon, although there is disagreement as to how well known those stories were to ancient audiences.

A common theory in criticism today is that the decline of °tragedy in the modern world stems from the lack of any significant modern myths or any unifying system of beliefs in contemporary society; we do not all believe in anything anymore. According to the theory of myths, perhaps the greatest of modern American tragedies, Arthur Miller's (1916–   ) *Death of a Salesman* (1949), seems to suggest that the predominant myth in our society is of economic success.

Many modern dramatists, faced with this paucity of contemporary myths, have resorted to the mythology of the past, in some cases retelling the ancient stories in updated words or °settings. A favorite subject for such works is the *Oresteia* °trilogy (458 B.C.) of Aeschylus (525 B.C.–456 B.C.). In 1943 Jean-Paul Sartre (1905–   ) used Aeschylus' characters of Orestes and Electra in his °existentialist drama *The Flies;* Eugene O'Neill (1888–1953) wrote a modern version of the *Oresteia, Mourning Becomes Electra* (1931), set in nineteenth-century New England; and T. S. Eliot (1888–1956), in *The Family Renuion* (1939), brought Orestes and his pursuing Furies into the drawing room of an English country house. Clearly, myths continue to be important to dramatists.

See also °mythic criticism and °ritual.

mythic criticism   The type of dramatic °criticism that explores a work in terms of °archetypes and archetypal patterns, often relating it to the ritualistic origins of drama in preliterary cultures. Mythic criticism is largely a product of the twentieth century, and its proponents are essentially interested in examining °tragedy in terms of basic patterns of °action that recur in one period after another, to see if the essential °rituals of tragic action are generic. One such critic is Francis Fergusson (1904–   ), who writes in *The Idea of a Theater* (1949) of the "tragic rhythm," formulated in the pattern of "Purpose, Passion, and Perception."

See also °analytical criticism, °archetype, °formal criticism, °historical criticism, °myth, °ritual, and °textual criticism.

mythos   The term in Aristotle's (384 B.C.–322 B.C.) *Poetics* (ca. 335 B.C.) usually translated as °plot, which see.

narration   In the drama, the relating of off-stage or °antecedent action by a dramatic character, either to other characters or directly to the audience. In all drama some amount of narration is always necessary, if only for aiding the °exposition, but the excessive use of narration can seriously detract from the effectiveness of a play. As Aristotle (384 B.C.–322 B.C.) so clearly recognized (in the *Poetics* [ca. 335 B.C.], Chapter III), drama accomplishes its °imitation of °action by showing (in the "dramatic manner"), not by telling (in the "narrative manner"). In °Greek drama, the amount of narrative material is usually fairly large, arising in part from the use of the °chorus. The narration, however, is made interesting by the poetic beauty and vivid °imagery of the language. Both Greek and °Roman Drama use narration through the conventional °messenger figure as well. One of the principal flaws in most French °neoclassical tragedy is excessive use of narration and a paucity of stage action. Fortunately, earlier English drama did not suffer from this problem.

See also °exposition, °messenger, and °narrator.

narrator   In general, one who relates a narrative or tells a story. In the drama the narrator is a °character who appears to be telling the story to the audience while it is being acted out by the other characters. Thus, the narrator is rarely involved directly in the action, and his presence serves as a technique for °distancing, by reminding the audience at all times that the play is, after all, a fiction. Bertolt Brecht (1898–1956) frequently used a narrator in his plays for this very purpose (see °alienation).

In addition to this distancing function, the narrator allows the playwright to comment directly to the audience, explaining the meaning or significance of the action. Obviously, overuse of this device is inartistic in that it detracts from the dramatic element and reduces the drama to the realm of narrative fiction—to story-telling. A well-known and skillful use of the narrator is found in Thornton Wilder's (1897–1976) *Our Town* (1938). Called the Stage Manager, Wilder's narrator introduces the action and sets the stage for each scene, but his interpretive comments are kept to a minimum. In addition, he frequently steps into the action himself, playing a variety of roles. The effect is enjoyable and quite theatrical.

See also °exposition and °narration.

naturalism   A movement in drama at the end of the nineteenth century calling for an end to °romanticism and advocating a new type of realistic drama that would reflect social and scientific developments. The leader of the naturalist movement was the French novelist Émile Zola (1840–1902), whose dramatization of his own novel *Thérèse Raquin* (1873) was an early example of the type. Zola strove for the scientific method in literature so that it would approach truth; he claimed that drama should illustrate the "inevitable laws of heredity and environment." He called for scientific detachment on the part of the writer, much as a physician would approach a patient. °Environmental determinism was a controlling doctrine of the naturalists, and their plays often dealt with downtrodden unfortunates—prostitutes, beggars, thieves, and so on.

The technique of the naturalist playwright was to avoid any appearance of design or plotting and to present on the stage a °"slice of life" in all its miserable randomness. The stage was to be thought of as a real room with the °fourth wall removed. Dialogue was to be earthy and realistic, liberally sprinkled with obscenities, and the contrived happy endings of °melodrama were unacceptable.

The naturalist techniques influenced dramatists throughout Europe well into the twentieth century. Perhaps the finest of naturalist plays is Maksim Gorki's *The Lower Depths* (1902), a powerful and moving portrait of human degradation, although not without some uplifting elements.

See also °environmental determinism, °fourth wall, and °slice of life.

necessity   See °probability and necessity.

negative capability The objective and impersonal quality of a writer's technique that prevents us from discerning the voice of the author in most of his work. The term was coined by the poet John Keats (1795–1821) in reference to the plays of Shakespeare. Keats admired Shakespeare's "innate universality." Negative capability has since been applied to other authors in speaking of the absence of a personal viewpoint in their work, but today the term is rarely, if ever, applied to dramatists.

neoclassical tragedy The seventeenth-century °tragedy of France and England that conformed to the rules of °neoclassicism. Neoclassical tragedy in France is best represented by the works of Pierre Corneille (1606–1684) and Jean Racine (1639–1699). Corneille essayed the neoclassical mode in France, although his most famous play, *The Cid* (1636), earned the contempt of the Académie Française for its violation of °decorum and °verisimilitude (see °*"Cid* controversy"). In the following generation Racine perfected neoclassical style and wrote the finest of French tragedies, including *Andromache* (1667), *Berenice* (1670), *Iphigenia* (1674), and *Phaedra* (1677).

English neoclassical tragedy was written in the years following the °Restoration of Charles II in 1660 and continuing into the eighteenth century. For the first fifteen to twenty years of this period English neoclassicism took the form of °heroic tragedy, a highly artificial genre generally viewed today as the nadir of English drama. The worthiest practitioner of heroic tragedy was John Dryden (1631–1700), whose *The Conquest of Granada,* parts 1 and 2 (1669–1700), and *Aureng-Zebe* (1675) are representative.

The tight grip of neoclassicism loosened in the later Restoration years, partly because of a renewed interest in the tragedies of the °Elizabethan and °Jacobean periods. In general, subsequent English tragedy exhibits mixtures of neoclassicism and native English °romanticism. In the eighteenth century various writers attempted to keep alive the neoclassical style, most notably Joseph Addison (1672–1719), whose *Cato* (1713) is possibly the finest eighteenth-century English tragedy.

See also °heroic tragedy and °neoclassicism.

neoclassicism The prevailing system of literary thought in Europe, including England, from the late-sixteenth century through at least the end of the seventeenth century. Neoclassical °criticism of the drama reached fruition in France, although it was based on earlier writings of the Italian critics, such as Julius Caesar Scaliger (1484–1558) and Lodovico Castelvetro (1505–1571). Essentially, the neoclassicists hoped to create in modern Europe a dramatic tradition to equal the highly respected body of ancient Greek and Latin works with which they were familiar. To this end they formulated certain guidelines, based on the ancient models and on their understanding of °Horatian and °Aristotelian criticism. These neoclassical guidelines quickly became critical dogma.

The neoclassical spirit revered order, reason, and rules. By imitating the practices of the Ancients, the neoclassicists felt that they could create drama exhibiting the ideals of order, logic, restrained or refined emotion, correctness, good taste, and °decorum. With the founding of the Académie Française in about 1629, the ideals of neoclassicism were set down in a prescriptive, legalistic framework, and virtually all French drama from that point on conformed to the rules.

In England, with the °Restoration of Charles II in 1660, the French standards were lauded by most English critics, and Restoration tragedians attempted to emulate French tragedy (see °heroic tragedy).

Among the canons of neoclassical criticism were the following stipulations:

1. °Comedy must be strictly separated from °tragedy, with the latter kept free from any frivolity, triviality, or comic appeal. Tragedy was to deal with elevated personages; comedy, with lower types. Tragedy was always to end in unhappiness; comedy, in joy. The language of tragedy was to be elevated; that of comedy, colloquial and pedestrian. This strict separation of °genres is subsumed under the larger doctrine of "decorum."

2. The °Three Unities of Time, Place, and Action must always be observed, in the interest of °verisimilitude.

3. All plays must be written in five °acts, each act to be composed of from four to seven °scenes (see °*liaison des scènes*). Each act must conclude with a turn of the action or the introduction of a new intrigue.

4. A tragedy must have a clearly defined °hero of noble bearing who is brought to misfortune by uncontrolled passion.

5. Tragedy must be "useful" in illustrating moral precepts and

showing the certain destruction of the wicked. This demand for °poetic justice clearly illustrates the neoclassical insistence upon °didacticism and is summed up in the French neoclassical motto, °"reason and good sense."

While neoclassicism in England gradually declined in importance during the eighteenth century, it retained its hold upon French drama well into the nineteenth century, until Victor Hugo's (1802–1885) °Preface to *Cromwell* (1827) finally made an effective case for an end to rules and advocated a new spirit of °romanticism.

See also °academies, °decorum, °"reason and good sense," °Three Unities, and °verisimilitude.

neorealism (German *Neue Sachlichkeit*) A movement in the German drama of the 1920s, which reacted against °expressionism by staging mundane topics of current interest. Neorealistic plays were numerous, although of little lasting merit, and they dramatized such concerns as the adjustment to peacetime, flaws in the legal system, and the problems of adolescent school children. Most successful of the neorealists was Carl Zuckmayer (1896–   ), whose *The Merry Vineyard* (1925) was quite popular.

New Comedy The predominant form of drama in the ancient world from 336 B.C. to approximately 150 B.C. With the collapse of Athenian democracy and the new world view that resulted from the conquests of Alexander in the fourth century B.C., the great age of Greek °tragedy ended and the drama turned entirely away from its Dionysian origins to a new style of cosmopolitan, Epicurean entertainment. This is called New Comedy, although its form is closer to what we today might call °melodrama.

Most of our knowledge of New Comedy is second-hand. Only one complete play, by Menander (ca. 342 B.C.–291 B.C.), survives, and we rely principally on the Roman adaptations by Plautus (ca. 254 B.C.–184 B.C.) and Terence (ca. 190 B.C.–159 B.C.). (See °Roman drama.) From them we know that New Comedy was a kind of °comedy of manners that appealed to an educated, leisure-class audience. Its subjects were domestic issues—lovers in distress, familial troubles, and so on. The personages were all °stock characters, such as the parasite, the courtesan, the knavish slave, the foundling, or the miser. The °chorus served only as an entertainment between the °acts, which were always five in number. Distressing and confusing situations always resulted in happy endings, and the satiric thrust of °Old Comedy was completely absent.

Menander has been called the "Father of New Comedy," and though *The Grouch,* discovered in the 1950s, is his sole surviving play, we know that he wrote over 100 plays in the style of New Comedy.

See also °Middle Comedy and °Old Comedy.

Noh drama (also **Nō**) The oldest of Japanese dramatic forms, which dates from the middle of the fourteenth century. There are some 500 extant Noh plays, all handed down from ancient times and performed today only by six companies or schools of Noh performers. Noh is perhaps the most nonrealistic theatrical style in the world. All plays are performed on a standard conventional stage with a minimum of props. °Masks and elaborate costumes are worn, and the dramatic roles are danced rather than acted, in a slow and restrained style. A °chorus chants the text as the performers dance to the accompaniment of one flute and two drums. A performance of Noh is, to the uninitiated, a ponderous and cryptic affair.

Noh dramas are solidly grounded in Buddhist thought and frequently depict the salvation of the soul of a dead person. Ghosts and tormented spirits encounter Buddhist monks and find peace. The texts of the plays themselves, unlike °Kabuki drama, are quite brief and essentially poetic rather than dramatic.

The plays can be classified into various types: "god plays," in which the principal dancer, or *shite,* portrays a god; "warrior plays," in which a battle is described; "women plays," with the *shite* dancing as a female character; "mad plays," which depict deranged ghosts; plays about "living persons"; and "demon plays," concerned with demons, devils, or other supernatural beings. As literature, the plays may seem, in translation, fairly simple and straightforward. It is in the performance, with its restraint and solemnity, that the Noh becomes, for the connoisseur, a deeply affecting and even spiritual experience.

A number of modern Western dramatists have been influenced by the Noh drama, principally the poet and playwright William

Butler Yeats (1865–1939) and the advocate of °epic theater, Bertolt Brecht (1898–1956).

See Arthur Waley, *The Nō Plays of Japan* (1921). See also °Bunraku and °Kabuki drama.

nuntius   See °messenger.

object (of imitation)   See °imitation.

objective correlative   A phrase coined by T. S. Eliot (1888–1965) to refer to the situations, objects, and events that a writer uses to evoke emotional response in the reader without simply describing the emotion. Eliot called it the "only way of expressing emotion in the form of art" and defined it as a "set of objects, a situation, a chain of events which shall be the formula of that *particular* emotion, such that when the external facts, which must terminate in sensory experience, are given, the emotion is immediately evoked." It was partly on the basis of Shakespeare's failure to find objective correlatives for Hamlet's feelings, according to Eliot, that he condemned *Hamlet* (1600–1601) as an artistic failure.

obligatory scene   According to William Archer (1856–1924) in *Play-Making* (1912), a scene "which the audience (more or less clearly and consciously) foresees and desires, and the absence of which it may with reason resent." Archer's concept is based on the theory of the French critic Francisque Sarcey (1828–1899), who wrote of the *"scène à faire,"* which was to satisfy the audience's sense of "expectation mingled with uncertainty." Archer describes five ways in which a scene can be said to be obligatory:
    1. It may be necessitated by the inherent logic of the theme. (His example is the final scene from Henrik Ibsen's *A Doll's House* [1879].)
    2. It may be demanded by the manifest exigencies of specifically dramatic effect.
    3. The author himself may have rendered it obligatory by seeming unmistakably to lead up to it.
    4. It may be required in order to justify some modification of character or alteration of will, too important to be taken for

granted. (Archer cites the third-act Othello-Iago "temptation scene" in Shakespeare's *Othello* [1604–5].)

5. It may be imposed by history or legend.

The concept of an obligatory scene has limited application to contemporary drama and is meaningful primarily in discussing the structure of the °well-made play.

ode In general, a type of lyric poem, exalted and dignified in tone, conforming to a fairly complicated structural form. The ode originated in ancient °Greek drama and was the lyric form employed by the tragic poets for the °*stasimon* in °tragedy. The tragic odes were sung by the °chorus to musical accompaniment. The chorus also danced as it sang, in the circular *orchestra* of the amphitheater.

The typical ode in a Greek tragedy is composed of °strophe and °antistrophe. The strophe may be viewed as a sort of stanza and the antistrophe as a structural parallel to it, presumably sung to identical music. It has been postulated that during the strophe the chorus danced around the *orchestra* in one direction and, at the antistrophe, changed directions, retracing their steps. This is largely conjecture, however. Some odes contain stanzaic portions that belong neither to the strophe nor to the antistrophe. One such portion is called an °epode. Any sung choral passage which does not conform to the strophe-antistrophe pattern is known as an °*astrophon*.

The choral odes comprise some of the most beautiful lyric poetry in Greek tragedy, even apart from the contributions they make to the action of the drama.

See also °chorus.

Old Comedy The °comedy of ancient Athens, from the fifth century B.C. The only extant comic works from this period are eleven comedies by Aristophanes (ca. 448 B.C.–ca. 380 B.C.); thus, Old Comedy is often called °Aristophanic comedy. Comedies were performed in ancient Athens beginning in about 487 B.C., as a part of festivals in honor of the god Dionysus. Each comedy was played after a group of three tragedies and an accompanying °satyr play. As in °tragedy, the actors wore °masks. The comic °chorus numbered twenty-four.

Since Old Comedy evolved from Dionysian revels in celebration of fertility, it retained an irreverent, bawdy tone. The plays were essentially poetic °musical comedy, suggestive of the modern topical °revue. The purpose of the plays was satiric, and contemporary morals, politics, and social customs came under fire with no holds barred. Even well-known personalities of the day were held up to merciless °ridicule. One of Aristophanes' favorite targets was the tragic poet Euripides (ca. 480 B.C.–ca. 406 B.C.), who appears as a character in some of his comedies. Much buffoonery and °slapstick were incorporated into the action, including exaggerated phalli attached to the front of some male characters' costumes. Sexuality and obscenity were exploited to the full.

The structure of Old Comedy was less refined than that of Greek tragedy. It was composed of °prologue, °*parodos,* and °episodes, like tragedy, but it also contained the °*agon,* a dramatized debate, and the °*parabasis,* a choral address made directly to the audience.

Pure Old Comedy was short-lived. Even the last plays of Aristophanes show a transition to °Middle Comedy.

See also °Greek drama, °Middle Comedy, and °New Comedy.

one-act play   A fairly short drama, usually with a continuous °action, complete in itself and achieving its effect through economy and intensity. The form of the one-act play developed at the turn of the century and served, particularly in America, as a method for encouraging new playwrights by allowing their works to be staged with a minimum expenditure of time and money. One master of the form was Eugene O'Neill (1888–1953). Other major writers in the °genre have been George Bernard Shaw (1856–1950), John Millington Synge (1871–1909), Sean O'Casey (1884–1964), Thornton Wilder (1897–1976), Noel Coward (1899–1973), and Tennessee Williams (1912–   ). Synge's *Riders to the Sea* (1904) is widely recognized as the finest one-act play in English.

Typically, the one-act play runs from a minimum of twenty minutes to about an hour, necessitating the inclusion of more than one play for an evening in the theater. The practice of offering programs of one-act plays originated with the °Little Theater Movement early in this century, and many writers have subsequently staged their one-acts in specified groupings. Noel Coward's *Tonight at 8:30* (1935) consists of nine one-acts that were performed three each on three successive evenings. O'Neill's short sea plays were staged in groups, and in 1955 Arthur Miller wrote *A Memory of Two Mondays* and *A View from the Bridge* (original version) for staging on a single bill. The one-act play is a fairly common form even today, particularly in the New York off-Broadway theater and in groups dedicated to experimentation.

onnagata In Japanese °Kabuki drama, a male actor who plays female roles. See °Kabuki drama.

opera A general term for any musical-dramatic composition in which the text is primarily sung rather than spoken. There have been a number of subspecies of opera, such as the English °ballad-opera, French °*opéra comique*, °operetta, and Wagnerian °music-drama. Opera, as it is known today, originated in Renaissance Italy around 1600 and was conceived of as principally a musical and scenic entertainment, rather than a dramatic one. Its most famous practitioner was Claudio Monteverdi (1567–1643), whose *Orpheus* (1607) serves as a fine example of early Italian opera.

From Italy the appreciation of opera spread quickly to France, to England, and throughout Europe. French opera flourished during the latter half of the seventeenth century, as the court of Louis XIV applauded the works of Jean-Baptiste Lully (1632–1687), called the founder of French opera. The English quickly followed suit, and opera was a dominant form of entertainment in the °Restoration theater.

The operatic repertory today contains major works by composers from Italy, France, Germany, Russia, and other countries. Contrary to popular stereotype, many of the works performed today have a fairly high degree of dramatic interest as well as musical excellence. In fact, many operas by Italian composers such as Gaetano Donizetti (1797–1848), Giuseppe Verdi (1813–1901), and Giacomo Puccini (1858–1924) took their texts from the °legitimate theater of their time. It is in operatic form that plays by the French dramatists Eugène Scribe (1791–1861),

Alexandre Dumas *fils* (1823–1895), and Victorien Sardou (1831–1908) are best known today. See also °ballad-opera, °comic opera, °musical comedy, °operetta, and °music-drama.

opéra comique The French variety of °comic opera, which evolved early in the eighteenth century and rose to great popularity in Paris during the nineteenth century, often exhibiting fairly serious subject matter. Technically, *opéra comique* may be distinguished from °opera in general by its use of spoken dialogue in addition to musical numbers. See also °comic opera, °opera, and °operetta.

operetta A form of light comic °opera, which utilizes spoken dialogue as well as song. Operetta, as a distinct form of musical theater, may be said to have evolved in France in the middle of the nineteenth century, its chief practitioner being Jacques Offenbach (1819–1880). Best known today for his serious opera *The Tales of Hoffmann* (1881), Offenbach gained fame in his own time with operettas like *Orpheus in the Underworld* (1858) and *The Beautiful Helen* (1865), works that relied on a combination of fantasy, buffoonery, and contemporary political and social satire for their appeal.

The operetta was a popular form in England and America in the early years of this century, having arrived in this country through the Viennese adaptations of the French form by such composers as Johann Strauss, Jr. (1825–1899) and Franz Lehár (1870–1948). Lehár's *The Merry Widow* (1905) enjoyed enormous popularity on the American stage.

Other notable composers of operettas were Victor Herbert (1859–1924), Rudolf Friml (1879–1972), and Sigmund Romberg (1887–1951). Operetta is principally a musical form, its dramatic values being secondary and generally inferior. The form lost popularity with the development of °musical comedy. See also °comic opera.

optique du théâtre Literally, "theater view"; a term introduced into English dramatic °criticism by George Henry Lewes (1817–1878), borrowed from the French actor François René Molé (1734–1802). *Optique du théâtre* requires that the spectator must understand and remember at all times that the play is a fiction and not reality. He must exercise, as Samuel Taylor Coleridge (1772–1834) phrased it, a °"willing suspension of disbelief," or he will perceive nothing but falseness and artifice, thus losing the pleasure of the fiction.

See also °dramatic illusion.

oxymoron   A poetic technique in which one thing is described in terms of its opposite; a bringing together of contradictory terms, such as "fiery ice," "wise fool," or "joyful sorrow." The term itself means "pointedly foolish," but oxymoron has been used in English drama to achieve sharp emphasis. The following example is taken from Act I, Scene 2, of Shakespeare's *Romeo and Juliet* (1594–95):

Why then, oh brawling love, oh loving hate,
Oh anything of nothing first create!
Oh heavy lightness, serious vanity,
Misshapen chaos of well-seeming forms,
Feather of lead, bright smoke, cold fire, sick health,
Still-waking sleep, that is not what it is!

pageant (1) A dramatic presentation staged in celebration of some historical or cultural event, usually of a civic nature. Pageants rely on °spectacle, great numbers of participants, and visual appeal. Frequently, pageants are staged out of doors as annual events commemorating some local hero. They are generally of little literary value and their texts may vary from year to year.

(2) Technically, the movable stage wagon on which English °liturgical drama was staged in the Middle Ages; but, by extension, the plays performed on such stages. These wagons were used for the great cycles of °miracle plays staged by the craft guilds of such towns as York, Coventry, and Chester. Each guild would construct a pageant for its single play, and the several wagons would then move in procession, stopping to perform the plays at various locations throughout the town.

See also °miracle play.

pantomime (1) A type of entertainment in which the performer relies totally on gesture, facial expression, and movement, rather than speech, for enactment of his material; silent acting. This use of the term derives from the dancelike performances of the ancient Roman theater, called pantomime.

(2) In the English theater, a form of elaborate and spectacular entertainment, dating from the eighteenth century, using a minimum of speech. Such pantomimes were staged frequently in London by John Rich at the Lincoln's Inn Fields Theatre in the middle of the century. According to Allardyce Nicoll (*British Drama*, 1925, p. 270):

> In the first place, there was usually a serious legendary story told by means of dancing and songs—in fact, a short opera. . . . In these plots moved the figures of the *commedia dell'arte*, burlesquing in silent movement the action of the more

serious tale. All of this was laid upon a background of the most spectacular description, with the lavish use of "machinery" and countless changes of scene to please the ravished spectators.

The English pantomime remained popular throughout the nineteenth century.
See also °extravaganza.

parabasis In Greek °Old Comedy, a portion of the play in which the °chorus addresses the audience directly, presenting the poet's views on a variety of subjects.
See °Old Comedy.

parallelism A structural principle in early English drama, especially notable in the plays of Shakespeare and his contemporaries. Parallelism derives mainly from the structure of the typical medieval °morality play and involves the repetition of °characters, °actions, or °themes in two or more simultaneous °plot lines within a single play. Shakespeare's *King Lear* (1605–6) illustrates the technique: the Gloucester plot is parallel to the Lear plot. Both characters are patriarchs, each with both loyal and ungrateful children. Each is brought to ruin by failing to recognize the true nature of his offspring. Each man is cast out and abused, and each comes to a final recognition of the truth in an ironic fashion. Gloucester is blinded and finally "sees," and Lear finds his reason in madness. (For a full discussion of structural parallelism, see David M. Bevington, *From "Mankind" to Marlowe*, 1962.)
See also °alternation and °compression.

parodos In °Greek drama, the early portion of the play during which the °chorus enters; also, that which they sing during their entrance. The *parodos* is named from the long ramplike entryway along which the chorus filed in entering or leaving the circular *orchestra* of the theater. Not all Greek dramas contain the *parodos*. In the *Eumenides* (458 B.C.) of Aeschylus (525 B.C.–456 B.C.), for example, the chorus is in the theater at the beginning of the play.
See also °episode, °exodos, °ode, and °prologue.

passion play In general, a religious play depicting the suffering of a god, such as the ancient Egyptian *Abydos Passion Play*, which dramatizes the death and resurrection of the god Osiris. More specifically, modern passion plays are those depicting the Passion of Christ. The most famous is one presented every ten years at Oberammergau, Bavaria; an American version is staged regularly in the Black Hills of South Dakota.

pastoral drama   In general, any play depicting shepherds and rustic life. In this sense, a play like the medieval °interlude, *The Second Shepherds' Play,* could be classed as pastoral. More specifically, the term is applied to English pastoral plays popular during the °Elizabethan period. They may be seen as a dramatic extension of the prose pastoral romance, as exemplified by Sir Philip Sidney's (1554–1586) *Arcadia* (1590) and Thomas Lodge's (1558–1625) *Rosalynde* (1590). The latter is, in fact, the source for Shakespeare's *As You Like It* (1599–1600), often classed as a pastoral °comedy. English pastoral plays were also written by Samuel Daniel (1562–1619), Ben Jonson (1572–1637), and John Fletcher (1579–1625). Fletcher's *The Faithful Shepherdess* (1609) is a fine example of the genre. Pastoral drama conventionally idealizes rustic life, and its simple shepherds and shepherdesses are often portrayed as astute natural philosophers. All is idyllic in such works, and the tone is decidedly escapist.

pathos   In Greek, the term for "suffering," "deep feeling," or "torment." Aristotle (384 B.C.–322 B.C.) claims in Chapter XI of the *Poetics* (ca. 335 B.C.) that *pathos* is one of three types of incidents in tragic °plots, the others being °recognition and °reversal. He defines an incident of *pathos* as one embodying "destructive or painful actions such as death on the stage, scenes of very great pain, the infliction of wounds, and the like."

In modern °criticism, "pathos" is used to denote elements in a drama that evoke feelings of pity, tenderness, or sorrow in the reader or spectator. The term implies a kind of suffering somewhat less heroic than that of a truly tragic character—an exploiting of the audience's emotions, as in °melodrama. A "pathetic" character is usually one who is helpless in the face of unmerited grief, such as Desdemona in Shakespeare's *Othello* (1604–5) or Ophelia in his *Hamlet* (1600–1601).

Peking Opera   The classical theater of China, which has its roots in the Ming dynasty (1368–1644) but which evolved into its present form, known as *ching hsi,* at about the middle of the nineteenth century. Peking Opera, like most classical Asian theater, is a performer's art, with strong emphasis upon vocal skills, °pantomime, dance movement, and even acrobatics. The texts of the dramas are of little literary value and are quite °episodic in structure. The staging utilizes virtually no scenery and a number of nonrealistic conventions, which must be understood by the spectator for full appreciation of the action. Costumes and makeup are also highly conventional, as well as lavish and colorful.

A number of modern Western dramatists have been influenced by the conventions and techniques of Peking Opera, most notably Bertolt Brecht (1898–1956), who advocated and practiced the theatrical °style known as °epic theater, which draws on some of the features of Peking Opera.

See A. C. Scott, *The Classical Theatre of China* (1957).

period piece A colloquial term for a play set in some historical period, especially one which is "dated" or lacking in relevance to modern times. The term is used also in reference to any play requiring historical costumes and °settings.

See also °costume piece.

peripety (Greek *peripeteia*) See °reversal.

phlyakes (singular *phlyax*) Ancient Italic °mimes, said to have been formulated first by Rhinthon, who lived in the first half of the third century B.C. Such mimes may have influenced the development of °Atellan farce.

pièce à thèse See °thesis play.

pièce bien faite See °well-made play.

pity and fear The chief emotions with which °tragedy is concerned, according to Aristotle (384 B.C.–322 B.C.). In Chapter XIII of his *Poetics* (ca. 335 B.C.) he tells us that the "plot of tragedy must be an imitation of pitiable and fearful incidents," and that "pity is aroused by someone who undeservedly falls into misfortune, and fear is evoked by our recognizing that it is someone like ourselves who encounters this misfortune." Thus, pity and fear are reciprocal emotions and may be thought of almost as a single complex feeling springing from the self-regarding instinct in all men. Aristotle is careful to point out that pity and fear are elements of °plot. They are integrated into the tragedy by the poet and are made manifest at all levels of the work—from °spectacle, through °diction, to °character.

Pity and fear have been closely associated with the concept of °catharsis, for Aristotle states (Chapter VI) that tragedy "achieves, through the representation of pitiable and fearful incidents, the catharsis of such pitiable and fearful incidents" (Leon Golden translation). The exact meaning of this passage has been much debated, but it is clear that pity and fear are key feelings in the appropriate subject matter of tragedy and that tragedy works some effect upon these emotions.

See also °catharsis.

Platonic criticism   Any system or work of °criticism that adheres to the method of Plato (427 B.C.–347 B.C.) in judging works of art not on their intrinsic merit but on extrinsic considerations, such as utilitarian value, moral content, historical accuracy, and so on. In this regard, Platonic criticism is distinguished from °Aristotelian criticism, which is concerned with formal aspects and intrinsic value. The Platonic spirit dominated dramatic criticism from the Renaissance well into the eighteenth century, with critics attempting to evaluate the drama in terms of its didactic worth or its usefulness in teaching moral and ethical values.

See also °criticism and °didacticism.

Plautine influence   The influence exerted on Renaissance writers of °comedy by their knowledge of the plays of the ancient Roman dramatist Plautus (ca. 254 B.C.–ca. 184 B.C.). The influence was made manifest chiefly in the comic °plots themselves; many of the best Renaissance comedies follow the Plautine plots rather closely. Molière's (1622–1673) *The Miser* (1668) is a reworking of *Pot of Gold;* Shakespeare's *The Comedy of Errors* (1592–93) recalls *Twin Menaechmi;* and Ben Jonson's (1572–1637) *The Alchemist* (1610) uses elements of the plot of *Haunted House,* to mention just a few.

Aside from comic plots, Plautus provided several °type characters that recur in Renaissance comedy—the °*miles gloriosus*

(braggart soldier), the parasite, the old lecher, and others. More-over, the later writers based their concepts of °dialogue, class of °character, and °dramatic structure on the models of Plautus. In all, Renaissance comedy, especially in England and France, was profoundly influenced by Plautine comedy.
See also °Roman drama and °Terentian influence.

play doctor The term given to a writer called in to help improve or "patch up" a new play before its official opening.

play-within-a-play A brief dramatization performed as a °scene or °episode within a larger drama, usually with the drama's char-acters serving as spectators. The play-within-a-play may be fairly brief, as is the Players' scene (Act III, Scene 2) in *Hamlet* (1600–1601), or it may occupy a considerable portion of the °ac-tion, as does the Characters' play in Luigi Pirandello's (1867–1936) *Six Characters in Search of an Author* (1921). The con-vention was fairly popular in the °Elizabethan drama and was often combined with the °dumb show, which see.
See also °induction.

plot A term which first appeared in dramatic °criticism in the *Poetics* (ca. 335 B.C.) of Aristotle (384 B.C.–322 B.C.) and which has since been used with various meanings. In Aristotle's usage, plot refers to the "arrangement of the incidents" and is called the "soul of tragedy." ("Soul" should be understood in the sense of "motive force," without spiritual connotations.) For Aristotle, plot (Greek *mythos*) is the most important of the six qualitative parts of °tragedy, the others being °character, °thought, °diction, °music, and °spectacle. The term is intended to refer to the constructing or ordering of the materials the story is composed of.

For Aristotle, plot is not the story of the play, but the drama-tist's way of telling the story. For example, the ancient Greek poet Sophocles (ca. 496 B.C.–406 B.C.) dramatized the well-known story of King Oedipus by beginning his *Oedipus* (ca. 430 B.C.) just before the king finds out that he is himself the murderer of Laius. All °antecedent action—the casting out of the infant Oedipus, his life in Corinth with his foster parents, his rash and impulsive killing of the arrogant wayfarer (Laius)—all this is accomplished through narrative °exposition. Sophocles could as well have ordered his plot differently, showing all these events one by one, and still have told the same story. Thus, the story of King Oedipus provides material for a number of possible plots.

In much modern criticism the term "plot" is often used to refer to the general story told by a drama, rather than to the ordering of that material by the dramatist. As such, it is quite different from the Aristotelian usage. If plot is to refer to the clarity or coherency of the story line, then one may speak of "plotless" plays—an absurdity in the Aristotelian sense—as has often been said of the plays of Anton Chekhov (1860–1904). But the mere fact that Chekhov determined which event should follow another evidences plotting. What is meant by a plotless play in modern criticism is one in which there is no easily grasped linear story line, or one in which the story is secondary to other considerations—language, °theme, °character, and so on.

According to Aristotle, whose precepts apply to drama even today, for the most effective drama a plot should conform to a number of requirements. A good plot must exhibit °wholeness. That is, it must have a beginning, a middle, and an end. Simplistic as this appears, it is a sound observation. A drama should portray a completed °action that effects a change, and this can be accomplished only by showing, as it were: (1) "how these things began"; (2) "what occurred next because of that beginning"; and (3) "how it all came out," leaving nothing more to be said. This constitutes a beginning, a middle, and an end—wholeness.

In addition to wholeness, a plot should portray incidents related to one another according to principles of °probability and necessity. That is, a series of incidents in itself is without meaning unless each occurrence is related to the others, either through direct causality or through their mutual relationship to some unifying principle. In a skillfully constructed plot, the separate incidents will seem to follow one another in a logical and believable fashion. The plot will seem credible.

A third principle of plotting is °unity. To understand this term, one must dismiss all one may have read of the °Three Unities (a Renaissance concept) and consider only the one definition of unity in the *Poetics*. According to Aristotle, unity exists when, "if any one part [of the plot] is transposed or removed, the whole will be disordered and disunified." Thus, in an effective plot, there should be no extraneous incidents, and the ordering of events should be so logical as to preclude transposition.

Skillful plotting, according to Aristotle, requires other considerations as well. There is an appropriate °magnitude for a drama; it should be neither too short nor too long. It should have a °complex plot rather than a °simple plot, thus incorporating both °recognition and °reversal in its action. And finally, the °resolution of a plot should not depend upon a °*deus ex machina* but should result from the plot's own °complications. For amplification on these points, consult separate entries under the various terms cross-referenced here.

See also °dramatic structure.

poesy An archaic term for poetry, including the art of making poems, or "poems" generally. The word appears frequently in the titles of older critical works—for example, Sir Philip Sidney's (1554–1586) *The Defense of Poesy* (1583) and John Dryden's (1631–1700) *An Essay of Dramatic Poesy* (1668).

See also °poetics.

poetic drama See °verse drama.

poetic justice The meting out of rewards and punishments at the conclusion of a drama, which satisfies our expectations by confirming moral and ethical ideals; the °hero is rewarded and the °villain is punished. The incorporation of poetic justice into a °plot is the business of the writer of °melodrama more than of °tragedy and is one of the features that differentiates the one from the other. In his *Poetics* (ca. 335 B.C.), Aristotle (384 B.C.–322 B.C.) noted that there is nothing tragic about °characters "perfect in virtue," nor are "extremely evil" characters who fall through "vice and depravity" fit for tragic °action. Such actions tell us nothing about the nature of the human condition. They are, rather, idealistic fantasy. They belong to melodrama. Tragedy, says Aristotle, deals with characters who are good but not perfect, and their fates are always comprehensible in terms of their actions. Tragic fate does not conform to the arbitrary system and simplistic ideals of poetic justice.

The desire for poetic justice in the drama dominated neoclassical criticism, which required that a tragedy serve to illustrate and reaffirm moral values. The case for poetic justice was stated most clearly by the English critic John Dennis (1657–1734) (as quoted in William F. Thrall et al., *A Handbook to Literature,* 1960, p. 362):

> I conceive that every Tragedy ought to be a very solemn Lecture, inculcating a particular Providence, and showing it plainly protecting the good, and chastizing the bad, or at least the violent: and that if it is otherwise, it is either an empty amusement, or a scandalous and pernicious Libel upon the government of the world.

See also °didacticism and °melodrama.

poetic truth A term used frequently in °romantic criticism to refer to a kind of truth that transcends empirical reality and resides in the mind and vision of the poet. The idea of poetic truth is essentially a plea for freedom from °verisimilitude and a justification for creative fantasy. Poetic truth is an idealized truth, and the romantic dramatists attempted to portray it by creating idealized characters in supercharged situations. The °hero of Victor Hugo's (1802–1885) *Hernani* (1830) is one such character. Unlike any person who ever lived, his virtue is perfect and his honor unassailable. In creating him, it was Hugo's purpose to picture man not as he is but as he might be. This is poetic truth as opposed to reality.

See °romanticism.

poetics Any system or theory of the art of poetry, the term "poetry" being used in the sense of "literature," including narrative prose and drama. Many works of dramatic theory and criticism have been called simply the Poetics of the writer, the most famous being that of Aristotle (384 B.C.–322 B.C.), written about 335 B.C. Aristotle's *Poetics* profoundly influenced the course of Western drama. Even today it is considered the foundation of dramatic theory.

See °Aristotelian criticism.

point of attack The point in a story at which the playwright chooses to begin his °action when constructing a °plot. In general, a drama will employ either an early point of attack and begin *ab* *ovo* (from the beginning) or a late point of attack, jumping into the story °*in medias res* (into the middle of things). Typically, the dramas of °romanticism utilize an °*ab ovo* point of attack. Many of Shakespeare's plays, for example, include incidents set very early in the story, thus creating a considerable amount of °dramatic time for the total action. The dramatic time for *The Winter's Tale* (1610–11) is more than sixteen years; the abandoned baby of Act III appears as the princess-heroine of Acts IV and V.

To begin *in medias res,* on the other hand, is the method of most °classical tragedy, °neoclassical tragedy, and much °modern drama. The action of Henrik Ibsen's (1828–1906) *Ghosts* (1881) opens less than twenty-four hours before Oswald goes insane (the °crisis of the plot), with the entire early history of the Alving family and of Oswald's life in Paris presented through °exposition.

See also °dramatic structure and °plot.

preface A brief statement by a dramatist that serves as an introduction to the printed version of his play. In a preface the writer can explain his purpose in writing the play, describe his method and theories of °dramaturgy, beg forgiveness for the work's shortcomings, attack his critics, and so on. The printing of prefaces became standard practice in the °Restoration drama and has continued to the present time. Frequently, a playwright's preface offers valuable historical and critical material, as is the case with Victor Hugo's (1802–1885) Preface to *Cromwell* (1827), a veritable manifesto of °romanticism, or August Strindberg's Preface to *Miss Julie* (1888), which paved the way for the drama of °realism. Perhaps the most famous writer of prefaces was George Bernard Shaw (1856–1950), whose lengthy introductions and commentaries not infrequently matched the length of the plays themselves.

prescriptive criticism Any work or system of °criticism that judges a work of art by relating it to a preconceived set of rules or requirements. The prescriptive critic measures a work against absolute standards for that kind of work. This method, the opposite of °descriptive criticism, is typical of most Renaissance and neoclassical criticism of the drama.

See °criticism.

presentationalism The theory and practice of drama as a frankly theatrical and fictional presentation, as against the opposite extreme of °representationalism, which attempts to create an illusion of the play as real life. Presentationalism is as much a matter of stage production as it is of writing, and a pure form of presentationalism is impossible, since some degree of illusion is unavoidable in the theater. Still, some styles of drama are heavily presentational, such as the ancient °Greek drama, the °Elizabethan drama, and the modern German playwright Bertolt Brecht's (1898–1956) °epic theater.

The more a theatrical style depends upon °dramatic conventions, asking its audience to exercise °"willing suspension of disbelief" and utilizing °distancing techniques, the more presentational it becomes. When °characters speak in rhymed verse, for example, artifice predominates over °realism. Nonrealistic °settings, °masks, °narrators, and sung or chanted °dialogue all obviously contribute to the impression of theatrical fiction and lessen the illusory aspects of a play.

See also °representationalism.

probability and necessity Two requisites for an effective tragic °plot, according to Aristotle (384 B.C.–322 B.C.) in Chapter IX of the *Poetics* (ca. 335 B.C.) Probability and necessity are properties or characteristics resulting from the dramatist's rendering of incidents not as they can happen in real life but according to universal principles. The poet, as opposed to the historian, writes of events as they *might* occur, given the circumstances that the plot presupposes. For example, it is impossible in real life for persons to become invisible and fly, yet these acts by Ariel in Shakespeare's *The Tempest* (1611–12) are made dramatically probable by the writer within the world of that play. The converse is also true. Some events happen in real life that would seem unmotivated and improbable if incorporated into a dramatic plot. In real life random or chance events occur. In the drama each event must be related to others and to the whole, according to the principles of probability and necessity.

See also °universality.

problem play A drama dealing seriously with some issue, usually social or ethical; a play in which the ideas are paramount. It is possible to identify plays of this nature from virtually every period—for example, the *Alcestis* (438 B.C.) of Euripides (ca 480 B.C.–ca. 406 B.C.), or Shakespeare's *Measure for Measure* (1604–5)—but the term "problem play" is usually applied to certain works from the °modern drama, especially to plays by Henrik Ibsen (1828–1906) and George Bernard Shaw (1856–1950). Both Ibsen and Shaw questioned the accepted values of their day and subjected certain social institutions to severe criticism. Both were concerned with the hypocrisy of Victorian society, particularly the inferior role of women and its accompanying "double standard." Ibsen's *A Doll's House* (1879) may be considered the first important modern problem play, and Shaw followed suit with plays like *Mrs. Warren's Profession* (1902).

See also °drama of discussion.

prologue (Greek *prologos*)   In general, any introductory speech or °dialogue preceding the °action of a play. In °Greek drama the *prologos* was simply the opening portion of the play and, in the plays of Aeschylus (525 B.C.–456 B.C.) and Sophocles (ca. 496 B.C.–406 B.C.), usually took the form of a long speech by a secondary character or a dialogue between two characters, by way of setting the scene and effecting the °exposition. Euripides (ca. 480 B.C.–ca. 406 B.C.) used the *prologos* differently, turning it into a frankly narrative introduction usually spoken by a god. Its chief purpose was expository. The Roman comic writers followed the tradition by writing prologues to their comedies. Those by Plautus (ca. 254 B.C.–184 B.C.), for example, are quite amusing and help to establish the comic tone of the plays.

Prologues were fairly common in the English drama, beginning with Shakespeare and his contemporaries, but they became an indispensable part of the drama during the °Restoration years (1660–ca. 1700) and through most of the eighteenth century. The typical Restoration prologue was usually spoken by one of the play's actors and was invariably a defense of the dramatist's work. It frequently insulted the audience by intimating that many of them lacked the wit and understanding to enjoy the play. Presumably, the Restoration audience found this amusing rather than offensive. In the eighteenth century it was not uncommon for writers of note to pen prologues for their colleagues' plays. Alex-

ander Pope (1688–1744), Samuel Johnson (1709–1784), and David Garrick (1717–1779) are known to have done so.
    See also °epilogue.

prose drama   Drama that is not written in a regular metric pattern (such as °iambic pentameter); the opposite of °verse drama. Many plays, those of Shakespeare for example, have been written in a combination of verse and prose passages, but they are still classed as verse drama. Pure prose drama first became firmly established in the Restoration period (1660–ca. 1700), when prose became the accepted medium for °comedy, but not for °tragedy. In the eighteenth century, serious prose drama evolved, and in the °modern drama, prose became the dominant medium for all drama, serious and comic.
    See also °verse drama.

prosody   The study of the art of versification, including metrical structures, °rhyme, stanza forms, and so on. Prosodic analysis can often be helpful in the study of °verse drama, as is the case with Shakespeare's plays. Such study has resulted in the "verse test" of his plays, a comparison of all the works in terms of their incidence of rhyme, kinds of rhyme, proportionate amount of °blank verse, and so on.
    See also °blank verse, °iambic pentameter, °rhyme, °scansion, and °verse drama.

protagonist   Originally, the first or chief °actor in °Greek drama. In the early stages of the evolution of °tragedy, the protagonist acted only with the °chorus, but when Aeschylus (525 B.C.–456 B.C.) added roles for a secondary actor, or °deuteragonist, to his plays, the potential for dramatic °action was greatly enhanced. Sophocles (ca. 496 B.C.–406 B.C.) is credited with adding roles for a third actor, the °tritagonist, and all subsequent Greek drama was played with only three actors who shared the various roles. Occasionally mutes were used as stand-ins for major characters if all three actors were needed on stage in other roles. In rare instances, a stand-in may have had the opportunity to speak a line or two.
    The term "protagonist" came to be associated with the dramatic °character, rather than with the actor, and today the word designates the central figure or °hero of a drama. When this character

is opposed by another in a situation of °conflict, the opposer is called the °antagonist. Such would be the case in Shakespeare's *Othello* (1604–5), for example, in which the title figure is the protagonist and Iago, the °villain, is the antagonist. In fact, however, the number of plays with a clearly identifiable antagonist is relatively small.

See also °conflict and °counterplayer.

psychological realism   A type of realistic drama that emphasizes °characterization, especially in terms of psychological °motivation and behavioral patterns. Psychological realism received much of its impetus from the new interest in psychology at the end of the nineteenth century, and its earliest important practitioner was August Strindberg (1849–1912). In the °Preface to his *Miss Julie* (1888) Strindberg outlined his new approach to characterization. Essentially, he rejected the concept of °type characters and pleaded for more °realism in drawing dramatic characters. In real life men's actions arise from complex motivations, he argued; therefore, they should be dramatized similarly. *Miss Julie* realizes his theories perfectly and presents some of the most fascinating character studies in the °modern drama. Strindberg led the way for subsequent dramatists, and much modern realism is strongly character-oriented. Playwrights like Eugene O'Neill (1888–1953) and Tennessee Williams (1912–   ) frequently have written in the style of psychological realism.

See also °characterization and °realism.

psychomachia   A term, derived from a fourth-century work by Prudentius (348–410?), describing the "soul struggle" of the °hero in a typical medieval °morality play. The term was applied by David M. Bevington (*From "Mankind" to Marlowe,* 1962) to the structural pattern of most of the moralities, in which the central Mankind-hero is torn between forces of good and evil, each personified by dramatic characters—for example, Charity, Conscience, Folly, Pride. The psychomachia is perhaps best represented in English drama in the title character of Christopher Marlowe's (1564–1593) *Doctor Faustus* (ca. 1588). Faustus suffers battles of conscience dramatized as struggles between the Good Angel and the Evil Angel, two other dramatic characters.

See also °allegory and °morality play.

pun A play on words in which the use of one word suggests another that is pronounced similarly but has a distinctly different meaning. Puns were popular in °Elizabethan drama, as is exemplified in this passage from the opening scene of Shakespeare's *Twelfth Night* (1599–1600):

> *Curio.* Will you go hunt my lord?
> *Duke.*   What, Curio?
> *Curio.* The hart. [punning on *heart*]
> *Duke.* Why so I do, the noblest that I have.

See also °quibble.

Punch-and-Judy show A traditional and popular form of °puppet theater in England, in which the character of Punch (descended from the °*commedia dell'arte* character of Pulcinello) quarrels with and physically abuses his wife Judy, to the great amusement of the spectators.

puppet theater In general, any form of dramatic entertainment performed not by live °actors but by dolls, puppets, or marionettes. Technically, a puppet is a doll manipulated on the hand of the operator, while a marionette is a doll detached from the operator and controlled by strings or wires. Some important forms of puppet theater are the °Bunraku of Japan, the °shadow plays of Southeast Asia, and the °Punch-and-Judy shows of England, all of which see for further discussion.

Puritan Period See °Dark Period.

pyramidal structure See °Freytag Pyramid.

quarto   The size and format of one type of book in early printing, in which a single sheet of "foolscap" (size 17″ x 13½″) was printed on both sides as eight pages, folded in quarters, and bound with other sheets similarly treated. Thus, the quarto of a Shakespeare play is an early edition printed in this fashion. The dating of certain Shakespeare quartos, and the determining of their authenticity, is a task that even today occupies scholars.

'See also °folio and °textual criticism.

"Quem Quaeritis"   The opening words of a °trope inserted into the Catholic Easter Mass in some English and Continental cathedrals, beginning in the late ninth century. The oldest extant example dates from around 925 and reads (as translated in Oscar Brockett, *History of the Theatre,* 1974, p. 73):

> *Angels.* Whom seek ye in the tomb, O Christians?
> *The Three Marys.* Jesus of Nazareth, the crucified,
>   O Heavenly Beings.
> *Angels.* He is not here, he is risen as he foretold.
>   Go and announce that he is risen from the tomb.

From this early form, which was probably chanted antiphonally, emerged more elaborate dramatizations of the confrontation between the Marys and the Angel. A version dating from around 970 in the *Regularis Concordia* of the Winchester Cathedral (England) is a small drama with complete staging directions. The expansion of the *"Quem Quaeritis"* trope of the tenth century into °liturgical dramas led to the fully expanded dramatic tradition of great cycles of °miracle plays during the fourteenth and fifteenth centuries. Thus, the *"Quem Quaeritis"* is often said to represent the beginning of English and modern European drama.

See also °miracle play and °trope.

quibble A type of word play common in °Elizabethan drama, especially in the comedies of Shakespeare. The quibble is an elaborated °pun in which varying meanings for key words are explored in °dialogue, leading the reader or listener from one °image to another. Although quibbling may have delighted the audiences of Shakespeare's time, the meanings are usually lost to readers and audiences today. For an example of quibbling, see *Love's Labor's Lost* (1594–95) (Act V, Scene 2, lines 242–55) and any accompanying editorial comment upon the passage.

See also °pun.

raillery A style of °dialogue featuring witty banter and °repartee, common in the °comedy of the °Restoration period (1660–ca. 1700). Raillery is almost always engaged in by a gentleman and a lady, and the tone is often decidedly sexual. In such cases, raillery serves as a cover-up for mutual romantic interest. Another type of raillery is directed, by way of criticism and °ridicule, against absent characters, as it is in typical Restoration gossip scenes. For an example, see the beginning of Act II of William Wycherley's (1640–1715) *The Plain-Dealer* (1676).

See also °repartee.

raisonneur Any dramatic °character who serves as a voice of reason or as a mouthpiece for the playwright; one who communicates to the audience the truths that the other characters may not see. The *raisonneur,* also called a °chorus character, is particularly valuable in °modern drama for assuming functions that the °chorus of ancient °Greek drama was able to perform. Examples of the use of a *raisonneur* include the Fool in Shakespeare's *King Lear* (1605–6), Cléante in Molière's (1622–1673) *Tartuffe* (1664), and Laudisi in Luigi Pirandello's (1867–1936) *Right You Are, If You Think You Are* (1916).

rant Wild, violent language, especially as used in the °dialogue of much °Elizabethan drama, such as the °tragedy of blood.

See °bombast.

realism In general, the mode in drama that attempts to place on the stage a convincing replica of real-life situations and engage its audience by creating an illusion of reality. Specifically, realism was a movement in theater and drama during the last quarter of the nineteenth century. It represented a reaction against °romanticism, and its playwrights aimed at replacing the superhuman

°heroes of the romantic °melodrama with ordinary, recognizable
characters. The exoticism of romantic drama was to be replaced
by the commonplaces of the drawing room, and exaggerated poetic dialogue was to give way to realistic prose.

The leader of the realistic revolution was the Norwegian writer
Henrik Ibsen (1828–1906), often called the father of the °modern
drama. The plays of Ibsen, and of the realists who followed his
lead, generally avoid the grand crises and sensational °catas-
trophes of romantic drama. Their concern is often with domestic
problems and social issues, and their characters tend to discuss
their problems rather than stab and shoot one another.

Realism has continued to advance in twentieth-century drama,
and the bulk of the important American plays from the 1920s to
the present are essentially realistic. The major American playwrights Eugene O'Neill (1888–1953), Tennessee Williams
(1912–   ), Arthur Miller (1916–   ), and Edward Albee
(1928–   ), in spite of occasional experiments in other forms,
are all essentially realistic.

See also °naturalism and °psychological realism.

realistic comedy   In general, any type of °comedy employing the
techniques of dramatic °realism, although the term is used more
specifically to refer to a type of °Elizabethan and °Jacobean comedy opposite in approach to °romantic comedy. This type of realistic comedy portrayed the immediate and recognizable in London life. It tended toward the satiric and the cynical, its character
types were frequently °humours, and the dialogue was fairly colloquial, prosaic, and coarse. The °comedy of humours was essentially realistic comedy, as were those plays that contained elements
of the °comedy of manners.

Some notable writers of English realistic comedy were George
Chapman   (1559?–1634),   Thomas   Middleton   (1580–1627),
Thomas Dekker (1572?–1632?), and Ben Jonson (1572–1637).
Jonson's *humours* comedies, such as *Every Man Out of His Humour*
(1599) and *Bartholomew Fair* (1614), draw upon the eccentric types
in London middle-class life and satirize them mercilessly. Dekker's
The Shoemakers' Holiday (1599) and Middleton's *A Trick to Catch the
Old One* (1606) are other notable examples, the former especially
for its blending of both realistic and romantic elements. Shakespeare was given to writing primarily romantic comedy, although

the Falstaff plot of *Henry IV* (1597–98) is an outstanding example of realistic comedy.
See also °comedy, °comedy of humours, °comedy of manners, and °romantic comedy.

"reason and good sense" A motto embodying the ideal of most French neoclassical literature, including the drama. The proper function of °tragedy, according to the doctrine of °neoclassicism, was to illustrate the triumph of reason over the destructive effects of uncontrolled passion (meaning, usually, love) and the harmony with the natural world resulting from the exercise of "good sense," meaning moral temperance. "Reason and good sense" in the drama were achieved through the passion for rules, regularity, and formal control which characterized most °neoclassical tragedy, and which the French referred to as *les* °*bienséances*.
See °neoclassicism.

recognition (Greek *anagnorisis,* also translated **discovery**) A necessary element of the °complex plot in °tragedy, according to Aristotle (384 B.C.–322 B.C.) in Chapter X of the *Poetics* (ca. 335 B.C.), and a significant test of the skill of the dramatist. By "recognition," Aristotle meant principally the incident of the °plot in which the central °character discovers some major piece of information that profoundly affects his actions—usually the recognition of a familial relationship or identity. Thus, in Euripides' (ca. 480 B.C.–ca. 406 B.C.) *Iphigenia in Tauris* (ca. 413 B.C.), at the crucial moment when the priestess Iphigenia is about to have the unknown stranger sacrificed, she learns that he is her brother Orestes, and he is spared.
In addition to this major sort of recognition between blood relations, tragedy also contains, Aristotle says, various kinds of minor recognitions—recognitions of "things" (signs and portents), and recognition of events that have or have not taken place. But the finest form, and the one leading to °reversal of fortune, is the recognition of persons, such as that in *Iphigenia in Tauris.* This major recognition must "develop directly from the construction of the plot itself, so that [it occurs] from prior events either out of necessity or according to the laws of probability."
See also °reversal.

regular play   A term used frequently in seventeenth-century dramatic °criticism to describe a drama that conforms to the rules and regulations established for the form of °tragedy, according to the ideals of °neoclassicism. These rules include adherence to the °Three Unities, the observance of °decorum, the utilization of the appropriate verse forms, the proper amount of °didacticism, and so on. Any tragedy not conforming to these precepts was termed "irregular." This was the fate accorded the plays of Shakespeare during the °Restoration and eighteenth century, for he was the least "regular" of the English playwrights.

See °neoclassical tragedy.

Renaissance drama   European drama from roughly the middle of the sixteenth to the end of the seventeenth centuries. Renaissance scholarship was predominantly concerned with classical culture and ideals, and the Renaissance drama of Italy, France, Spain, and England reflected an interest in, and emulation of, ancient °Greek and °Roman drama.

Italy was the first country whose dramatists and critics exhibited classical ideas in their writings. Italian Renaissance dramatic criticism originated in the 1540s, although Italian dramatists had before that attempted to write plays in the classical mode. There are no dramas of major worldwide importance from the Italian Renaissance; the criticism of the period clearly overshadows the practice in importance. The most noteworthy playwrights from the period were Niccolò Machiavelli (1469–1527), whose *The Mandrake* (ca. 1515) is often cited as an exemplary Italian Renaissance °comedy; Lodovico Ariosto (1474–1533), whose comic *The Casket* (1508) is still studied today; Giangiorgio Trissino (1478–1550), writer of the first important Italian °tragedy, *Sophonisba* (1515); Giambattista Giraldi Cinthio (1504–1573), a writer of °Senecan tragedies; and Torquato Tasso (1544–1595), who essayed °pastoral drama in *Aminta* (1573).

In France the Renaissance drama took root in the next century, beginning roughly in the 1620s and reaching fruition during the reign of Louis XIV (1643–1715). The French critics followed the lead of the Italians, formulating strict principles for playwriting, and French drama closely adhered to these neoclassical rules (see °neoclassicism). The chief writers were Pierre Corneille (1606–1684), whose tragedy *The Cid* (1636) occasioned one of the most lively critical battles in history (see °*"Cid* controversy"); Thomas Corneille (1625–1709), his younger brother, who wrote over forty plays; Jean Racine (1639–1699), perhaps the greatest of all French tragedians; Jean Galbert de Campistron (1656–1723), whose seven tragedies, written between 1683 and 1691, earned him a considerable reputation; and the great Molière (1622–1673), surely one of the finest comic writers the world has ever known. Molière was popular from 1658 to his death in 1673, and he stands today as the greatest of French dramatists.

In Spain, too, the Renaissance produced a body of drama of considerable merit, chiefly between 1580 and 1680, the hundred years known as the °*Siglo de Oro* (Golden Age) of Spanish culture. Spanish drama was far less influenced by the restrictions of neoclassicism than was French, and it more closely resembles the English °Elizabethan drama with which it is roughly contemporary. The Spanish spirit was decidedly romantic rather than neoclassic. The leading dramatist of the *Siglo de Oro* was Lope de Vega (1562–1635), the most prolific playwright the world has ever known. It is thought that he may have written as many as 1,800 plays. Some 450 of them survive. Lope de Vega was a master of the °*comedia,* a type of °tragicomedy the Spanish favored. His best known play is *Fuente Ovejuna* (ca. 1614). After Lope de Vega, the Spanish drama is best represented by Pedro Calderón de la Barca (1600–1681), whose *Life Is a Dream* (ca. 1636), his most famous play, is occasionally performed even today. Spanish Renaissance playwrights produced an estimated 30,000 plays by 1700, an astounding output. But the Spanish drama, while similar in feeling to the English, never attained the excellence of the works of Renaissance England. (See also °*autos sacramentales,* °*capa y espada,* and °*comedia*)

In England, the Renaissance drama is considered to be that which flourished from the beginning of the Tudor dynasty (roughly 1500) to the closing of the public theaters by the Puritans in 1642. The Renaissance drama of England is discussed elsewhere under the individual headings (chronologically) of °Tudor drama, °Elizabethan drama, °Jacobean drama, and °Caroline drama.

repartee A witty exchange of dialogue, usually between characters in a °comedy of manners. Repartee is prevalent in °Restora-

tion drama, where witty rejoinders abound. In the °modern drama, the outstanding master of repartee was Oscar Wilde (1856–1900), whose *Lady Windermere's Fan* (1892) and *The Importance of Being Earnest* (1895) amply illustrate his genius in this kind of dialogue. The term "repartee" itself is derived from fencing terminology, and the image of thrusting and parrying is particularly apt.
See also °raillery.

repertory (French *repertoire*) In general, a roster of works; in theatrical parlance, a list of plays, either as performed by a particular company or as representing a style or movement ("the classical repertory"). A repertory company is one that regularly performs a number of plays in rotation.

repraesentatio A general Latin term for a play in °medieval drama.

representationalism The theory and practice of drama as a representation of the real world, emphasizing the illusion of reality and asking the audience to believe that the stage action is real life. Representationalism is as much a matter of stage production as of writing, and the complete illusion of reality on stage is, of course, impossible. Still, much drama is written with the idea of creating just such an illusion—for example, the plays of °realism and °naturalism that dominated the European theater at the turn of the century. The French producer André Antoine (1858–1943), at the Théâtre Libre in Paris, first attempted the ultimate in representationalism by putting real props on his stage and asking his actors to turn their backs to the audience. The American producer David Belasco (ca. 1854–1931) likewise strove for absolute literal realism in his productions. As a starting point for a theory of theatrical art, representationalism fails to account for the fact that the audience always knows that stage life is a fiction and, indeed, expects it to be.
See also °fourth wall, °presentationalism, and °slice of life.

resolution In °dramatic structure, that portion of the °action of a play from the moment of °crisis to the end. The terms °falling action, °*dénouement,* and °catastrophe are frequently used for resolution, but each of these terms has more specific meanings. The resolution of the °plot makes clear the implications and significance of all that has come before in the °complication. It has been likened to the "untying of the knot" of the °rising action.

See °dramatic structure.

Restoration drama   The drama of England from the Restoration of Charles II in 1660 to roughly the end of the seventeenth century. During the Puritan interregnum (1649–60) there was virtually no legitimate theatrical activity in London, but Charles encouraged a rebirth of the drama in 1660 by issuing Patents Royal for the operation of professional theaters, and the English drama quickly revived. The three chief °genres of Restoration drama were °opera, °tragedy, and °comedy, the latter being the type for which the period is best known.

The Restoration opera evolved from the musical-dramatic entertainments that had served as substitutes for °legitimate theater during the Commonwealth years. Its popularity was due in large part to the new mode of extravagant staging that the English quickly adopted from the French after 1660. It was much like tragedy set to music, with songs, dance, and spectacle, and it replaced Italian recitative with spoken dialogue. Frequently, adaptations of Shakespeare's plays were rendered in operatic form.

Restoration tragedy, although popular with its original audiences, is generally viewed today as the nadir of English drama. In the first fifteen to twenty years of the period, the accepted style was known as °heroic tragedy, a highly artificial, self-conscious imitation of French °neoclassical tragedy. It succeeds only in illustrating the futility of attempting to force the English romantic spirit into the mold of °classicism. Fortunately, a shift in tragic style occurred in the late 1670s, due largely to the leadership of the period's chief literary figure, John Dryden (1631–1700). In *All for Love* (1677) Dryden broke away from the strict neoclassical mold, and subsequent tragedians followed the example. Chief among them was Thomas Otway (1652–1685), whose *Venice Preserved* (1682) mixes romantic and neoclassical styles and is, aside from *All for Love,* the only Restoration tragedy of any merit.

Restoration comedy took many forms, chief among them the °comedy of humours, °farce, the °intrigue comedy, and the °comedy of manners. Humours comedy recalled the popular type of the pre-Puritan era (the °Elizabethan and °Jacobean periods), and its chief practitioner in the Restoration was Thomas Shadwell (1642–1692), whose *The Squire of Alsatia* (1688) nicely illustrates the type. The comedy of intrigue (especially sexual intrigue) was quite popular, and most of the successful dramatists essayed the form. The plots involved trickery, sexual liaisons, infidelities, and cuckoldry. Mrs. Aphra Behn (1640–1689) and Thomas D'Urfey (1653–1723) were among the successful practitioners of comedy of intrigue. Although most Restoration comedy contained farcical elements, pure farce is best represented by Edward Ravenscroft (ca. 1650–ca. 1700), whose *The London Cuckolds* (1681) and *The Anatomist* (1696) both lasted well into the eighteenth century. It is the comedy of manners, however, which above all is thought of as "Restoration comedy" and which embodies the best of the period's drama. The three leading writers of the type were Sir George Etherege (ca. 1633–1691), William Wycherley (1640–1715), and William Congreve (1670–1729). (See °comedy of manners.)

The character of Restoration drama began to change at the end of the century, partly because of a treatise by the Reverend Jeremy Collier (1650–1726), *A Short View of the Immorality and Profaneness of the English Stage* (1698), which attacked the licentiousness and amorality of Restoration comedy, and partly because of a rising middle class and a monarch less tolerant of—and patronizing toward—theatrical activity, the sober William of Orange (reign 1689–1702). By 1700, the shift toward °sentimental comedy was well under way.

revenge tragedy   A type of °tragedy popular in the °Elizabethan period of English drama, best exemplified by Thomas Kyd's (1558–1594) *The Spanish Tragedy* (ca. 1587). Revenge tragedy was influenced primarily by the subject matter of the plays of Seneca (ca. 4 B.C.–A.D. 65), the ancient Roman dramatist. Seneca's tragedies were filled with °plots of revenge and retribution, as well as acts of murder, insanity, ghosts, and sensational and bloody deeds. The Elizabethans incorporated these elements into their revenge tragedies, notably Shakespeare's *Titus Andronicus* (1593–94) and *Hamlet* (1600–1601), Cyril Tourneur's (1580–1626) *The Revenger's Tragedy* (ca. 1606), and George Chapman's (1559?–1634) *Bussy D'Ambois* (ca. 1604). *Hamlet* displays elements of revenge tragedy brought to a high level of artistry, with its ghost seeking retribution, a prince bent on avenging his father's murder, °suspense created through delayed revenge, mental derangement of the °hero, a crafty °villain, an incestuous marriage, and several on-stage deaths, leaving the stage strewn with a number of corpses at the final curtain.

See also °Senecan influence and °tragedy of blood.

reversal (Greek *peripeteia*) A major incident in the °complex plot of °tragedy, according to Aristotle (384 B.C.–322 B.C.) in Chapter X of the *Poetics* (ca. 335 B.C.); it results from a °recognition on the part of the characters of some hitherto unknown piece of information. The reversal, which Aristotle does not treat at any length, is a "change of fortune in the action of the play to the opposite state of affairs" and may be a change either from good fortune to bad or from bad to good. The first type is illustrated by the *Oedipus* (ca. 430 B.C.) of Sophocles (ca. 496 B.C.–406 B.C.), in which a just and prosperous king is reduced to the unhappy state of an exiled blind beggar. The latter type is seen in the *Iphigenia in Tauris* (ca. 413 B.C.) of Euripides (ca. 480 B.C.–ca. 406 B.C.), in which Orestes, destined for certain death at the hands of the Taurian priestess, is spared when it is revealed that his would-be executioner is his sister Iphigenia. The siblings are reunited, Orestes is saved, and the two escape together. While such happy endings strike us today as inappropriate for tragedy, they were perfectly allowable within the genre as the Greeks knew it and as Aristotle defined it.

See also °recognition.

revue A light entertainment, musical and dramatic in nature, featuring songs, dance, comic °sketches, and a generous amount of scenic display. The revue differs from the °musical comedy in that it lacks a unified dramatic story line. The revue is a peculiarly modern theatrical form and was quite popular in America between the two World Wars, often serving as a showcase for particular performers and personalities. Perhaps the most famous of all revues were the annual *Ziegfeld Follies,* performed in New York every year between 1907 and 1931.

See also °burlesque, °extravaganza, and °vaudeville.

rhyme   The similarity or identity of sounds in successive lines of verse, usually at the ends of the lines. Rhyme was an important feature of medieval and Renaissance °verse drama, although it was unknown in ancient °Greek and °Roman drama. In the English drama rhyme is found in abundance in °miracle plays, °morality plays, and the works of the °Tudor dramatists. The use of rhyme in drama became less frequent in the °Elizabethan period as °blank verse gained in popularity. Shakespeare used a great deal of rhyme in his early plays (for example, *Love's Labor's Lost* [1594–95]) but almost none toward the end of his career. *The Winter's Tale* (1610–11), one of his last plays, is without rhyme, except for its songs. Rhymed verse reappeared briefly in the °heroic tragedies of the Restoration years, but since then it has played almost no role in the composition of verse drama.

Rhyme may be classified according to where it falls within the verse line. End rhyme, the most frequent variety, involves only the final syllable or syllables of the lines and is said to be "masculine" when the correspondence involves only the final syllable ("sing" and "ring," "reply" and "defy") and "feminine" or "double" when two syllables are involved, the second being unaccented ("story" and "glory," "manner" and "banner"). Internal rhyme occurs when a syllable within the poetic line rhymes with one in a corresponding position in the following line. Shakespeare occasionally employed internal rhyme:

> Above the sense of *sense;* so sensible
> Seemeth their conf*erence;* their conceits have wings
> *(Love's Labor's Lost,* V, 2)

Beginning rhyme, in which the initial syllable of a line rhymes with that of the following, is rare in English dramatic verse.

See also °blank verse and °verse drama.

ridicule   The act of making someone or something the object of contemptuous laughter by exposing faults and shortcomings. Thus, ridicule is at the heart of nearly all °comedy, particularly °critical comedy and °satire. Aristotle (384 B.C.–322 B.C.), in Chapter V of the *Poetics* (ca. 335 B.C.), was the first to recognize that comedy "imitates" men characterized by the "ridiculous," which he calls a species of the "ugly."

See °comedy and °comic theory.

rising action In °dramatic structure, according to the °Freytag Pyramid, the second major portion of the °plot, in which most of the °complication occurs; also used synonymously with "complication." Gustav Freytag (1816–1895) asserted that the rising action begins with the °exciting force and represents the entanglement of incidents and the °conflict between the °hero and the opposing forces. This leads to the °climax, the highest pitch of excitement. See °dramatic structure and °Freytag Pyramid.

ritual In general, an act or observance with a set form which is based upon custom and which has the effect of lending meaning and order to an essentially chaotic world. The subject of rituals is important in dramatic °criticism because of modern theorists who see, in all great drama, certain rituals recurring from century to century. One such writer is Francis Fergusson (1904–   ), who in *The Idea of a Theater* (1949) finds what he calls the "tragic rhythm" in most great °tragedy, as a result of the nature of the basic tragic ritual.

Ancient °Greek drama is known to have evolved from religious rituals in worship of the god Dionysus, and the theory is that all tragedy re-creates some basic ritual having to do with growth, death, and regeneration—an analogue to the winter-spring cycle of nature.

Many modern dramatists have attempted to restore ritual to the theater by using well-known rituals in their plays or re-creating the rituals of the classical world. An example is *The Balcony* (1956) by Jean Genet (1910–   ), in which rituals of the church, the law, and the military are central to the action.

See also °archetype and °myth.

Roman drama The Latin drama of ancient Rome, which was based principally on Greek models and flourished largely between 240 B.C. and 140 B.C. The only extant works from this period are the comedies of Plautus (ca. 254 B.C.–184 B.C.) and Terence (ca. 190 B.C.–159 B.C.), although there were many other active playwrights in this Golden Age of Roman drama. The tragic poet Seneca (ca. 4 B.C.–A.D. 65), of a later period, is the only other Roman dramatist whose works have survived (see °Senecan influence).

Prior to this period, which is characterized primarily by the strong Greek influence, there was a variety of indigenous, Italic, preliterary theatrical forms, such as the °*fabula Atellana* (°comedy improvised around °stock characters) and the °mime. But in the third century B.C. the influx of Greek culture gave rise to a literary drama based, like all Roman art, on Greek models. The comic writers, like Plautus and Terence, drew upon the °New Comedy of the Greek Menander (ca. 342 B.C.–291 B.C.), closely following his plots in a style known as °*fabula palliata* ("comedy in Greek dress"), while the tragic poets took their plots from Aeschylus (525 B.C.–456 B.C.), Sophocles (ca. 496 B.C.–406 B.C.), and especially Euripides (ca. 480 B.C.–ca. 406 B.C.). There are no extant Roman tragedies from this period.

The comedies of Plautus and Terence are characterized by broad, farcical action, improbable °plots, °type characters, and the inclusion of music and dance. They are written in colloquial, snappy dialogue filled with °puns, some obscenity, and topical Roman allusions, in spite of their Greek °settings. Their characters are always middle-class and their situations are frivolous, aimed at entertaining. Terence differs from Plautus in greater fidelity to the spirit of the Greek originals, the practice of °*contaminatio* (combination of plots), a more subtle verbal style, greater skill in plot construction (including the °double plot), and a more sophisticated humor. The plays of both men had a profound effect upon the Renaissance concept of comedy, influencing major comic dramatists such as Shakespeare, Ben Jonson (1572–1637), and Molière (1622–1673). (See °Plautine influence and °Terentian influence.)

Roman drama began to decline in the second century B.C. The *fabula palliata* of Plautus and Terence gave way to the °*fabula togata*, or "comedy in native dress," a cruder, rustic variety of °farce. Tragedies ceased to be written for the stage because of a shift in taste of the Roman public. Legitimate dramatic activity was replaced by spectacle, sensationalism, and public displays of blood (executions, animal-baiting, and so on). Mime and °pantomime continued as popular entertainments, but even they degenerated during the imperial period until, in the sixth century A.D., the emperor Justinian bowed to the demands of the Christians and abolished all theatrical activity in the Roman Empire.

romantic comedy In general, any type of °comedy dealing chiefly with romance and love interests in a sympathetic fashion. Specifically, romantic comedy refers to a comic tradition of the °Elizabethan drama, as best exemplified in the plays of Robert Greene (1558–1592) and Shakespeare. Greene's *Friar Bacon and Friar Bungay* (ca. 1589) is an excellent example of the type, as are most of Shakespeare's comedies—for example, *The Two Gentlemen of Verona* (1594–95), *A Midsummer Night's Dream* (1595–96), *As You Like It* (1599–1600), and *Twelfth Night* (1599–1600).

The features of romantic comedy include: romantic love as the central °action; pastoral, out-of-doors, or idealized °settings (for example, the Forest of Arden); multiple sets of lovers; idealized °heroines, frequently disguised as boys; lovers beset by great difficulties and separation; reconciliations and the reform of the °villain; and happy endings, with all the lovers united.

During the °Jacobean period romantic comedy largely gave way to types of °realistic comedy, such as the °comedy of humours and other forms stressing the mode of °satire.

See also °realistic comedy.

romantic criticism In general, any °criticism that views a work of art as a free expression of the creative impulse and attempts to evaluate it in terms of its own nature, without recourse to prescriptive rules or definitions. Specifically, romantic criticism of the drama flourished in the late-eighteenth and nineteenth centuries and represented a revolt against the spirit of °classicism with all its rules and restraints.

The Germans, who had no really significant neoclassical tradition in their native literature, may be said to have led the way for romantic criticism. The early writings of Friedrich Schiller (1759–1805) and Johann Wolfgang von Goethe (1749–1832) advocated freedom for the dramatist. The °Preface to Schiller's *The Robbers* (1782) is an important piece of romantic criticism, and Goethe's drama *Götz von Berlichingen* (1773) clearly disregards neoclassical rules. (See °*Sturm und Drang*.) It was largely due to the admiration of the nineteenth-century Germans for the plays of Shakespeare that this greatest of all English romantics was rescued from the neglect he had suffered during the age of classicism and restored to his rightful position as one of the world's great writers.

In England romantic criticism may be traced back to Dr. Samuel Johnson (1709–1784), essentially a classicist but one of the first to champion Shakespeare's romantic style. In his Preface to Shakespeare's plays (1765) Johnson recognized Shakespeare's genius for °characterization and freed subsequent English dramatists from the bugbear of the °Three Unities. And, in the next century, Samuel Taylor Coleridge (1772–1834) continued to elevate Shakespeare in a number of critical works.

French romantic criticism may be said to have originated with Victor Hugo (1802–1885), whose Preface to *Cromwell* (1827) served as a romantic manifesto and dealt a death blow to French °neoclassicism. Throughout Europe, dramatic criticism continued in the romantic vein, until the last quarter of the nineteenth century, when °realism came to defeat it.

See also °romanticism.

romantic tragedy °Tragedy characterized by freedom of artistic expression and a lack of adherence to formal precepts such as those found in °classical tragedy. Generally, romantic tragedy differs from classical tragedy in its looser structure (including sometimes °multi-plotting); its emphasis upon °character and heroic behavior, at the expense of controlled plotting; the freedom and extravagance of its language, which may be either °prose or °blank verse; and its inclusion of elements of the comic and the °grotesque. Most °Elizabethan tragedy, including Shakespeare's, exemplifies the romantic spirit, but the great age of romantic tragedy was during the late-eighteenth and nineteenth centuries. A fine example from this period is Victor Hugo's (1802–1885) *Hernani* (1830).

See also °melodrama and °romanticism.

romanticism A movement in late-eighteenth- and nineteenth-century drama that marked a departure from the formal restraints of °classicism and advocated freedom of creative expression. The shift from classicism to romanticism is difficult to trace with any precision, as it occurred at different times in various countries. Germany was perhaps the first country to experience the spirit of romanticism, with its °*Sturm und Drang* drama of the 1770s and 1780s, represented by the early plays of Friedrich Schiller (1759–1805) and Johann Wolfgang von Goethe

(1749–1832). In England the romantic period in literature is generally dated from 1798, the year of the publication of William Wordsworth's (1770–1850) and Samuel Taylor Coleridge's (1772–1834) *Lyrical Ballads*. Many English poets of the period—Coleridge, Wordsworth, John Keats (1795–1821), Percy Bysshe Shelley (1792–1822), Lord Byron (1788–1824), and others—wrote romantic dramas, although few of their works were actually produced on the stage. English theatrical taste during the nineteenth century favored °melodrama, itself a form of romantic drama. In France the romantic spirit was definitely established with Victor Hugo's (1802–1885) melodrama *Hernani* (1830), which deeply offended the neoclassical sensibilities of the Académie Française and occasioned riots at its initial performances.

Essentially, romanticism displays a contempt for rules and precepts. A premium is placed upon the creative act, with terms such as "talent," "imagination," and °"poetic truth" dominating the °criticism. Romantic plays are conceived as idealizations of life, in which °heroes perfect in virtue and honor come into conflict with cataclysmic forces, often personified in a °villain. Romantic drama pictures man in an ideal harmony with nature, finding there a revelation of truth. Its concerns are often with the mystical and the spiritual in human life, and it incorporates the strange and the °grotesque into its action. For the romantics, imagination overshadowed rules and reason.

See also °romantic tragedy.

run-on line   A line of verse whose sense and structure continue on to the following line, preventing a pause or rhythmic break at the end of the line; the opposite of an °end-stopped line. The bulk of English °verse drama is composed mostly of run-on lines. They allow for more effective stage delivery and for rhythms more closely approximating normal speech. An examination of the Shakespeare °canon reveals that he moved progressively away from the use of end-stopped lines toward run-on lines as his career advanced. The following example of run-on lines is from *The Winter's Tale* (1610–11), Act IV, Scene 4:

> Your heart is full of something that does take
> Your mind from feasting. Sooth, when I was young
> And handed love as you do, I was wont

To load my she with knacks. I would have ransack'd
The pedlar's silken treasury and have pour'd it
To her acceptance; you have let him go
And nothing marted with him.

See also °blank verse and °end-stopped line.

Russian realism   The name given to a general movement that
occurred in Russian drama and theater, beginning in the middle
of the nineteenth century. Among the leaders in this movement
toward °realism in the drama were Ivan Turgenev (1818–1883),
Aleksandr Ostrovski (1823–1886), Leo Tolstoi (1828–1910), and,
somewhat later, Maksim Gorki (1868–1936). Russian realism cul-
minated in the four great plays of Anton Chekhov (1860–1904):
The Sea Gull (1896), *Uncle Vanya* (1899), *Three Sisters* (1901), and
The Cherry Orchard (1904).

Russian realism is often associated with the °Moscow Art Theater, founded in 1898 by Vladimir Nemirovich-Danchenko
(1858–1943) and Konstantin Stanislavski (1863–1938). In its early
years the Moscow Art Theater was dedicated to the reform of
Russian theater by throwing out the artificial conventions in-
herited from the eighteenth century and introducing a new spirit
of realism in playwriting, acting, and production. Stanislavski
was a leader in this respect, giving realistic stagings to the plays of
writers like Chekhov and Gorki, and developing a new method of
acting, which is known and practiced even today as the °Stani-
slavski System.

See also °realism.

sacra rappresentazione A general Italian term for a play in the °medieval drama.

saint's play See °miracle play.

Sankskrit drama The traditional drama of India, dating from roughly the fourth century A.D. and written in Sanskrit, the classical language of India. Sanskrit drama found its origins in, and always reflects, the tenets of the Hindu religion. Its literary principles are far different from those of Western drama, with °plot and °characterization given little attention. Sanskrit plays mix the comic with the serious and are epic in scope, drawing upon stories of love, adventure, and the supernatural.

In Sanskrit dramatic theory, the dominant principle is known as *rasa,* meaning "flavor" or "sentiment." An individual play is a pageant or kaleidoscope of emotions, images, and °episodes, all reflecting and reinforcing the one central *rasa.*

The two Sanskrit plays that have found the widest audience among Western readers and audiences are *Shakuntalā* by the greatest of Sanskrit dramatists, Kālidāsa (late fourth–early fifth centuries) and the anonymous *The Little Clay Cart,* from roughly the same period.

See A. B. Keith, *The Sanskrit Drama: Its Origin, Development, Theory and Practice* (1924).

"Sardoodledom" An amusing term coined by the great English dramatist and critic George Bernard Shaw (1856–1950) in reference to the slick, superficial type of °melodrama practiced so ably by the French dramatist Victorien Sardou (1831–1908). This kind of work, also known as the °well-made play, dominated the European stage before the advent of the °modern drama and its serious °problem plays.

See °well-made play.

satire In general, a mode of writing that utilizes °wit and humor to criticize or °ridicule human institutions and behavior, with a view to correction or improvement. In the drama, satire has been a popular mode since the °Old Comedy of Aristophanes (ca. 448 B.C.–ca. 380 B.C.). Comic dramatists have always felt compelled to expose human folly, although the intensity of the attack has varied.

There are two principal approaches to satire, named for their classical practitioners: Horatian satire, which is gentle, smiling, and fairly sympathetic; and Juvenalian satire—biting, angry, and bitterly contemptuous of corruption. In the first category one can place the works of the greatest of all French dramatists, Molière (1622–1673), whose essential faith in human nature triumphed over his disappointment in its shortcomings. The great George Bernard Shaw (1856–1950) might also qualify as a Horatian satirist. Juvenalian satire, on the other hand, is the mode of the leading Elizabethan satirist, Ben Jonson (1572–1637), of England's Noel Coward (1899–1973), and of the masters of American dramatic satire, George S. Kaufman (1889–1961) and Moss Hart (1904–1961).

In English drama the era dominated by the satiric mode was that of the °Restoration drama with its °comedy of manners, most of it strongly Juvenalian.

See also °comedy and °comic theory.

satyr play In °Greek drama, a °mock heroic play with an admixture of comic and serious material, performed at the conclusion of a tragic °trilogy in the Athenian dramatic competitions. Satyrs were mythical worshipers of Dionysus, and the satyr plays recalled the wildness of Dionysian revelry as a reminder of the origins of the drama. It is also believed that the lightness of the satyr play provided an uplift for the audience after the unrelieved seriousness of the three °tragedies. The only extant satyr play is the *Cyclops* (ca. 423 B.C.) of Euripides (ca. 480 B.C.–ca. 406 B.C.). Occasionally, the satyr play was replaced in fourth position by a play of a different nature, such as Euripides' °tragicomedy *Alcestis* (438 B.C.).

See °Greek drama.

scansion The determining of the meter of a passage of verse by dividing the lines into metric feet, counting syllables, and indicating accents. This analytical process, when applied to the study of °verse drama, is often valuable in understanding the structure of the poetry and appreciating the skill and craftsmanship of a great poetic dramatist, such as Shakespeare.

Once scansion has been performed, the meter of the verse is labeled according to the type of metric foot (iambic, trochaic, anapestic, dactyllic, and so on) and the number of feet to the line (monometer for one, dimeter for two, trimeter for three, tetrameter for four, pentameter for five, and so on).

The normal meter for English dramatic verse is °iambic pentameter, discussed in a separate entry. The following example of scansion, performed upon the three opening lines of Shakespeare's *Love's Labor's Lost* (1594–95), utilizes a slash mark (/) to separate the metric feet, a macron (—) to indicate accented syllables, and a breve (◡) for an unaccented syllable.

> Lĕt fāme, / thăt āll / hŭnt āf- / tĕr īn / thĕir līves,
> Līve rēg- / ĭstēred / ŭpōn / ŏur brā- / zĕn tōmbs,
> Ănd thēn / grăce ūs, / ĭn thē /dĭsgrāce / ŏf dēath.

See also °iambic pentameter and °verse drama.

scenario An outline of the °action of a drama, indicating the order of incidents, entrances, and exits; the skeleton of the °plot. The scenario was widely used in the °*commedia dell'arte,* in place of a fully realized script with dialogue. The performers knew when they were to enter and the direction the scene was to take, but the lines themselves were largely improvised.

Scenario is used in the cinema to denote a filmplay in script form.

See also °argument.

scene A subdivision of a play, or of an °act of a play; a unit of dramatic °action in which a single point or effect is achieved. Scene is also used to refer to the location or °setting in which the action is supposed to occur. The concept of what constitutes a scene has varied from period to period and from one culture to another.

In the English dramatic tradition, beginning with Shakespeare and his immediate predecessors, a scene, as Sir Edmund Chambers has pointed out (*The Elizabethan Stage*, 1923), was a "continuous section of action in an unchanged locality." When the stage was emptied of players, the scene was completed and the following action could be supposed to occur in a new location. There are some exceptions to this, but the general principle obtains. Thus, in a play like Shakespeare's *Antony and Cleopatra* (1606–7), there are some forty-two separate scenes, some containing only a speech or two, and a great number of °locales.

The French tradition is different. Beginning with °neoclassical tragedy, the scene was established as that portion of the drama during which the "composition" of °characters on stage remained the same. When an important character left the stage, a scene had concluded, and if a new character entered, a new scene had begun. This occurred, of course, with no break in the action and without a change of locale. It was a literary concept rather than a theatrical one. The French stage was never empty of actors during a single act, and each act, according to the rules, was to be composed of from four to seven scenes. This principle of continuity of action within an act was referred to as *liaison des scènes*. When the plot required a lapse in °dramatic time, the elapsed period was considered to have passed between the acts.

In much °modern drama, scene is defined more in the English sense, and the labeling of acts is not always observed. Tennessee Williams (1912–   ), for example, is inclined to write in a succession of scenes, with no attention to act division. °Episodic drama, such as that of Bertolt Brecht (1898–1956), also follows this practice.

The term "scene" is often used with a qualifying adjective to describe the function of a dramatic unit—"love scene," "expository scene," "transitional scene," "°messenger scene," and the like.

See also °act and °dramatic structure.

scène à faire   A term coined by the French critic Francisque Sarcey (1828–1899) and translated by William Archer (1856–1924) as °obligatory scene, which see.

school plays   Plays of the English °Tudor period (1485–1603) which were written originally for presentation at boys' schools and which played a role in the general development of the English drama. The curricula of these schools emphasized classical studies, and performance by the boys of plays in Latin (and to a lesser extent Greek) was intended to supplement their education in those languages.

As the tradition of school performances evolved, some schools became noted for the proficiency of their boy actors and were invited to perform at court. The boys of Westminster Grammar School are known to have acted before Elizabeth in 1564–65, and the boys of St. Paul's Choir School were frequent performers at her court. A further evolutionary step was the acting of plays in English rather than in the classic languages, and then the writing of plays in the vernacular especially for the boy performers. One well known schoolmaster-playwright was Nicholas Udall (1505–1556), whose rollicking comedy *Ralph Roister Doister* (ca. 1540) is a fine example of the school-play type.

Both the school dramas and the boys' companies remained popular throughout the °Elizabethan period, and many plays by important Elizabethan dramatists—such as John Lyly's (ca. 1554–1606) *Campaspe* (1584)—are known to have been performed by, if not written expressly for, boy actors.

See also °Elizabethan drama.

scriptural drama   See °miracle play.

Senecan influence   The influence exerted upon English Renaissance writers of °tragedy by the characteristics and the °dramatic conventions of the plays of Seneca (ca. 4 B.C.–A.D. 65), the ancient Roman dramatist. Seneca's tragedies were written as °closet dramas, though this was not recognized by the Renaissance writers, who set out to follow the models Seneca had provided. Shakespeare and his contemporaries were greatly influenced by Seneca.

The Senecan influence in °Elizabethan drama includes: (1) °plots based on revenge for the murder of a parent or child; (2) the inclusion of ghosts, especially those seeking vengeance; (3) distraction and insanity, either real or pretended; (4) on-stage murders, torture, maimings, and other displays of carnage; (5) long, vivid descriptions of offstage action by a °messenger; (6) exaggerated dialogue filled with rant and °bombast; (7) frequent allusions to classical °myths and deities; (8) five-act structure; (9) occasional use of the °chorus and °prologue; (10) use of the °soliloquy; and (11) employment of °stichomythia for intensification of dramatic effect.

See also °revenge tragedy and °tragedy of blood.

sensibility   An eighteenth-century term for emotionalism (as opposed to rationalism) in response to a literary or theatrical experience; an extreme reliance upon feelings and sentiment.

See °sentimental comedy.

sentimental comedy   A type of °comedy that dominated the English stage during the middle of the eighteenth century, also referred to as °"weepy comedy." The aim of sentimental comedy was to depict on the stage ordinary human beings beset by misfortune, caught up in distressful situations, but ultimately triumphing over seemingly insurmountable difficulties, thanks to their virtue. The ability of the spectator to respond (emotionally and even tearfully) to such fictional situations was known as °sensibility.

All this represented a sharp departure from the traditional view of comedy as a depiction of the ridiculousness of human folly. In fact, the rise of sentimental comedy can be seen as a reaction against the callousness of the °comedy of manners of the °Restoration period (1660–ca. 1700), which brutally satirized the sexual and social affectations of the London leisure class.

Sentimental comedies typically feature "virtuous" (virginal) young girls in financial difficulties who are loved by honorable young men. The couple cannot declare their mutual love because of various demands of honor. She has no dowry; their parents disapprove; the young man has a "duty" (usually financial) to another lady; and so on. Often, a villainous guardian keeps them apart by concealing the girl's true identity as a wealthy heiress. But in the end, after much self-denial and wailing about "unkind Fate," all is resolved. The lovers are united; the virtuous are rewarded; and any wrongdoing is suitably punished. Such plays are extremely didactic, drawing heavily upon °poetic justice for their °resolutions.

Sentiment began to creep into English comedy during the Restoration period; Colley Cibber's (1671–1757) *Love's Last Shift* (1696) is often cited as an early example. But the greatest shift toward sentiment occurred after the Reverend Jeremy Collier's

(1650–1726) scathing indictment of Restoration comedy, *A Short View of the Immorality and Profaneness of the English Stage,* appeared in 1698. The resulting disenchantment with the amoral, leisure-class comedy of the Restoration, coupled with a rising London middle class, turned the tide in the early part of the eighteenth century. Sir Richard Steele (1672–1729) began to gain popularity on the London stage with his sentimental comedies as early as 1701, and by the time he wrote *The Conscious Lovers* (1722), the finest example of the type, sentimental comedy had completely triumphed over the style of the Restoration comedy. In the °Preface to *The Conscious Lovers,* Steele asserts:

> Any thing that has its foundation in happiness and success, must be allowed to be the object of comedy; and sure it must be an improvement of it, to introduce a joy too exquisite for laughter, that can have no spring but in delight.

Although the type continued well into the nineteenth century, the popularity of sentimental comedy began to decline in the last quarter of the eighteenth century, thanks to the revival of °laughing comedy as written by Oliver Goldsmith (1728–1774) and Richard Brinsley Sheridan (1751–1816). The sentimental impulse has never since been entirely absent from the drama, for sentiment lies at the heart of °melodrama, and melodrama of one kind or another has been the dominant serious genre of the nineteenth and twentieth centuries.

See also °laughing comedy.

set speech   An extended speech by a single °character, in which a number of points are made, with no interruption by other characters. The set speech does not conform to the demands of °realism in that others listen to a carefully developed train of thought before responding with questions or comments. When the response comes, it addresses itself in logical fashion to the points made in the set speech. The device is especially prevalent in °verse drama.

See also °*tirade.*

setting   The fictional location of a dramatic °action as it is represented on the stage; also, the theatrical scenery and properties with which it is realized. The setting of Sophocles' (ca. 496

B.C.–406 B.C.) *Oedipus* (ca. 430 B.C.) is before the palace at Thebes, but the settings of *Hamlet* (1600–1601) vary—from throne room, to graveyard, to Gertrude's closet, and so on. The time period in which an action is placed also can be considered as a part of the setting—"a medieval setting," "an eighteenth-century setting," and so on.

See also °locale.

shadow play   A traditional form of entertainment in some parts of Southeast Asia, principally Java, Malaya, and Bali. Shadow plays are presented on a large translucent screen, which the audience views from the front. Behind it, flat cut-out figures are manipulated by wires and sticks before a strong light. These shadow °puppets are often quite detailed and can present startling effects when operated by skilled artists.

See also °puppet theater.

she-tragedy   A °tragedy in which the central character is a woman. The term came into use in reference to the plays of the English dramatist Nicholas Rowe (1674–1718), such as *The Fair Penitent* (1703) and *The Tragedy of Jane Shore* (1714).

Shrovetide play   A type of medieval German °farce, written probably for the apprentices' revels of the pre-Lenten carnivals. Those that survive display considerable crudeness, although Hans Sachs (1494–1576) wrote some sixty-four that are above the norm. One of his best is *The Wandering Scholar and Exorcist*. The Shrovetide plays paralleled the development of farce in other countries at the same time, such as the °*sotties* of France and the English °interludes.

See °farce.

Siglo de Oro   Literally, "Century of Gold" or "Golden Age"; the hundred years roughly between 1580 and 1680 in Spain, during which Spanish drama flourished and the greatest of Spanish dramatists wrote. The principal playwrights of the Golden Age were Lope de Vega (1562–1635), Pedro Calderón de la Barca (1600–1681), Miguel de Cervantes (1547–1616), and Tirso de Molina (ca. 1584–1648).

See the section on Spain under °Renaissance drama.

simple plot According to Aristotle (384 B.C.–322 B.C.) in Chapter X of the *Poetics* (ca. 335 B.C.), a tragic °plot lacking a °recognition and resulting °reversal and concerned solely with the depiction of suffering (°pathos). The simple plot is inferior to the °complex plot, which contains both recognition and reversal. Classical examples of simple plots might include *The Persians* (472 B.C.) and *Prometheus* (after 468 B.C.) of Aeschylus (525 B.C.–456 B.C.) and *The Trojan Women* (415 B.C.) of Euripides (ca. 480 B.C.–ca. 406 B.C.).
See also °Aristotelian criticism and °complex plot.

situation comedy (also **"sitcom"**) A °comedy whose °action depends almost exclusively upon contrivances of °plot and the exploitation of ludicrous situations, as opposed to °wit or °characterization. Situation comedies serve as standard fare on television, but they have also been popular on the stage throughout the history of the drama. Situation comedy is a variety of °farce. Brandon Thomas's (1849–1914) *Charley's Aunt* (1892) is a well-known modern example.
See °farce.

sketch (also **skit**) A very brief comic °scene, often a part of a variety show or °revue.

slapstick Wild, knockabout stage humor based upon broad visual and physical action. The term derives from an actual stick used by stage comedians to slap one another, dating back at least to the Renaissance. The slapstick was constructed of two narrow slats which produced a loud noise when struck together, as against someone's head or chest. The standard components of slapstick action are beatings, pratfalls, chases, and so on.
The term "slapstick" is often confused with °farce, a dramatic °genre. While much farce does utilize slapstick action, the two terms are distinct.
See °farce and °low comedy.

slice of life (French *tranche de vie*) A structural concept in the drama of °naturalism, referring to the rendering of a stage action as an exact replica of reality. According to the naturalists, a drama should not exhibit a clearly constructed and whole °plot, in the

°Aristotelian sense, for that contradicts true life. The playwright should, rather, show a random selection of °scenes as they might occur in reality. Thus, the °dramatic structure of a naturalistic play appears random. Maksim Gorki's (1868–1936) *The Lower Depths* (1902), for example, begins with the line, "And then?", suggesting that the audience is eavesdropping on a conversation already in progress.

See also °fourth wall and °naturalism.

soap opera   Originally, a form of domestic °melodrama on radio and television, usually serialized, and so named for the soap-manufacturing companies that served as commercial sponsors. Use of the term has been extended to include stage drama exhibiting many of the same features—distressed housewives, marital crises, medical problems, sexual rivalries, class struggles, and so on. The soap opera may be seen as a direct descendant of eighteenth-century °sentimental comedy and °domestic tragedy.

See also °melodrama.

Socialist Realism   The official state doctrine and style of Soviet art and drama, beginning in 1934. Socialist Realism dictates that all plays must serve as didactic illustrations of the virtues of collectivism and other Communist ideals, while illustrating the evils of the capitalist system. It forbids experimentation in nonrealistic "formalism." The strict adherence to Socialist Realism began to decline in the 1960s, but it is still recognized in the Soviet Union as a valid mode of artistic expression. Examples of early plays of this persuasion are *The Muscovite Character* (1949) by Anatoly Safronov; Konstantin Simonov's (1915–   ) *Alien Shadow* (1949), an anti-American polemic; and A. Stein's *Prologue* (1952), a glorification of Stalin.

soliloquy   A speech made by a °character while he is alone on the stage, presumed to be an externalization of his thoughts or emotions; a "thinking out loud," as it were, for the benefit of the audience. As such, the soliloquy is a nonrealistic °dramatic convention and is largely absent from the drama of °realism.

The soliloquy derives from ancient °classical tragedy and was widely utilized in the °Renaissance drama. Some of the more notable passages in Shakespeare's plays are soliloquies, including the

famous "To be or not to be" speech in *Hamlet* (1600–1601). The soliloquy, while it has largely passed from stage usage, has become a perfectly acceptable feature of film technique, through the device of "voice-over." The actor's lips remain still, but we hear his thoughts on the sound track.
See also °aside.

sonnet A form of lyric poetry found occasionally in the °Renaissance drama, including some of the plays of Shakespeare. The sonnet is the most regularized of lyric forms, containing exactly fourteen lines of °iambic pentameter, with a set °rhyme scheme. There are two principal varieties of sonnet: the Italian, best exemplified by the works of Petrarch (1304–1374), and the English or Elizabethan, of which Shakespeare was a master. A sonnet, when employed within the text of a °verse drama, can serve to heighten the poetic effect and intensify the dramatic impact of an action. A particularly fine example is the initial meeting, in Shakespeare's *Romeo and Juliet* (1594–95), of the two lovers (Act I, Scene 5), in which, after a mere fourteen lines, the two strangers fall hopelessly in love.

sottie A type of medieval French °farce, popular in the late-fifteenth and early-sixteenth centuries. The *sotties* evolved from the earlier celebrations of the Feast of Fools and were frequently thinly disguised political, social, or religious °satires whose characters were fools. The Parisian *sotties* were staged by two groups, the Basoche du Palais and Les Enfants sans Souci. The best known *sotties* were written by Pierre Gringoire (1475–ca. 1539). His *The Prince of Fools* (1512), a good example, satirized the quarrel between Louis XII and Pope Julius II.

soubrette The °type character of a young woman, especially a flirtatious maid-servant involved in intrigues. The type goes back at least to the °stock character of Columbina in the °*commedia dell'arte*.

"speaking name" See °tag name.

spectacle One of the six qualitative parts of °tragedy, according to Aristotle (384 B.C.–322 B.C.) in Chapter VI of the *Poetics* (ca.

335 B.C.), the others being °plot, °character, °thought, °diction, and °music. The term is used by Aristotle not in the modern sense of "spectacular" or "extravagant," but to indicate the whole of those elements included in a play because it is intended for staging. Spectacle is not the production itself or the theatrical realization; it is inherent in the structure of the play.

Elements of spectacle in the script cause us to visualize the action when we read it and are often so obvious that we take them for granted. For example, if a line of dialogue reads, "Here she comes now; doesn't she look beautiful?", at least two visual considerations are included: that a female character is entering the stage, and that she must appear beautiful. Again, if one reads in an °Elizabethan drama, "Fie, fie, rain not these blows upon my head!", there is no question but that the speaker is being beaten on the head. These lines contain spectacle. Spectacle is the sum of the visual implications in a drama and is, as Aristotle pointed out, one of the integral parts of a play. It permeates every aspect of the action, beginning with the words of the dialogue.

speech tag In a play script, the name of the speaker preceding a line of dialogue. In performance, of course, it is not spoken, since it is obvious who the speaker is. Technically, speech tags are °stage directions.

stage business Physical activity, usually in °pantomime, incorporated into the performance of a play; stage action outside the °dialogue. A piece of stage business may be as simple as an actor scratching his head, or it may be a fully developed routine or sequence of actions. In the Italian °*commedia dell'arte* the stage business improvised by the performers was extremely important and was known as a °*lazzo* or °*burla*.

stage direction Any portion of a dramatic script not intended to be spoken in performance. Such material includes °speech tags (assigning the lines to the speakers), entrances, exits, physical descriptions of characters, descriptions of °setting, and commentary on line readings (*"hesitantly," "with conviction," "angrily,"* and so on).

In earlier drama stage directions are normally minimal. The ancient texts of Greek °tragedy, for example, include no stage directions, the necessary action being indicated in the dialogue itself.

In a few instances, it is unclear even which characters are speaking the lines. Modern plays, on the other hand, tend to include a substantial number of stage directions. George Bernard Shaw (1856–1950) was particularly generous in including not only elaborate and extensive descriptions of setting (sometimes running to pages!) but also quite detailed explanations of why his characters said what they were saying, as well as what he, the author, felt about it.

Several stage directions, some still in use today, are descended from Latin origins: *exit* (he or she goes off), *exeunt* (they go off), *exeunt* severally (they go off in different directions), *solus* (alone), *manent* (remaining), *omnes* (speaking together), and so on. Renaissance playwrights were particularly fond of including Latin stage directions as a proof of erudition.

stage time The actual time required for the performance of a drama; not to be confused with °dramatic time, which is the fictional time covered by the °action. Normal stage time is from two to four hours.
See also °dramatic time.

Stanislavski System A method of realistic acting developed by Konstantin Stanislavski (1863–1938), which is grounded in the belief that acting is an art. Stanislavski advocated rigorous training, discipline, and self-knowledge in developing character portrayal that is totally truthful and believable. His methods are still employed today in most actor-training institutions, and the system, somewhat modified by the acting teacher Lee Strasberg (1901–   ), is referred to simply as the "Method." The work that best explains Stanislavski's approach to acting is *An Actor Prepares*, which he wrote in 1936.
See also °Moscow Art Theater and °Russian realism.

stasimon In ancient °Greek drama, the term for a choral passage. The *stasima* (plural) alternated with the °episodes in the °plot of a drama.
See °ode.

static drama A concept of dramatic °action espoused by Maurice Maeterlinck (1862–1949) and other French °symbolists in the

1890s. The drama of stasis, also called the Theater of Silence, was an attempt to avoid the furious bustle and activity characteristic of the typical nineteenth-century °melodrama and to evoke the essence of the tragic—the mystic and secret activities of the soul. Maeterlinck's *Pelléas and Mélisande* (1892) is the outstanding example of static drama. The author explained his idea of static drama in an article entitled "The Tragical in Daily Life" (1896), which reads in part:

> I have grown to believe that an old man, seated in his armchair, waiting patiently, with his lamp beside him; giving unconscious ear to all the eternal laws that reign about his house, interpreting, without comprehending, the silence of doors and windows and the quivering voice of the light, submitting with bent head to the presence of his soul and his destiny . . . I have grown to believe that he, motionless as he is, does yet live in reality a deeper, more human and more universal life than the lover who strangles his mistress, the captain who conquers in battle, or "the husband who avenges his honor."

See also °symbolism.

stichomythia A poetic device originating in ancient °classical tragedy, in which individual lines of verse °dialogue are assigned to alternate speakers. Character A is assigned one verse line, Character B takes the following line, Character A takes the next, and so on. Stichomythia was used by the °Greek and °Roman tragedians as a technique for providing contrast to lengthy speeches and choral passages, of which their plays are principally composed. Ordinarily, the passages of stichomythia occur at moments of high tension or °conflict between the characters.

Stichomythia may be used to present thesis and counter-thesis, question and answer, or argument and refutation. In its best form, the structure of the lines is nearly parallel, and cue words lead the thought from one speech to the next. A variation of the technique is °*antilabe,* in which a single verse line is broken up between alternate speakers. This creates an even more intense dramatic effect.

Renaissance dramatists, in imitation of the Ancients, utilized stichomythia in their °tragedies to good effect. A particularly fine example can be found in Act IV, Scene 4 of Shakespeare's *Richard III* (1592–93):

> *Richard.* Say I will love her everlastingly.
> *Elizabeth.* But how long shall that title "ever" last?
> *Richard.* Sweetly in force unto her fair life's end.
> *Elizabeth.* But how long fairly shall her sweet life last?
> *Richard.* As long as heaven and nature lengthens it.
> *Elizabeth.* As long as hell and Richard likes of it.
> *Richard.* Say I, her sovereign, am her subject love.
> *Elizabeth.* But she, your subject, loathes such sovereignty.
> *Richard.* Be eloquent in my behalf to her.
> *Elizabeth.* An honest tale speeds best, being plainly told.
> *Richard.* Then plainly to her tell my loving tale.
> *Elizabeth.* Plain and not honest is too harsh a style.

See also °*antilabe* and °distichomythia.

stock character   Any traditional dramatic stereotype with immediately identifiable characteristics, usually named and costumed according to the prototype. The most famous group of stock characters is descended from the Renaissance Italian °*commedia dell'arte* tradition, which in turn has its origins in the °Atellan farce of ancient Rome. These °characters are immediately known by their names and °masks, and they continue to delight audiences even today. Some of the better known are Arlecchino (Harlequin in French), Pantalone, Columbina, and Pulcinello, who evolved into the puppet character of Punch in the English °Punch-and-Judy tradition.

See also °*commedia dell'arte* and °type character.

strophe   A part of the choral °ode or °*stasimon* of °Greek drama. The strophe is a structural unit of lyric singing and dancing, much like a stanza, which is then duplicated in form by the °antistrophe, rather like an antiphonal response. It has been theorized that the °chorus in a °tragedy, during the singing of the strophe, danced around the circular *orchestra,* then turned and danced in the opposite direction during the antistrophe.

See also °chorus and °ode.

structure   See °dramatic structure.

Stuart drama   See °Jacobean drama and °Caroline drama.

***Sturm und Drang* (Storm and Stress)**   A movement in German drama during the last quarter of the eighteenth century; the beginnings of German °romanticism. The name derives from a play by Friedrich Maximilian Klinger (1752–1831) entitled *Sturm und Drang* (1776). Essentially, the movement was a reaction against °classicism, rather than a unified, organized approach to dramatic form. Thus, there is great variety in the plays representative of *Sturm und Drang*. Generally, however, the plays are loosely constructed (Goethe's *Götz von Berlichingen* [1773] has 54 scenes!), extravagantly emotional in tone and language, and frequently sensational or shocking in subject matter. Other examples of *Sturm und Drang* plays are *The Tutor* (1774) by Jacob M. R. Lenz (1751–1792), *The Child Murderess* (1776) by Heinrich Leopold Wagner (1747–1779), and two well-known early plays of Friedrich Schiller (1759–1805), *The Robbers* (1782) and *Intrigue and Love* (1783). The °Preface to *The Robbers* is often considered an important piece of German °romantic criticism.

Few of the *Sturm und Drang* plays were actually produced, and the chief value of the movement was in weakening the grip of classicism and paving the way for a more mature German drama, after 1785, in the plays of Schiller, Goethe, Heinrich von Kleist (1777–1811), Georg Büchner (1813–1837), and others.
See also °romanticism.

style   The sum of the characteristic techniques a playwright uses to express his ideas; "how" he writes. Critics often write of the style of Aeschylus (525 B.C.–456 B.C.), or of Shakespeare's style. By this they mean the playwright's unique handling of °dramatic structure, °characterization, °diction, versification, °imagery, and so on. Style, then, is what makes a dramatist distinctive and individual, regardless of the qualities he may share with others of his period, philosophical outlook, or school.

Style is used similarly to refer to movements and distinctive types of plays. "Expressionist style" refers to those qualities of a body of works that make °expressionism different from other types of drama.

subplot (also **double plot** or **under-plot**)   A minor or secondary line of °action in a drama that usually either contrasts with or reinforces the major °plot. The subplot is a distinguishing feature of English drama from its beginnings in the °Tudor period through at least the mid-nineteenth century. It is present in almost all °comedies and °tragedies of the °Elizabethan and °Jacobean periods, and in the °Restoration drama it is not unusual to find a play with two and even three subplots interwoven with the main plot.

The subplot can function as a contrasting action, as in Shakespeare's *Love's Labor's Lost* (1594–95), in which the plot of the rustic buffoons serves to set off the elegance and grace of the main plot's courtly figures; or it may serve as a thematic reinforcement of the main plot, as does the Gloucester plot in *King Lear* (1605–6), perhaps the most skillful employment of the subplot in English drama. The use of subplots was definitely discouraged in neoclassical °criticism, accounting for its total absence from French drama. While the French, and even some English neoclassicists, were quick to criticize English drama for its °multi-plotting, it was certainly the device of the subplot that gave to English drama much of its variety and richness.

subtext The life, thoughts, and feelings of a dramatic °character that are not expressed in the °dialogue but can be inferred from suggestive evidence in the text. As a kind of "unwritten life" of a character, subtext is of most value to the actor; the term comes from the °Stanislavski System of acting. Still, the concept of subtext is of considerable value in the critical analysis of °characterization, especially in plays like those of Anton Chekhov (1860–1904), in which the dialogue is often fragmentary and full of nonsequiturs, only suggesting what the characters are presumed to be thinking.

subtitle The secondary or explanatory title of a drama. Subtitles were assigned regularly to seventeenth-century English plays and were usually considered a part of the full title, joined to the main title by the conjunction "or." Examples are *Philaster; or, Love Lies a-Bleeding* (1609) by Francis Beaumont (1584–1616) and John Fletcher (1579–1625), *The Man of Mode; or, Sir Fopling Flutter* (1676) by Sir George Etherege (ca. 1633–1691), and *All for Love; or, The World Well Lost* (1677) by John Dryden (1631–1700). In the °Restoration period (1660–ca. 1700) it was not uncommon for popular plays to be known by their subtitles rather than their main titles.

suffering A rendering of the Greek °*pathos,* an important term in the *Poetics* (ca. 335 B.C.) of Aristotle (384 B.C.–322 B.C.). It also means "deep feeling" or "torment."
See °pathos.

surrealism A reaction against °realism in the arts, including the drama, that flourished in the 1920s and 1930s, principally in Europe. In drama the surrealists, inspired by the works of Alfred Jarry (1873–1907) and Guillaume Apollinaire (1880–1918), issued a "manifesto" in 1924. It defined the form as "pure psychic automatism, by which is intended to express, verbally, in writing, or by other means, the real process of thought. Thought's dictation, in the absence of all control exercised by the reason and outside all esthetic or moral preoccupation" (quoted in Oscar Brockett, *History of the Theatre,* 1974, p. 531). Thus surrealism drew upon the subconscious mind and dreamlike psychic states.

The best example of a surrealist drama is Apollinaire's *The Breasts of Tiresias* (1903, revised for production in 1917), which involves a fantastic transformation of a woman into a man when her breasts float away, balloon-like. She/he then becomes the parent, through sheer willpower, of over forty thousand offspring. The surrealist movement was short-lived, although it did contribute toward the general trend away from realism.
See also °Dadaism.

suspense A state of uncertainty and heightened interest in a reader or spectator, brought about by the playwright's engaging his interest in the play's development; an excited anticipation. Suspense is particularly effective when it involves the fate of a character in whom the audience has become deeply interested.

In the drama suspense is generally of two kinds, one characteristic of °melodrama, the other of °tragedy. In the first instance, suspense is achieved when the audience is uncertain of what the outcome will be. The writer of melodrama teases his audience by making them wonder "who, what, and how." The more surprising and unexpected the outcome, the more effective the work. In tragedy, on the other hand, the suspense resides not in the outcome but in the process whereby the more-or-less inevitable conclusion occurs. It is this suspenseful anticipation of "when" that helps to arouse the °pity and fear of which Aristotle (384 B.C.–322 B.C.) wrote in the *Poetics* (ca. 335 B.C.).

symbolism   A late-nineteenth-century movement in drama and theater that emphasized subjectivity, spirituality, and the mystic internal forces of existence, to the exclusion of direct, external representation. The symbolists, who held sway in Paris in the 1880s and 1890s, paralleled in poetry and drama the movement in painting and music known as impressionism, as represented by the painters Renoir, Monet, and Manet, and the composers Ravel and Debussy.

The symbolists were inspired chiefly by Edgar Allan Poe (1809–1849), Charles Baudelaire (1821–1867), Fyodor Dostoevski (1821–1881) and Richard Wagner (1813–1883). The bulk of their work was in lyric poetry, and their original spokesman was the poet Stéphane Mallarmé (1842–1898). The most successful dramatist to emerge from the symbolist movement was Maurice Maeterlinck (1862–1949), whose *Pelléas and Mélisande* (1892) remains the definitive symbolist drama.

To arrive at a higher level of truth, the symbolists utilized legends, °myths, evocations of mood, and symbols, all of which were to communicate indirectly and even subconsciously with the reader or spectator. While their direct impact on the course of the drama was minimal, the symbolists significantly influenced twentieth-century poets such as William Butler Yeats (1865–1939) and T. S. Eliot (1888–1965). Their influence on modern stage production also was considerable, because of the staging techniques they developed for symbolist plays. They shunned realistic, representational settings and concentrated upon evocations of mood, drawing upon the impressionist painters for their inspiration.

See also °static drama.

synaesthesia   In poetic drama, a technique whereby an appeal is made to two or more of the senses through a single image; the description of one kind of sensation in terms of another. "Wet roses," "velvety music," and "icy green" are examples of the device. Synaesthesia is a common technique in lyric poetry, and it was used by the French symbolists in drama as well. Maurice Maeterlinck's (1862–1949) *Pelléas and Mélisande* (1892), a symbolist drama, contains many examples of synaesthesia.

synopsis   A narrative summary of the °action of a drama; an abstract or resume of the °plot. In printed theatrical programs, synopsis often refers to the scene-by-scene description of the drama's time and place—the °setting of each °scene.
See also °argument and °scenario.

tableau A pose or picture presented by living actors; a device often used at the ends of the °acts of a play in nineteenth-century theater. The *tableau vivant* (living picture) was a more elaborate form of the same device, incorporated into dramatic entertainments in the °medieval theater.

tag line The closing line of a °scene, an °act, or an entire drama. In much nineteenth- and twentieth-century drama, including the °well-made play, the effect of the tag line was thought to be particularly important. A brilliant example is the final line of Ben Hecht's (1894–1964) and Charles MacArthur's (1895–1956) *The Front Page* (1928). Walter Burns, a big Chicago newspaper editor, bids farewell to his star reporter, Hildy Johnson, who is leaving on his honeymoon. Burns, who is determined not to lose Johnson, presents him with his watch as a memento and cheerfully wishes him well. The audience is puzzled by Burns's good nature at the seeming loss of his best reporter until, after Johnson's exit, Burns calmly telephones the sheriff and orders Johnson's arrest. The tag line to the sheriff: "The son of a bitch stole my watch!" The laughter is sure-fire.

tag name A name given to a dramatic character that in some way describes or comments upon his nature. Such names in ancient Roman comedy are sometimes referred to as "speaking names." Tag names are most common in °comedy, especially the English °comedy of humours and °comedy of manners. Some notable examples from the former type are found in the plays of Ben Jonson (1572–1637): Dol Common (a whore), Sir Politick Wouldbe (a pretentious knight), and Zeal-of-the-land Busy (a hypocritical clergyman). Perhaps the most famous of all tag names is in Richard Brinsley Sheridan's (1751–1816) *The Rivals* (1775)—Mrs.

Malaprop, the dowager aunt who always chooses the wrong word, oblivious of her mistakes (see °malapropism).

The fact that comic characters are so frequently given tag names indicates that in comedy character is based chiefly on well-known and easily recognizable types. Tragic characters are seldom named for the traits they possess; their names are more individual—Oedipus, Hamlet, King Lear, and so forth. Even apart from comedy, however, character names can be chosen to make subtle commentary—for example, Willy Loman (low man?) in Arthur Miller's (1916–   ) *Death of a Salesman* (1949) and Dion Anthony (combining Dionysus and St. Anthony) in Eugene O'Neill's (1888–1953) *The Great God Brown* (1926).

Terentian influence   The influence exerted upon Renaissance writers of °comedy by certain characteristics of the plays of Terence (ca. 190 B.C.–159 B.C.), the ancient Roman dramatist. Although there are only six extant comedies by Terence, he was much admired by Renaissance writers. He, along with Plautus (ca. 254 B.C.–184 B.C.), determined the form of comedy from the sixteenth century forward.

The style of Terence was more refined and elegant than that of Plautus, and the Renaissance comic writers, following his lead, strove for refinement of expression. Terence's skill in integrating two Greek °plots into one comedy (called °*contaminatio*) contributed to the English tradition of comic °multi-plotting. The epigrammatic dialogue of the Roman poet also was emulated in the witty speech of the later comic characters, and the Terentian practice of writing polemical °prologues was much imitated. Although his influence was not as strong as that of Plautus, Terence contributed much to the course of modern comedy, especially in England.

See also °Plautine influence and °Roman drama.

tetralogy   A group of four plays, each complete in itself, which together tell a larger story, or which are related by some unifying °theme or idea. Unified tetralogies are rare, but the °chronicle plays of Shakespeare can serve as examples. The history of the houses of York and Lancaster is dramatized in two tetralogies: (1) *Richard II* (1595–96), the two parts of *Henry IV* (1597–98) and

Henry V (1598–99); and (2) the three parts of *Henry VI* (1590–92) together with *Richard III* (1592–93).
  See also °trilogy.

textual criticism The study and analysis of all available texts of a work, by way of establishing as accurately as possible the writer's original intention and of explaining any variants between existing texts. Textual criticism of the drama is extremely important in cases in which the author's manuscript is not available and the original printings of the plays are inaccurate or suspect. Nowhere is this more ably illustrated than in the case of Shakespeare. Textual critics are still at work on some of the more knotty problems raised by variant texts of his plays.
  For futher reading into the problems and techniques of textual criticism, see Fredson Bowers, *The Principles of Bibliographical Description* (1962).
  See also °folio and °quarto.

Theater of Cruelty A phrase coined by the French theorist Antonin Artaud (1896–1948) to describe his concept of what the theatrical experience should be. Artaud's theater represents a revolt against all that is conventional in Western drama in an attempt to capture the mystical and metaphysical qualities of Oriental theater—especially of the Balinese dance-drama.
  In his writings Artaud denounced the theater of language. He sought other means of communication. The Theater of Cruelty was to be spectacular and mythic in scope, drawing upon subjects violent, passionate, and occasionally bloody. There was to be no separation between spectator and performance. Indeed, Artaud advocated seating the audience in the center of the spectacle, with the action surrounding them on several stages interconnected by elevated catwalks. The emphasis was to be upon the nonverbal— upon visual spectacle, startling and expressive lighting, and a full range of sounds, from vocal incantation to exotic, quasi-musical noises. The appeal of the Theater of Cruelty was always to be to the senses, not to the intellect or to the rational instincts. It was in this sense—in its force, its violence, its attack upon the sensibilities—that his theater was to be "cruel."
  Artaud's ideas were articulated in the 1930s, and although his

ideal has not come to pass, his writings have had some influence upon the course of twentieth-century theater. There have recently been notable experiments in nonverbal theater (Jerzy Grotowski's [1933–   ] work), new sound and light media have been developed (as in the rock-musical *Hair* [1967]), and the proscenium stage is no longer the norm. The British director Peter Brook has staged productions much in the spirit of what Artaud advocated.

Some of Artaud's writings were collected in 1938 under the title *The Theater and Its Double,* published in English in 1958.

Theater of Fact   See °documentary drama.

Theater of Silence   See °static drama.

Theater of the Absurd   The name given by the contemporary critic Martin Esslin (1918–   ) to a body of dramatic works, mainly French, which arose in the 1950s and which were closely allied to existentialist thought. Absurdism in the drama is the depiction of the randomness and meaninglessness of life, rendered in nonrealistic and unorthodox forms. The absurdists, who have been concerned with the irrationality of human experience, often utilize chaotic structure, incongruous events, seriocomic and ironic effects, and irrational language.

The roots of absurdism in France can be found as far back as Alfred Jarry's (1873–1907) *King Ubu* (1896), but the first major work of the genre was *Waiting for Godot* (1953) by Samuel Beckett (1906–   ), possibly the finest of absurdist dramas. Other major playwrights associated with absurdism, according to Esslin (*The Theatre of the Absurd,* 1961), are Eugène Ionesco (1912–   ), whose *The Bald Soprano* (1949) and *Rhinoceros* (1960) have enjoyed great popularity; Jean Genet (1910–   ), author of *The Balcony* (1956); Arthur Adamov (1908–1971); and a number of other dramatists less purely absurdist but significantly influenced by the style: Max Frisch (1911–   ) in Switzerland, Harold Pinter (1930–   ) in England, and Edward Albee (1928–   ) and Arthur Kopit (1938–   ) in America, among others.

See also °existentialist drama.

Theater of the Grotesque   A short-lived movement in Italian drama during World War I, which emphasized the ironic and the macabre in contemporary life. The movement was named after a play by Luigi Chiarelli (1884–1947), *The Mask and the Face* (1916), which was billed as "a grotesque in three acts." This ironic comedy contrasts a man's role as seen by the public and his private identity. Luigi Pirandello (1867–1936), the greatest of modern Italian dramatists, is said to have been influenced by this "grotesque" movement, and many of his comedies reflect its concern with identity and °masks. Notable in this respect are his *Right You Are, If You Think You Are* (1916) and *Henry IV* (1922).

theme   In general, the central or dominating ideas with which a drama is concerned; the abstract concept which is made concrete through a specific °action and its °characters. Theme is a fairly imprecise and much overused term in dramatic °criticism. It is highly questionable that any major dramatist ever began writing with the intent of illustrating a theme. The theme is, rather, something which we infer from the °plot, the characters, the language, the °imagery, or a combination of all these. It is a result or an end product of the total work.

Theme is often used in contradistinction to "thesis," the former denoting the general concern of a work and the latter a specific message or didactic viewpoint.

thesis play   (French *pièce à thèse*)   A play posing some social problem and advocating particular solutions to it. Such plays were common during the last quarter of the nineteenth century.

See °drama of discussion and °problem play.

thought   (Greek *dianoia*)   One of the six qualitative parts of °tragedy, according to Aristotle (384 b.c.–322 b.c.) in Chapter VI of the *Poetics* (ca. 335 b.c.), the others being °plot, °character, °diction, °music, and °spectacle. By "thought," Aristotle meant those speeches in the play that are not directly related to the characters' actions and purposes but are rather meant to convey general or abstracted truths, philosophical observations, motives, and attitudes. Thought is the "ability to say whatever is pertinent and fitting to the occasion. . . . Thought we find in those speeches in which men show that something is or is not, or utter some universal proposition."

Three Unities A prescriptive theory of dramatic construction
that evolved from Renaissance Italian and French °criticism, and
dominated the criticism of drama until at least the nineteenth century. The theory of the Three Unities stated that an acceptable
°tragedy must conform to the Unities of Time, Place, and Action.
Unity of Time meant that the °dramatic time of the °action could
not exceed one day, though a day was variously understood to
mean anything between twelve and twenty-four hours. Unity of
Place confined the dramatic action to one °locale, although there
were variable allowances here, too. "One place" could be considered, for example, as one city. Unity of Action decreed that the
use of °subplots or a °double action was not allowed, and that a
tragic action should concern only one central °hero.

The theory of the Three Unities grew from poor translations
and misinterpretations of the *Poetics* (ca. 335 B.C.) of Aristotle (384
B.C.–322 B.C.) in the sixteenth century, but it quickly took on an
authority of its own and was virtually unquestioned on the Continent. Only in Elizabethan England, where native dramatic traditions outweighed esoteric theories, were the Unities usually ignored.

Of the Three Unities, Unity of Action is the only one acknowledged by Aristotle. Aristotelian °unity does not, however, preclude the use of subplots, and English drama has proved that
°multi-plotting can be handled artistically. The theory of Unity of
Time derived from the observation that most °Greek drama
shows a coincidence between °dramatic time and °stage time—
that the action is continuous and time is supposed to pass without
interruption. Unity of Time stemmed also from a statement in the
Poetics (Chapter V) that tragedy endeavored to confine its action
within "one circuit of the sun." However, this Aristotelian phrase
had nothing to do with a discussion of unity. Unity of Place arose
as a corollary of Unity of Time, thanks largely to the Italian critic
Lodovico Castelvetro (1505–1571) (*On Aristotle's Poetics,* 1570). According to Castelvetro, if dramatic action is continuous, so that
dramatic time and stage time are identical, it is impossible to sup-
pose that the locale or °setting has changed. Therefore, the action
can occur in only one place. ·

Once the theory of Three Unities became critical dogma, it was
almost universally defended and justified in many ways—on the
basis of °verisimilitude, by example in the Greek models, on the

grounds of morality and °didacticism, and so on. French dramatists observed the Unities almost without exception until the early-nineteenth century, when °romanticism partly defeated neoclassical attitudes. English tragedy during the °Restoration and eighteenth century strove to adhere to the doctrine of the Three Unities, in spite of its foreignness to all that was good in the English tradition (for example, the plays of Shakespeare).

Of course, there is no artistic justification for the limitations imposed on °dramatic structure by the Three Unities, and they eventually lost currency. Dr. Samuel Johnson (1709–1784), in the famous Preface to his edition of Shakespeare (1765), struck an effective blow against the Unities, as did Victor Hugo (1802–1885) in France in the following century (the Preface to *Cromwell*, 1827). With the growing impulse toward romanticism, the theory of the Three Unities passed from dramaturgical practice, and it is today chiefly an interesting phenomenon in the history of dramatic criticism. (Oddly enough, in his recently published *Memoirs* [1975], the American dramatist Tennessee Williams [1912–   ] cites *Cat on a Hot Tin Roof* [1954] as the favorite of all of his plays "because of its classic unities of time and place." The specter of the Three Unities refuses to be laid to rest.)

See also °neoclassicism, °unity, and °verisimilitude.

tirade   An extended speech by a single character in a drama, especially in French romantic drama of the nineteenth century. Such *tirades* were usually designed to give a popular actor the opportunity to impress the audience with his skillful delivery, much like an aria in °opera. For examples, see Victor Hugo's (1802–1885) *Hernani* (1830), in Act III of which the king, Don Carlos, engages in a °soliloquy of several minutes' duration; or see Edmond Rostand's (1868–1918) *Cyrano de Bergerac* (1897), which contains at least three *tirades* for the title character.

See also °set speech and °soliloquy.

tragedy   A form of drama, in either prose or verse, profoundly serious in nature, possessing the power to affect the reader or viewer, which generally deals with the stressful nature of the human condition and the nobility of the human spirit in the face of such stress. A precise definition of tragedy is impossible, since the word has different meanings in various critical systems and the °genre is exemplified by widely varying works from several periods.

Tragedy originated in Athens in the fifth century B.C. and was defined a century later by Aristotle (384 B.C.–322 B.C.) in his *Poetics* (ca. 335 B.C.). Both the characteristics of the Greek plays themselves and Aristotle's commentary upon them have affected all subsequent concepts of the nature of tragedy and of the principles to which it should conform. To the Greeks, however, tragedy (which means simply "goat song," from the original °dithyrambs sung by goatskin-clad worshipers of Dionysus) was simply any serious drama, as distinguished from °comedy. The diversity evident in the extant Greek plays is so great as to make any simple definition of "Greek tragedy" impossible.

Aristotle defines the best form of tragedy as that which deals with the fortunes and misfortunes of characters who are "good" but who suffer because they commit some error (°*hamartia*) unknowingly. Further, he states that tragedy deals with sufferings among blood relations. Children bring misfortune upon parents, brother harms brother, and so on. When a tragedy is skillfully constructed, Aristotle states, it portrays events that are pitiable and fearful, and it is these incidents of °pity and fear and their °catharsis that account for the affective power of tragedy and the concomitant pleasure it provides for us. (The subject of catharsis is a difficult one; see the discussion under the separate entry.)

Tragedy declined in the fourth century B.C., being superseded by °New Comedy and forms that we today would identify as °melodrama. It was not until the Golden Age of °Elizabethan drama that great tragedy appeared once more, as written by Shakespeare and his contemporaries. Elizabethan tragedy was based upon many influences but drew heavily for its models on the plays of Seneca (ca. 4 B.C.–A.D. 65), the ancient Roman dramatist. For this reason, the English plays are filled with action—deeds of blood, deaths, revenge, and the supernatural. They also differ vastly from Greek tragedy in structure, encompassing greater spans of °dramatic time and diversity of °locales, and eliminating almost entirely the °chorus, which was an integral part of the classical works. Nevertheless, the basic seriousness of intent remains. The great writers of Elizabethan tragedy show us as much about the human spirit as did the Greeks, and the English plays can be profoundly moving even today. Again, tragedy declined as English drama fell into the °decadence of the °Jacobean and °Caroline periods.

The French poets wrote °neoclassical tragedies in the seventeenth century, but their works strike us today as artificial, essentially literary, and inhibited by the many rules of °neoclassicism to which the writers were forced to adhere. The best of the period are those by Jean Racine (1639–1699), who drew heavily upon the Greek °myths, but even Racine's tragedies seem little more than copies of the ancient originals. At best, it can be said that French neoclassical tragedy reflects the spirit of its time, championing the ideal of °"reason and good sense" and warning against the excesses of passion in human conduct.

A peculiar variety of tragedy emerged in eighteenth-century England. A type of °bourgeois drama called °domestic tragedy, it depicted the sorrows and trials of middle-class life, intentionally avoiding the heroic tone of the traditional tragic plays. Such works were written in prose and were largely aimed at moral instruction. The intent was to teach the middle-class audience of the perils of sinful ways and of the joyful rewards with which Providence would bless the virtuous. As such, it may be dismissed as sentimental °melodrama, although its practitioners identified it as tragedy. A good example is George Lillo's (1693–1739) *The London Merchant* (1731).

Tragedy largely disappeared from the European stage during the late-eighteenth and nineteenth centuries, and melodrama was the dominant serious form of drama until roughly the 1870s, when Henrik Ibsen (1828–1906) began writing serious plays of great merit. Ibsen's tragedies, and those of the playwrights who have followed him, tend to draw upon common, recognizable figures for their central characters, and these figures are usually depicted as victims of external forces—the environment, society, heredity, and so on. These middle-class and sometimes lower-class characters, in the better plays, are seen to struggle against oppressive circumstances with all the seriousness and determination of the ancient Greek °heroes. In such plays, modern tragedy speaks to its audience and can be profoundly moving. A notable example is Arthur Miller's (1916–   ) *Death of a Salesman* (1949) with its tragic common Everyman, Willy Loman.

Although its precise forms and styles have varied from period to period, tragedy in every age is the dramatic form in which writers have expressed their deepest concerns and their insights into the human condition.

tragedy of blood   A type of popular °revenge tragedy in °Elizabethan and °Jacobean England, filled with sensational and bloody events, such as murders, mutilations, torture, and so on. The character of the tragedy of blood owes much to the °Senecan influence. The tragedies of the ancient Roman writer Seneca (ca. 4 B.C.–A.D. 65) were filled with descriptions of horrible and bloody incidents, since they were intended for reading and not for the theater. The Elizabethan dramatists transferred this sensational material to the stage in their plays, much to the delight of their audiences, who were accustomed to bear-baitings, public executions, and the like.

Some of the better known tragedies of blood of this period are Shakespeare's *Titus Andronicus* (1593–94), in which hands are cut off, a tongue is cut out, and several characters are brutally murdered; Thomas Kyd's (1558–1594) *The Spanish Tragedy* (ca. 1587); and John Webster's (ca. 1580–ca. 1630) *The White Devil* (1609–12) and *The Duchess of Malfi* (1613–14).

See also °revenge tragedy and °Senecan influence.

tragic dilemma   A situation frequently found in °tragedy, especially that of the classical period, in which a character is put in the position of choosing between two alternative courses of action, neither of which will spare him an unhappy fate. A good example of the tragic dilemma is found in *The Libation Bearers* (458 B.C.) of Aeschylus (525 B.C.–456 B.C.), in which Orestes is commanded by the god Apollo to avenge his father's death by murdering his slayer, Clytemnestra, who is Orestes' mother. To the Greeks, matricide was clearly an act of pollution. Thus, Orestes will be guilty of offending the gods, whether or not he acts to avenge his father's murder.

tragic flaw   See °*hamartia.*

tragic irony   See °dramatic irony.

tragic waste, doctrine of   The °dramatic convention in early English °tragedy of increasing the effect and significance of the death of the °protagonist by surrounding it with subsidiary deaths. Thus, in Shakespeare's *Hamlet* (1600–1601), the impact of the tragic action is meant to be heightened by the slaughter of Laertes, Gertrude, and Claudius, in addition to the death of Hamlet, in the play's final scene.

tragicomedy In general, a type of play mixing serious and comic material, especially when the °plot is mainly suitable to °tragedy but results in a happy ending. Tragicomedy may be traced back to the ancient °Greek drama; plays like Euripides' (ca. 480 B.C.–ca. 406 B.C.) *Alcestis* (438 B.C.) and *Helen* (412 B.C.) exemplify the type. The English tragicomedy of the °Elizabethan and °Jacobean drama was quite popular and generally employed all the elements of tragedy, leading up to a surprise turn of events resulting in good fortune for the characters. Shakespeare employed this structure in *Cymbeline* (1609–10) and *The Winter's Tale* (1610–11), and Francis Beaumont (1584–1616) and John Fletcher (1579–1625) had much success with it. Fletcher defined the form in the introduction to *The Faithful Shepherdess* (1609):

> A tragicomedy is not so called in respect of mirth and killing, but in respect it wants deaths, which is enough to make it no tragedy, yet brings some near it, which is enough to make it no comedy, which must be a representation of familiar people, with such kind of trouble as no life be question'd; so that a god is as lawful in this [tragicomedy] as in a tragedy, and mean people as in a comedy.

In the twentieth century the term "tragicomedy" has taken on a different meaning, due in part to the development of the °Theater of the Absurd.' In modern parlance a tragicomedy is essentially a deeply serious play which includes elements of comic interest and which often causes one to laugh at the very moments in which one experiences the most profound sense of the serious. ' *Waiting for Godot* (1953) by Samuel Beckett (1906–   ) is a play of this sort. Modern tragicomedy, if it continues to evolve, may make the traditional historical distinctions between tragedy and comedy meaningless in the dramatic literature of the future.

tranche de vie See °slice of life.

transformational drama   A type of nonrealistic °presentational play, developed in the 1960s, in which the actors are required to shift dramatic identities during the play and assume a number of different roles, one after the other. Occasionally, the actors may even "transform" themselves into inanimate objects. Transformational drama evolved largely from improvisational work by actors in training, but it was formalized by dramatist Megan Terry (1932–   ) in some of her plays, such as *Keep Tightly Closed in a Cool Dry Place* (1966) and *Calm Down, Mother* (1966).

trilogy   A group of three plays, each complete in itself, unified by their relationship to a larger narrative or to a central °theme or idea. In the formative years of °Greek drama, poets wrote their °tragedies in trilogies, plus a fourth work of less seriousness, called a °satyr play. The only extant trilogy is the *Oresteia* (458 B.C.) of Aeschylus (525 B.C.–456 B.C.). Composed of *Agamemnon, The Libation Bearers,* and *Eumenides,* it dramatizes the curse on the House of Atreus. In Aeschylus' time the practice of writing unified trilogies was abandoned, although poets continued to submit groups of three individual plays for competition.

In the °modern drama, the outstanding example of a trilogy is Eugene O'Neill's (1888–1953) *Mourning Becomes Electra* (1931), a modern retelling of the Oresteian °myth. Shakespeare's three *Henry VI* plays (1590–92) provide an early English example.

See also °tetralogy.

tritagonist   In °Greek drama, the third actor. Sophocles (ca. 496 B.C.–406 B.C.) is credited with the addition of a third actor to play a variety of minor roles. The evidence indicates that such actors were highly skilled in fast changes of costume and °masks.

See °protagonist.

trope   A phrase or musical passage interpolated into the liturgy of the Catholic church, beginning in the eighth and ninth centuries. Such passages originated as simple musical embellishments, evolved to include verbal content, and finally took on °dialogue form, serving as the basis for °liturgical drama and eventually for the great cycles of °miracle plays that flourished throughout the Continent and England during the Middle Ages. The most famous trope, often called the beginning of modern drama, is the °"*Quem Quaeritis*" from the Easter Mass. See °miracle play and °"*Quem Quaeritis*."

Tudor drama The drama produced in England under the Tudor monarchs: Henry VII (reign 1485–1509), Henry VIII (1509–1547), Edward VI (1547–1553), Mary I (1553–1558), and Elizabeth I (1558–1603). The Tudor period marks the beginning of English drama.

The variety of types of Tudor drama is great, including °school plays, °morality plays, °masques, °pageants, °court comedy, °romantic comedy, °tragedy, and others. The greatest dramatic works of the Tudor dynasty were produced during the reign of Elizabeth I and are discussed under °Elizabethan drama.

The most important playwrights of the early Tudor period were Henry Medwall (flourished 1490–1500), author of the first English secular comedy, *Fulgens and Lucrece* (ca. 1497); John Heywood (ca. 1497–ca. 1580), whose best-known comedies are *The Play of the Weather* (1533) and *The Four PP* (ca. 1530); Nicholas Udall (1505–1556), whose comedy *Ralph Roister Doister* (ca. 1540) is still read and occasionally performed; and Thomas Sackville (1536–1608) and Thomas Norton (1532–1584) whose co-authored *Gorboduc* (1562) is acknowledged as the first English tragedy.

See also °Elizabethan drama and separate entries under the various subjects cross-referenced here.

type character A dramatic °character exhibiting well-known characteristics of a general class of characters, rather than seeming to emerge as a distinctly individual creation. In serious drama, such as °tragedy, characters who tend toward type are generally said to be badly written, but in °comedy the most effective characters seem to be clearly identifiable types—the parasite, the hypocrite, the glutton, the miser, and so forth. Even so, many great tragic characters can be assigned to distinct type categories. Hamlet, for example, conforms to the type of the avenger in much °revenge tragedy.

Aristotle (384 B.C.–322 B.C.) recognized (*Poetics* [ca. 335 B.C.], Chapter IX) that whereas the characters and titles of tragedy are generally named for individuals (*Antigone, Hamlet, Phaedra*), comedy is more often named for the type that the central character illustrates (*The Miser, The Imaginary Invalid, The Odd Couple*). Clearly, all drama, to some extent, is concerned with illustrating generalized or universal types of behavior.

See also °stock character.

under-plot See °subplot.

Unities See °Three Unities.

unity The essential organizing principle in a drama that assures
its cohesiveness, its completeness, and its oneness. Aristotle (384
B.C.–322 B.C.) first recognized the necessity for unity in his *Poetics*
(ca. 335 B.C.). In Chapter VIII he states:

> It is necessary that the parts of the action be put together in
> such a way that if any one part is transposed or removed, the
> whole will be disordered and disunified. For that whose pres-
> ence or absence has no evident effect is no part of the whole.

What is implied is that unity consists of a correctness and appro-
priateness in the way that the parts of a work are arranged. The
superfluous has no place, and the arrangement cannot be random. Ordering and selection, as in any artistic creation, are necessary. The *Poetics* considers no other kind of unity.

Renaissance critics, misinterpreting Aristotle, proposed a theory
of °Three Unities (Time, Place, and Action). Their writings affected the course of dramatic literature for centuries, though
today the theory of Three Unities wields little influence. Unity, to
the modern writer or critic, is considered much in the Aristotelian
sense as stated above, and there are various ways of achieving
such unity in the drama.

A play can be unified through its °theme, all of its component
parts contributing necessarily to a central idea or concept. Such
would be the unity of much philosophic drama, including the
plays of such dramatists as Samuel Beckett (1906–   ), Eugene
Ionesco (1912–   ), and Jean-Paul Sartre (1905–   ). Unity is
also achieved partly by tone. The tone or mood of a drama produces an emotional effect upon the audience, and that effect

should be unified. Finally, some dramatists today still strive for unity through intensification, as practiced by the Ancients. They limit the °dramatic time of the °action and keep it within one °locale. Many modern dramatists also limit the number of characters, even to the point of keeping the central ones always before us. This, too, achieves the effect of unity. A good example is Arthur Miller's (1916–   ) *The Price* (1968), an uninterrupted two-hour action with only four characters.

See also °wholeness.

universality That quality of a dramatic work which makes it seem applicable to all men at all times, regardless of the particulars of the period and culture which might seem to limit it. According to Aristotle (384 B.C.–322 B.C.), universality is a characteristic of artistic literature and is absent from historical or factual writing. In Chapter IX of the *Poetics* (ca. 335 B.C.) Aristotle defines "the universal" as "what sort of man turns out to say or do what sort of thing according to probability and necessity." Universality, then, is a kind of general truth, according to what is observable in human nature as we know it—what would *probably* happen to this kind of °character, considering the circumstances as the poet has presented them. Universality reinforces credibility.

History on the other hand, says Aristotle, deals with the reporting of facts—"what Alcibiades did or experienced." And in history (real life) people often do things that are uncharacteristic, arbitrary, random, or inexplicable. Such individual or particular behavior tells us no universal truths about men, as does poetry (including drama). Thus, according to Aristotle, poetry is more "philosophical" than history and, for artistic considerations, superior.

See also °probability and necessity.

University Wits A term used by critics in reference to a number of young writers who came to London in the 1580s from the universities of Cambridge and Oxford and contributed to the literary life of Elizabethan England, especially in the drama. The University Wits included Robert Greene (1558–1592), George Peele (1558?–1597?), Thomas Nashe (1567–1601), Thomas Kyd (1558–1594), and the great Christopher Marlowe (1564–1593).

John Lyly (ca. 1554–1606), the major writer of °court comedy, is sometimes included in this group.

The University Wits contributed much to the development of °Elizabethan drama, establishing forms for °revenge tragedy (Kyd), °romantic comedy (Greene and Peele), and the °chronicle play (Marlowe), among others. Marlowe was particularly influential upon his contemporaries and successors, including Shakespeare. It may be said that Christopher Marlowe brought to full development English dramatic °blank verse. His tragedies, such as *Doctor Faustus* (ca. 1588) and *Tamburlaine* (1587–88), are ranked among the finest of the Elizabethan age.

See also °Elizabethan drama.

vaudeville A popular form of theatrical entertainment in Europe and America from the 1890s to about the 1930s. Essentially a refined form of °burlesque, vaudeville featured a series of variety acts, songs, °sketches, and short comic plays performed on a single bill. Animal acts, such as trained seals, were especially popular. Featured players were known as "headliners" and many notable twentieth-century entertainers began their careers in vaudeville. Vaudeville may be seen as the forerunner of the topical °revue and of many contemporary television variety shows.
See also °burlesque and °revue.

vehicle A term often used to refer to a play, when the work serves some particular purpose beyond pure entertainment. A play might, for example, serve as a vehicle for a starring actor or actress, or it might be a vehicle for the author's views on some subject.

Verfremdungseffekt See °alienation.

verisimilitude In general, the appearance in a literary work of truth and actuality; truth to life. In the drama verisimilitude became a controlling doctrine of °neoclassicism, dictating that the audience at a play would accept whatever was represented on the stage as truly happening, exactly as events happen in real life. Thus, the doctrine of verisimilitude represents one of the major misconceptions in the history of dramatic °criticism. It accounts in part for the wide acceptance of the theory of the °Three Unities, for according to verisimilitude an audience could not be expected to believe that a °scene had changed from, say, Athens to Rome, when they knew that they were still in the place they had originally come to—the theater. Nor could they be expected to accept a long span of °dramatic time, when they knew that they had been in the theater for only a few hours. Thus, Unity of Place and Unity of Time were corollaries of the belief in verisimilitude. This belief strikes us today as ludicrous, but it did indeed control neoclassical thought in regard to the nature of "truth" in the theater. The defeat of the doctrine of verisimilitude came slowly. John Dryden (1631–1700) was one of the earlier critics to assert that a "play is still a play; we know we are to be deceived, and we desire to be so" (*An Essay of Dramatic Poesy*, 1668). A century later, Dr. Samuel Johnson (1709–1784) in his famous Preface to Shakespeare's plays (1765) stated: "It is false, that any representation is mistaken for reality; that any dramatic fable in its materiality was ever credible, or, for a single moment, was ever credited." And in 1817 Samuel Taylor Coleridge (1772–1834) added his voice to the defeat of verisimilitude with his famous statement (*Biographia Literaria*, Chapter XIV) of the °"willing suspension of disbelief," which recognized that in matters of poetry one voluntarily chooses, for the moment, not to disbelieve what is obviously not real.

See also °neoclassicism and °Three Unities.

verse drama   Drama written in any poetic form and intended for performance, as distinguished from °closet drama (written for reading only) and °dramatic poetry (used most often to refer to lyric poetry with some dramatic elements, such as the °monologue).

Until the modern period, verse was universally accepted as the proper medium for drama, beginning with the poetic masterpieces of the °Greek drama. There have been exceptions, however. John Lyly (ca. 1554–1606) developed a comic prose style known as °euphuism in the Court of Elizabeth I, and some eighteenth-century °tragedy was written in prose. One notable example is George Lillo's (1693–1739) *The London Merchant* (1731), a middle-class °domestic tragedy. Moreover, the °comedy of the Restoration period (1660–ca. 1700) was written in prose, as was most comedy thereafter.

Notwithstanding these historical exceptions, it is only in the last hundred years or less that prose has become the dominant medium for dramatic composition. Today playwrights who attempt to restore verse drama to the stage—for example, Maxwell Anderson (1888–1959), T. S. Eliot (1888–1965), and Christopher Fry (1907–   )—are viewed by some as oddities.

By writing in verse, dramatists are able to heighten dramatic effect and achieve a greater affective power. Much of the beauty of Greek tragedy and of °Elizabethan drama is due to effects possible only in verse.

See also °prose drama, °blank verse, and °iambic pentameter.

Vice figure   A popular °type character in the medieval English °morality play who was eventually absorbed into the °Elizabethan drama. The Vice of the early moralities was the chief tempter of the Mankind-hero and an allegorical representation of evil. As such, he was the most important figure in the plays and a source of great delight to the audience. Frequently he was carried off the stage at the end of the play by a devil. His role became increasingly comic as the morality form evolved, and in the Elizabethan drama his vestigial remains can be seen in characters of °villains and °Machiavels, as well as in less evil (but no less entertaining) characters, such as the Falstaff of Shakespeare's *Henry IV* plays (1597–98).

See also °Machiavel, °morality play, and °villain.

villain   A type of dramatic °character who is predisposed to evil and commits acts harmful to the °hero or °protagonist. The term implies a degree of malevolence in the character that excludes any redeeming features, although in practice some dramatic villains are seen to reform or repent at the end of the play. Villains are inappropriate for high °tragedy, as Aristotle (384 B.C.–322 B.C.) noted in Chapter XIII of the *Poetics* (ca. 335 B.C.), and they are found almost exclusively in °melodrama, where questions of good and evil are simplified and rendered as absolutes.

See also °Machiavel.

weepy comedy A type of °comedy aimed not at producing laughter in the spectator but at causing him to weep over the happy events of the action. Such comedy, more frequently called °sentimental comedy, was extremely popular in France and England during the eighteenth century. According to Sir Richard Steele (1672–1729), a leading practitioner of the type, weepy comedy aimed at the depiction of a "joy too exquisite for laughter."
See °*comédie larmoyante* and °sentimental comedy.

Weimar classicism The style of dramatic composition and theatrical production fostered by Johann Wolfgang von Goethe (1749–1832) and Friedrich Schiller (1759–1805) in the court theater at Weimar (Germany) between 1798 and 1805. Goethe and Schiller attempted to turn away from the °romanticism then so dominant on the stage and restore to the theater some of the spirit, if not the form, of °classicism. Their thesis was that the drama should not merely create an illusion of real life but seek to transform experience through artistic means. To this end they wrote plays in verse, strove for carefully patterned structure, and stylized their productions. Weimar classicism, which became famous throughout Germany, is best represented in drama by Goethe's *Iphigenia in Tauris* (1787) and by Schiller's *Wallenstein's Camp* (1798), which opened the Hoftheater in Weimar under Goethe's direction.
See also °*Sturm und Drang.*

well-made play From the French *pièce bien faite,* a term that developed in late-nineteenth-century criticism to describe the type of tightly structured "formula" play written first by Eugène Scribe (1791–1861) and later by other Frenchmen such as Alexandre Dumas *fils* (1823–1895) and Victorien Sardou (1831–1908). Important English practitioners of the well-made play included Sir

Arthur Wing Pinero (1855–1934) and Henry Arthur Jones (1851–1929).

Essentially, the well-made play formula emphasizes principles of construction, at the expense of content or significant subject matter. It depends upon °suspense, excessive contrivance, and surprises. It is basically a formula for °melodrama, with its reliance on scenes of tearful emotion, secrets known to the audience but not to the characters, °discoveries, misunderstandings, °reversals, and °poetic justice.

With the advent of °naturalism, social drama, and the °problem play, the well-made play fell into critical disrepute, and the term is to this day used pejoratively to indicate a type of slick, superficial melodrama with trivial subject matter. Such major dramatists as George Bernard Shaw (1856–1950) and Henrik Ibsen (1828–1906) denounced the type, although ironically both were masters of play construction and utilized the better elements of the well-made play's structure. Shaw went so far as to coin the term °"Sardoodledom," from the name of Sardou, to ridicule the form.

wholeness   One of the requisites of °plot for an effective °tragedy, according to the *Poetics* (ca. 335 B.C.) of Aristotle (384 B.C.–322 B.C.). Aristotle defines "wholeness" of plot (Chapter VII) as the characteristic of having a beginning, a middle, and an end. As simplistic as this appears, his reasoning is sound, for he implies that an effective plot is not a random arrangement of incidents, but a purposeful ordering to create a completed °action. "Beginning" implies that °antecedent action is not necessary in order for the plot to commence; "middle" suggests that something develops after and because of the initiation of action; and "end" means that at the conclusion nothing is left unfinished. The action is completed; this is wholeness.

See also °dramatic structure and °plot.

"willing suspension of disbelief"   A phrase coined by the English poet Samuel Taylor Coleridge (1772–1834) in his *Biographia Literaria* (1817, Chapter XIV) to identify the basis upon which "poetic faith" operates. Coleridge's contention, which is in accordance with much modern aesthetic theory, is that in the reading of literature (including the drama) we do not accept as realistically possible those actions that are portrayed. Instead, we voluntarily choose not to disbelieve them—to suspend "for the moment" our disbelief and accept the poet's vision as an artistic representation. Coleridge's idea of willing suspension of disbelief can be extended to include the theatrical event, as an explanation of our faith in the truth of a representation on the stage. We do, indeed, suspend our disbelief in viewing a play and share for the moment the artistic transformation of reality offered us. Never for a moment do we believe that what we see in the theater is really happening or, for that matter, that it could ever happen.

See also °aesthetic distance and °*optique du théâtre.*

wit and humor Two words used frequently in °criticism in reference to the fundamental material of °comedy and the sources of comic delight, although their exact meanings and the distinction between them are not always clear. It was roughly in 1800 that these terms became associated with the laughable, each one designating a more-or-less distinct comic source.

Wit is primarily intellectual, appealing to the mind's ability to perceive conceptual relationships, similarities, and comparisons. Thus, it is essentially verbal and expresses itself in °puns, °quibbles, epigrams, the *bon mot,* and other forms of word play. According to the *Oxford English Dictionary,* wit is:

> that quality of speech or writing which consists in the apt association of thought and expression, calculated to surprise and delight by its unexpectedness; . . . later always with reference to the utterance of brilliant or sparkling things in an amusing way.

The writers of the Restoration °comedy of manners were masters of wit, as was Oscar Wilde (1856–1900) in plays like *Lady Windermere's Fan* (1892) and *The Importance of Being Earnest* (1895).

Humor (an American spelling of °humour) was originally a physiological term which took on psychological implications and came to mean, roughly, "eccentricity" (see °comedy of humours). Thus humor seems to refer more to the nature of character as a source of laughter—specifically, the exhibition of characters in circumstances that reveal their foibles and follies. Thus, most of Molière's (1622–1673) great comedies—for example, *Tartuffe* (1664), *The Misanthrope* (1666), and *The Imaginary Invalid* (1673)—

depend principally upon humor, although they are certainly not devoid of wit.

See also °comedy and °comic theory.

wittol   A favorite °type character in English drama of the seventeenth century. The wittol is a man who knows that his wife is unfaithful to him but either does not care or pretends not to. The wittol is a figure of contempt, even more than an ordinary cuckold. Cuckoldry was, of course, a popular subject of °ridicule in °Restoration comedy.

zanni A group of characters in the Italian °*commedia dell'arte* who conform to the type of the comic servant. The term derives from a corruption of *Gianni* (Johnny) and has been anglicized to "zany," denoting a madcap °clown. Probably the best known of the *zanni* today is Harlequin (or Arlecchino).

See °*commedia dell'arte* and °stock character.

zarzuela A form of Spanish °lyric theater in which music is combined with spoken dialogue, dating back to the °*Siglo de Oro* or Golden Age of Spanish culture (roughly 1580–1680). Named for one of Philip IV's palaces, La Zarzuela, at which many of them were originally performed, the *zarzuelas* were first made popular by the Spanish dramatist Pedro Calderón de la Barca (1600–1681). The tradition continued into the eighteenth century, the musical and dramatic values of the form improving, chiefly through the work of dramatist Ramón de la Cruz (1731–1794), who developed the *zarzuela* into a type of °ballad-opera.

The *zarzuela* declined in popularity in the early-nineteenth century, largely attributable to an influx of Italian influences on Spanish musical theater, but with the founding of the Teatro de la Zarzuela in 1856 the *zarzuela* gained the stature of a national lyric theater form. Influential in this development was Tomás Bretón (1850–1923), whose *Dolores* (1895) serves as an excellent example of the *zarzuela* brought to a high degree of artistry. The *zarzuela* continues to be written and performed today throughout the Spanish-speaking world.

A Chronology of Dramatic
Theory and Criticism

Each entry in the following chronological list of critical works is generally considered to be a milestone in the history of dramatic criticism. The list is not exhaustive; doubtless, some important works have been omitted, particularly from the modern period. Still, these works taken together represent an account of the history and development of Western thought on the drama as a literary art form, from Aristotle through the present century.

Each entry contains a brief note on the content or significance of the work, together with cross-references to relevant articles in the body of this handbook (where applicable) and a citation of a volume in which the work itself may be found. These bibliographical citations have been selected as the sources most probably available to the average reader. Usually the critical work will be found in its entirety, although in some cases the citation is of a volume in which only key selections from the work may be found.

ca. 335 B.C. Aristotle. *Poetics.*
This ancient work by one of the greatest of Greek philosophers has been the foundation for Western literary and dramatic criticism for over 2,000 years. It is an extremely difficult work—fragmentary, possibly incomplete, and subject to a number of varying translations. It may be called a definition of the form of tragedy, and it approaches the subject through an analysis of the constituent parts of the form and a comparison of tragedy with epic narrative. The *Poetics* profoundly influenced all subsequent writings on the drama and is even today an extremely important critical work.
See °Aristotelian criticism.
Suggested reference: Leon Golden, tr., and O. B. Hardison, commentator. *Aristotle's Poetics.* Englewood Cliffs, N.J., 1968.

ca. 4th–2nd centuries B.C. *Tractatus Coislinianus.*
This anonymous work is virtually the only treatise on comedy from the ancient world. It is quite fragmentary, being a schematic diagram rather than a developed essay. Lane Cooper has translated this work and used it as the basis for a reconstruction of a theory of comedy as it might have been written by Aristotle.

Suggested reference: Lane Cooper. *An Aristotelian Theory of Comedy.* New York, 1969.

24 B.C.–20 B.C. Horace (Quintus Horatius Flaccus). "Epistle to the Pisos," also called *Art of Poetry.*
Horace's epistle on poetry is the single most important piece of literary criticism from the ancient Roman world. It stands in sharp contrast to Aristotle's *Poetics* in its loose organization and its prescriptive tone. Its influence upon Western drama has been considerable; it became an authoritative source for Renaissance critics even before the discovery of Aristotle's work.
See °Horatian criticism.
Suggested reference: Edward H. Blakeney, ed. *Horace on the Art of Poetry.* London, 1928.

ca. 350 A.D. Aelius Donatus. "Comedy and Tragedy."
The Middle Ages were nearly devoid of dramatic criticism, but Donatus, one of the last Roman scholars, is typical of the intermittent attempts to preserve the critical tradition, even in an era in which the theater was largely dormant. Donatus' emphasis upon the distinctions between tragedy and comedy was to be picked up in most Renaissance criticism.
Suggested reference: Barrett H. Clark, ed. *European Theories of the Drama,* rev. ed. New York, 1966.

1536. Bernardino Daniello. *Poetics.*
Daniello was the earliest of the Italian Renaissance critics to formulate a theory of poetry based on classical authority. His *Poetics* presents a mixture of Aristotelian and Horatian ideas, a phenomenon which was to characterize all subsequent Renaissance criticism.
See °neoclassicism.
Suggested reference: Selections in Barrett H. Clark, ed. *European Theories of the Drama,* rev. ed. New York, 1966.

1543. Giambattista Giraldi Cinthio. *Discourse on Comedies and Tragedies.*
Cinthio, a writer of prose narratives as well as tragedies, was the first critic to formulate the idea of Unity of Time, based upon a statement in Aristotle's *Poetics.* He exerted a considerable influence upon subsequent Italian theorists, leading eventually to the statement of the Three Unities in the writing of Lodovico Castelvetro.
See °neoclassicism and °Three Unities.
Suggested reference: Selections in Bernard F. Dukore, ed. *Dramatic Theory and Criticism.* New York, 1974.

1548. Franciscus Robortellus. *On Comedy.*
Robortellus was one of the first thoroughly Aristotelian critics in

Renaissance Italy, and his comments on Unity of Time were respected and emulated in subsequent criticism. This work also reinforced Renaissance ideas on the strict separation of comedy and tragedy.

See °neoclassicism and °Three Unities.

Suggested reference: Marvin T. Herrick. *Comic Theory in the Sixteenth Century.* Urbana, Ill., 1964.

1561. Julius Caesar Scaliger. *Poetics.*

The most influential of Italian Renaissance critics apart from Castelvetro, Scaliger relied heavily upon Aristotle, contributing to the idea of the Three Unities and planting the misconception of verisimilitude in the minds of subsequent commentators.

See °neoclassicism, °Three Unities, and °verisimilitude.

Suggested reference: Frederick Morgan Padelford, ed. *Select Translations from Scaliger's "Poetics."* New York, 1905.

1570. Lodovico Castelvetro, *On Aristotle's "Poetics."*

Castelvetro's commentary on Aristotle represents the culmination of Italian Renaissance dramatic criticism. Here are summarized all the ideas that were to influence criticism for at least another 200 years: the Three Unities, separation of comedy and tragedy, verisimilitude, and so on. Castelvetro is surely the most important of all the Italian Renaissance critics.

See °neoclassicism, °Three Unities, and °verisimilitude.

Suggested reference: H. B. Charlton. *Castelvetro's Theory of Poetry.* Manchester University Press, 1913.

1572. Jean de la Taille. "The Art of Tragedy."

Although the seventeenth century was the great age of French dramatic criticism, Jean de la Taille represents an earlier, sixteenth-century viewpoint—one that pretty much follows the Italian lead. This critical essay advocates the Three Unities and confirms the influence of Aristotle in French criticism.

See °neoclassicism and °Three Unities.

Suggested reference: Barrett H. Clark, ed. *European Theories of the Drama,* rev. ed. New York, 1966.

1579–80. Thomas Lodge. *A Defence of Poetry, Music, and Stage Plays.*

One of the earliest pieces of English dramatic criticism, Lodge's defense of the theater, although fairly conventional and unimaginative, anticipated the tone of subsequent English critics. The English seemed devoted principally to the defense of the drama in the face of adverse criticism from neoclassical scholars.

Suggested reference: G. Gregory Smith, ed. *Elizabethan Critical Essays,* Vol. I. Oxford, 1904.

1583 (published **1595**). Sir Philip Sidney. *The Defense of Poesy.*
Sidney's essay is the most important piece of English dramatic criticism before the seventeenth century. Sidney was writing before the Golden Age of Shakespeare and his contemporaries, and his defense of literary art is based on neoclassical ideals: the Three Unities, decorum, verisimilitude, and moral usefulness. Sidney represents the beginning of a pseudo-Aristotelian critical tradition in England.
See °decorum, °Three Unities, and °verisimilitude.
Suggested reference: Katherine Duncan-Jones and Jan Van Dorsten, eds. *Miscellaneous Prose of Sir Philip Sidney.* Oxford, 1973.

1600–25. Ben Jonson. Brief introductory passages from selected plays, such as: the Induction to *Every Man Out of His Humour* (1599); the Preface to *Sejanus, His Fall* (1603); the Dedication to *Volpone* (1606). Also, Jonson's major critical work, *Timber; or, Discoveries Made upon Men and Matter* (1620–25).
Jonson was the most neoclassical of all the successful English playwrights of his time, and his criticism reflects this inclination. In *Timber* Jonson advances the cause of Aristotle. He was the first to write critically of Shakespeare's plays.
Suggested reference: C. H. Herford and Percy and Evelyn Simpson, eds. *Ben Jonson,* Vol. VIII. Oxford, 1947.

1609. Lope de Vega. *The New Art of Writing Plays.*
Lope de Vega, the most prolific playwright the world has ever known, explains here, in an offhand and charming manner, his approach to dramaturgy, which violated nearly every rule of neoclassicism. The Spanish, like the English, largely ignored the rules and restrictions of which the French were so fond. Lope de Vega defends the mixture of comic and serious material, dismisses the Three Unities, and claims that the ultimate test of the worth of a drama is its popularity with its audience.
See °*comedia,* °Renaissance drama (section on Spain), and °*Siglo de Oro.*
Suggested reference: Brander Matthews, ed. *Papers on Playmaking.* New York, 1957.

1637. Georges de Scudéry. *Observations on "The Cid."*
Scudéry's indictment of the popular Corneille tragedy *The Cid* (1636) was typical of the attacks leveled at that drama by those who objected to Corneille's violation of the neoclassical rules. Scudéry objects to *The Cid* on five counts: (1) its trivial plot; (2) its violation of the rules; (3) its "irregularity"; (4) its inferior verse; and (5) its lack of originality. All in all, this critical work expresses the typical French neoclassical viewpoint.

See °"*Cid* controversy" and °neoclassicism.
Suggested reference: Bernard F. Dukore, ed. *Dramatic Theory and Criticism*. New York, 1974.

1637. Pierre Corneille. "Apologetic Letter."
This is Corneille's answer to Scudéry's indictment of his tragedy *The Cid* (1636). It is important only as a rebuttal to the absurd objections raised by the neoclassical Scudéry.
See °"*Cid* controversy."
Suggested reference: Bernard F. Dukore, ed. *Dramatic Theory and Criticism*. New York, 1974.

1638. Jean Chapelain et al. *The Opinions of the Académie Française* . . .
Chapelain was designated by the members of the Académie Française to write the definitive assessment and condemnation of Corneille's *The Cid* (1636), probably under the close supervision of Cardinal Richelieu, France's "aesthetic legislator." Chapelain neatly summarizes the viewpoint of the French neoclassicists in this essay, defending verisimilitude, the Three Unities, decorum, and the didactic value of tragedy.
See °academies, °"*Cid* controversy," and °neoclassicism.
Suggested reference: Bernard F. Dukore, ed. *Dramatic Theory and Criticism*. New York, 1974.

1657. François Hedelin, Abbot of Aubignac. *The Whole Art of the Stage*.
D'Aubignac's work is perhaps the first practical manual of playwriting, though it essentially echoes the beliefs of the French neoclassicists, sometimes to the extent of absurdity. D'Aubignac defends the neoclassical rules, insists upon the instructive value of drama, and recognizes the effect of plays in production, rather than as mere literary works.
See °neoclassicism.
Suggested reference: Selections in Bernard F. Dukore, ed., *Dramatic Theory and Criticism*. New York, 1974.

1660. Pierre Corneille. *Discourses*.
In a series of fairly perceptive essays, Corneille attempts to reconcile his own knowledge of what succeeds on the stage with the accepted rules and restrictions of neoclassicism. Corneille's criticism is perhaps the most valid and artistically astute of all French neoclassical writings on the drama, from the modern viewpoint. This is the work of a practicing playwright who sensed the disparity between prescriptive theories and successful practice.
See °"*Cid* controversy" and °neoclassicism.
Suggested reference: Selections in Bernard F. Dukore, ed. *Dramatic Theory and Criticism*. New York, 1974.

1668. John Dryden. *An Essay of Dramatic Poesy.*
Dryden was the giant of his age—the greatest of English Restoration
literary figures. His tragedy *All for Love* (1677) is perhaps the only
Restoration tragedy of any worth. In this essay Dryden considers the
relative merits of ancient and modern drama and of French and English drama. The essay is cast as a dialogue between four writers,
each arguing a different position. The final speaker, Neander (Dryden himself), defends the "variety and copiousness" of English
drama over the coldness and severity of French neoclassical drama.
This work, although written by an English neoclassicist, is one of the
first to question the doctrine of verisimilitude and to recognize the
worth of native English techniques.
See ° neoclassicism and ° Restoration drama.
Suggested reference: Samuel Hynes, ed. *English Literary Criticism:
Restoration and Eighteenth Century.* New York, 1963.
Other significant critical works by Dryden: *A Defense of an Essay of
Dramatic Poesy* (1668); Preface to *All for Love* (1678); Preface to
Troilus and Cressida (1679).

1668–77. Jean Racine. Various brief prefaces to his plays, including: First
Preface to *Andromache* (1668); First Preface to *Britannicus* (1670); Preface
to *Berenice* (1674); Preface to *Phaedra* (1677).
A successful dramatist rather than a critic, Racine nevertheless offered in his prefaces a glimpse of his ideas on the drama. He was a
thorough neoclassicist, and the sum of his comments in these selections reveals the French neoclassical attitude from a practical standpoint.
See ° neoclassical tragedy and ° neoclassicism.
Suggested reference: Selections in Bernard F. Dukore, ed. *Dramatic Theory and Criticism.* New York, 1974.

1672. Charles de Marguetel de Saint-Denis, Seigneur de Saint-Évremond.
Of Ancient and Modern Tragedy.
Saint-Évremond may be called one of the first comparative critics.
His exposure to English drama allowed him to adopt an approach to
dramatic criticism far less prescriptive and rigid than that of his
French contemporaries. He questioned Aristotle, championed Cor-
neille, and appealed to success in the theater as a criterion of good
drama.
Suggested reference: Bernard F. Dukore, ed. *Dramatic Theory and
Criticism.* New York, 1974.

1674. Nicholas Boileau-Despréaux. *The Art of Poetry.*
Boileau, an extremely influential critic in his time, wrote his *Art of Poetry* in rhymed couplets and in defense of the neoclassical rules for

drama. It is an interesting work for its dogmatic and prescriptive approach to drama, but its importance lies in its great influence in neoclassical France rather than in any intrinsic merit as criticism. See °neoclassicism.

Suggested reference: Albert S. Cook, ed. *The Art of Poetry: The Poetical Treatises of Horace, Vida, and Boileau.* Boston, 1892.

1693. Thomas Rymer. *A Short View of Tragedy.*
Rymer, much respected in Restoration England, represents the extreme of neoclassical pedantry. His adherence to dramatic rules was almost fanatic, and his criticism is of value today chiefly for its entertainment value. In *A Short View of Tragedy* Rymer lashes out at Shakespeare, measuring *Othello* against neoclassical rules and arriving at the opinion that this great Shakespearean tragedy is worthless claptrap.

See °neoclassicism and °Restoration Drama.

Suggested reference: Joel E. Spingarn, ed. *Critical Essays of the Seventeenth Century,* Vol. II. Bloomington, Ind., 1957.

1698. Jeremy Collier. *A Short View of the Immorality and Profaneness of the English Stage.*
Collier's lengthy indictment of the licentiousness of the Restoration drama was instrumental in bringing an end to the comedy of sexual intrigue and turning public tastes toward sentimental comedy. Collier, a clergyman, found sympathetic readers in London society. As a result of this work, some leading dramatists were indicted for writing obscenity. The work also sparked a number of rebuttals from several playwrights. *A Short View* is generally considered a turning point in the course of English drama and makes for interesting reading.

See °comedy of manners, °Restoration drama, and °sentimental comedy.

Suggested references: Jeremy Collier. *A Short View . . . ,* ed. Arthur Freeman. New York, 1972; and Sr. Rose Anthony. *The Jeremy Collier Stage Controversy: 1698–1726.* New York, 1966.

1698. John Dennis. *The Usefulness of the Stage to the Happiness of Mankind, to Government, and to Religion.*
Dennis's work is notable for its advocacy of poetic justice in dramatic writing. Dennis saw the drama as a useful instrument of moral improvement, a view common among the neoclassical critics.

See °poetic justice.

Suggested reference: Edward Niles Hooker, ed. *The Critical Works of John Dennis,* 2 vols. Baltimore, 1939–43.

1711–12. Joseph Addison and Richard Steele. *The Spectator* (nos. 39, 40, 51, 65, and 290).

These selections give a sampling of enlightened eighteenth-century criticism, as represented by two major essayists of the period. Both men were fond of the theater and wrote primarily in defense of the drama. Addison wrote the finest of eighteenth-century classical tragedies, *Cato* (1713), and Steele contributed a number of sentimental comedies to the English stage, most notably *The Conscious Lovers* (1722).

See °classical tragedy and °sentimental comedy.

Suggested reference: Gregory Smith, ed. *The Spectator*. New York, 1907.

1723. Richard Steele. Preface to *The Conscious Lovers*.

Steele's comedy, performed in 1722, is today considered the best example of eighteenth-century English sentimental comedy. In the Preface, Steele explains his aim in writing the play and makes the case for this peculiar style of comedy that dominated the stage in the eighteenth century. This is a brief but important critical document.

See °sentimental comedy.

Suggested reference: Samuel Hynes, ed. *English Literary Criticism: Restoration and Eighteenth Century*. New York, 1963.

1731. George Lillo. Dedication to *The London Merchant*.

The London Merchant is the most famous example of eighteenth-century English domestic tragedy. In its dedication, Lillo states the case for bourgeois drama better than any other writer of the period. This brief epistle dedicatory is important as an indication of the writer's faith in the didactic value of drama.

See °bourgeois drama and °domestic tragedy.

Suggested reference: John Gassner and Ralph G. Allen, eds. *Theatre and Drama in the Making*, Vol. I. Boston, 1964.

1731. Voltaire (François Marie Arouet). *A Discourse on Tragedy*.

Voltaire's essay represents the continuation of a strict, conservative neoclassical approach to drama brought forward into eighteenth-century France. Voltaire has been called a reactionary classicist, and his advocacy of rhymed verse, the Three Unities, and other neoclassical ideals helped to keep France in the grip of classicism for the entire century.

See °classicism.

Suggested reference: John Gassner and Ralph G. Allen, eds. *Theatre and Drama in the Making*, Vol. I. Boston, 1964.

1758. Denis Diderot. *On Dramatic Poetry*.

Diderot was one of the first major critics to question the dominance of neoclassicism in France and to advocate greater freedom in dramatic composition. His own plays are decidedly in the middle-class, sentimental mode, and he contributed to the gradual decline of classicism in the eighteenth century.

See °*drame.*

Suggested reference: Selections in John Gassner and Ralph G. Allen, eds. *Theatre and Drama in the Making,* Vol. I. Boston, 1964.

1765. Samuel Johnson. Preface to *The Plays of William Shakespeare.*

Dr. Johnson, the leading literary figure of his age, was one of the early champions of Shakespeare's art. This preface to Johnson's own edition of Shakespeare's plays is extremely important as a recognition, by a noted classicist, of the beauties of the romantic mode of playwriting. Johnson praises Shakespeare's art of characterization, catalogues his faults, and calls for an end to the reverence for the Three Unities. This last feature is perhaps the most significant aspect of the entire Preface. It may be considered the beginning of the end of classicism in England.

See °classicism and °romanticism.

Suggested reference: D. Nichol Smith, ed. *Eighteenth Century Essays on Shakespeare.* New York, 1962.

1769. Gotthold Ephraim Lessing. *Hamburg Dramaturgy.*

Lessing was the first and perhaps the greatest of German dramatic critics. With him, the German drama may be said to have been born. In this work he renounces the French models and theories, advocating the romantic style of dramaturgy practiced in England by Shakespeare and his successors. Lessing also advocated—and practiced—a form of bourgeois drama depicting common types of characters. *Hamburg Dramaturgy,* actually a collection of separate essays, is an extremely important critical document in support of romantic drama.

See °*Sturm und Drang,* °romanticism, and °romantic tragedy.

Suggested reference: G. E. Lessing. *Hamburg Dramaturgy,* tr. Helen Zimmern. New York, 1962.

1772. Oliver Goldsmith. "An Essay on the Theatre; or, A Comparison Between Sentimental and Laughing Comedy."

This brief essay states succinctly and convincingly the case for humorous, critical comedy over the maudlin sentimental comedy that dominated the English stage during the first three-quarters of the eighteenth century. Goldsmith questions whether the mission of comedy ought to be the exhibition of human distress or the exposure of human folly. The latter is the course advocated by Goldsmith, both in this essay and in his own plays. This work in some measure contributed to the demise of sentimental comedy and the restoration of "laughing comedy" to the English stage.

See °comedy, °comic theory, °laughing comedy, and °sentimental comedy.

Suggested reference: Samuel Hynes, ed. *English Literary Criticism: Restoration and Eighteenth Century.* New York, 1963.

1782–92. Friedrich Schiller. Various brief critical works including: Preface to *The Robbers* (1782); *The Stage as a Moral Institution* (1784); and *On the Tragic Art* (1792).

Schiller continued Lessing's lead in advocating and practicing a romantic style of dramaturgy. Generally Schiller rejects the distilled sublimity of French neoclassicism and favors mixtures of the grotesque with the sublime, the common with the noble, the sensual with the rational. Schiller, along with Goethe, was a motivating force in the *Sturm und Drang* movement as well as a founder of Weimar classicism.

See °romanticism, °*Strum und Drang,* and °Weimar classicism.

Suggested reference: Nathan Haskell Dole, ed. *The Complete Works of Friedrich Schiller.* Boston, 1910.

1809–11. August Wilhelm von Schlegel. *Lectures on Dramatic Art and Literature.*

Schlegel has been recognized as a founder of the romantic school in German literature, and this series of lectures, delivered in 1808 and published in 1809 and 1811, contrasts classic and romantic drama. Schlegel translated Shakespeare and greatly admired the English dramatic style. In these lectures he considers the combination of the poetic with the theatrical, the nature of tragedy and comedy, the Three Unities, and other important aspects of dramaturgy.

See °ideal spectator and °romanticism.

Suggested reference: A. W. von Schlegel. *A Course of Lectures on Dramatic Art and Literature,* tr. John Black, 2nd ed. London, 1889.

1818–36. Samuel Taylor Coleridge. Various essays on the drama including: "The Progress of the Drama" (1818); "Greek Drama" (1818); "On the Characteristics of Shakespeare's Plays" (1836); "Notes on *Hamlet*" (1836); "Notes on *The Tempest*" (1836); and "Shakespeare's English Historical Plays" (1836).

Coleridge was the leading English romantic critic of the drama, and in his essays he praises the heterogeneity of dramatic material in romantic drama, especially as represented in the plays of Shakespeare. Coleridge's statement of the "willing suspension of disbelief" may be said to have begun modern aesthetic criticism of the drama.

See °romanticism and °"willing suspension of disbelief."

Suggested reference: Henry Nelson Coleridge, ed. *The Literary Remains of Samuel Taylor Coleridge,* Vol. II. London, 1836–39.

1819. William Hazlitt. *Lectures on the English Comic Writers.*

Hazlitt's *Lectures* constitutes the first major inquiry into comedy by an

English critic. The subject of comedy subsequently received much critical attention. Hazlitt cites incongruity as the source of the ludicrous and establishes a differentiation between "wit" and "humor." His observations have served as a point of departure for many subsequent comic theorists.

See °comedy, °comic theory, and °wit and humor.

Suggested reference: William Hazlitt. *Lectures on the English Comic Writers.* London, 1951.

1822. Charles Lamb. "On the Artificial Comedy of the Last Century."

In this brief essay Lamb makes a significant contribution to dramatic criticism by examining the comedy of manners of the Restoration years and attempting to justify it to a society that largely ignored it. Lamb's observations on the amorality of the Restoration comedies shed light upon the nature of comedy in general.

See °comedy, °comic theory, °comedy of manners, and °Restoration drama.

Suggested reference: Paul Lauter, ed. *Theories of Comedy.* New York, 1964.

1823–30. Johann Wolfgang von Goethe. *Conversations of Goethe with Eckermann and Soret.*

Goethe is certainly the literary giant of Germany, but his critical commentaries are scattered and difficult to characterize. A staunch romantic in his early years, he tended later toward classicism. Eckermann's account of the *Conversations* brings together many of Goethe's ideas and is the single most complete source of Goethe's critical statements on the theater.

See °romanticism and °*Sturm und Drang.*

Suggested references: John Oxenford, tr. *Conversations with Goethe by Eckermann* . . . New York, 1951; and Joel E. Spingarn, ed. *Goethe's Critical Essays.* New York, 1921.

1827. Victor Hugo. Preface to *Cromwell.*

This important critical document is a veritable manifesto of French romanticism and was largely responsible for the defeat of neoclassical ideals in French drama. Hugo was an iconoclast, and his Preface calls for an end to all rules and complete freedom for the creative spirit. Hugo advocates a mixture of the "grotesque" with the sublime and posits a rather far-fetched theory of the evolution of literary art.

See °grotesque and °romanticism.

Suggested reference: John Gassner and Ralph G. Allen, eds. *Theatre and Drama in the Making,* Vol. II. Boston, 1964.

1849 and **1871.** Richard Wagner. "The Art Work of the Future," and "The Purpose of the Opera."

Wagner, best known for his music-dramas, was one of the earliest writers to advocate the synthesis of all the disparate theatrical arts into one composite art form. Music and poetry were to become one, realized by technical means—staging and lighting—under the control of one central artistic consciousness. These essays, among others, express many of the ideas that had a profound effect upon such successive theater figures as Adolphe Appia and Edward Gordon Craig.
See °music-drama.
Suggested references: Edward L. Burlingame. *Art, Life, and Theories of Richard Wagner.* New York, 1875; and William Ashton Ellis, tr. *Richard Wagner's Prose Works,* Vol. I. London, 1892.

1863. Gustav Freytag. *Technique of the Drama.*
Freytag's work was one of the more influential of modern inquiries into the structure of drama. Using essentially romantic tragedy as a basis for discussion, Freytag posited the famous "Freytag Pyramid," which identified the structural function for each act of a five-act play. Freytag's analysis of dramatic structure is interesting, although his work has been superseded by more creditable works on the subject.
See °Freytag Pyramid.
Suggested reference: Gustav Freytag. *Technique of the Drama.* New York, 1894.

1871. Friedrich Nietzsche. *The Birth of Tragedy.*
Influenced by Wagner's ideas of artistic synthesis, Nietzsche advanced the idea that tragedy is the result of the fusion of two basic impulses in human conduct—the Apollonian, representing the rational instincts, and the Dionysiac, representing the impulsive and the inspirational. This statement of the Apollonian-Dionysiac duality influenced subsequent philosophers who attempted to explain the absence of great tragedy from the modern dramatic tradition.
See °Apollonian-Dionysiac duality.
Suggested reference: Friedrich Nietzsche. *The Birth of Tragedy, and The Genealogy of Morals,* tr. Francis Golffing. New York, 1956.

1873 and **1880.** Émile Zola. Preface to *Thérèse Raquin* (1873) and "Naturalism on the Stage," from *The Experimental Novel* (1880).
Zola was chief spokesman for the naturalist movement, which dominated European drama in the late-nineteenth century. His play *Thérèse Raquin,* adapted from his own novel, exemplifies all that the naturalists believed in, and the Preface summarizes these beliefs. "Naturalism on the Stage" attacks both the romantic drama and the popular well-made play in advocating the techniques of naturalism.
See °fourth wall, °naturalism, and °slice of life.
Suggested references: Émile Zola. *The Experimental Novel, and Other*

Essays, tr. Belle M. Sherman. New York, 1893; and John Gassner and Ralph G. Allen, eds. *Theatre and Drama in the Making,* Vol. II. Boston, 1964.

1877. George Meredith. *An Essay on Comedy.*
Meredith, an English novelist, displayed a serious interest in the nature of comedy, and this essay is an excellent work on the civilizing effect of high comedy. Meredith differentiates among satire, irony, comedy, and humor. He further establishes the idea that comedy is a manifestation of the intellect and cultivation of the society from which it springs and that it attests to the equality of the sexes.
See °comic theory and °high comedy.
Suggested reference: Wylie Sypher, ed. *Comedy.* Garden City, N.Y., 1956.

1888. August Strindberg. Preface to *Miss Julie.*
The Preface to Strindberg's masterpiece of psychological realism may be considered a manifesto of dramatic and theatrical realism. Strindberg objects to all that is artificial and conventional in playwriting and staging, and advocates a new spirit of realism in the theater. This essay is an extremely important document in modern dramatic criticism as well as a fascinating glimpse into Strindberg's own methods.
See °psychological realism and °realism.
Suggested reference: Bernard F. Dukore, ed. *Dramatic Theory and Criticism.* New York, 1974.

1894. Ferdinand Brunetière. *The Law of the Drama.*
Of interest today chiefly as a curiosity, Brunetière's work was devoted to isolating the one element of dramatic composition that distinguishes the drama from all other literary genres, and this one element was "conflict." Brunetière attempted, moreover, to distinguish between comedy, tragedy, farce, and melodrama on the basis of the nature of the conflict. "Brunetière's Law," as it came to be called, exerted considerable influence upon subsequent critics and would-be dramatists, but his Law is of little value from the modern viewpoint.
See °Brunetière's Law and °conflict.
Suggested reference: Ferdinand Brunetière. *The Law of the Drama,* tr. Philip M. Hayden. New York, 1914.

1896. Maurice Maeterlinck. "The Tragical in Daily Life."
Maeterlinck was chief spokesman for the Theater of Silence or the static drama. In this brief but interesting essay Maeterlinck advances the idea that true tragedy resides in the silent, private musings of the secret soul rather than in the overt, sensational catastrophes of traditional drama. Maeterlinck's *Pelléas and Mélisande* (1892) came closer

than any other play to the realization of his somewhat esoteric ideas on the drama of stasis.

See °static drama and °symbolism.

Suggested reference: Maurice Maeterlinck. *The Treasury of the Humble,* tr. Alfred Sutro. New York, 1900.

1900. Henri Bergson. *Laughter.*

Of the many modern inquiries into the subject of comedy, Bergson's small book is perhaps the most penetrating and the most thought-provoking. Starting with the very basic mechanical patterns that induce laughter in human beings, Bergson expands his theory to encompass an entire concept of dramatic comedy. At the core of his work is the theory of inelasticity in human conduct or rigidity of character. Bergson's carefully developed theory should be of interest to any student of comic writing.

See °comedy and °comic theory.

Suggested source: Wylie Sypher, ed. *Comedy.* Garden City, N.Y., 1956.

1912. William Archer. *Play-Making.*

This was one of the first of many twentieth-century manuals on playwriting. Archer analyzes dramatic structure and techniques, touching upon such subjects as "point of attack," "climax," "exposition," and "obligatory scene." Archer's work is based almost exclusively upon his observations of the well-made play and represents a fairly old-fashioned approach to playwriting. Archer, incidentally, disputes "Brunetiere's Law."

Suggested reference: William Archer. *Play-Making.* Boston, 1912.

1913. George Bernard Shaw. *The Quintessence of Ibsenism.*

Shaw's critical accomplishments are staggering, but this particular work is especially significant for its recognition of the new style of drama pioneered by Henrik Ibsen in the last quarter of the nineteenth century. This work examines all of Ibsen's plays with a particular view to the technical accomplishments Ibsen innovated.

See °modern drama.

Suggested reference: George Bernard Shaw. *The Quintessence of Ibsenism.* New York, 1959.

ca. 1930. Bertolt Brecht. "The Modern Theatre Is the Epic Theatre."

Brecht is unquestionably one of the great playwrights and dramatic theorists of the twentieth century. This essay explains in capsule form his concept of epic theater, a mode of writing and staging that has had a profound influence upon dramatists and directors of our time.

See °alienation, °epic theater, and °presentationalism.

Suggested reference: John Willett, tr. *Brecht on Theatre*. New York, 1964.

1938. Antonin Artaud. *The Theater and Its Double.*
This is a collection of the writings of Antonin Artaud, one of the more interesting theorists of the twentieth century. Artaud advocated the "Theater of Cruelty" and totally mistrusted the written drama as a basis for theatrical art. His theories, though extreme, have greatly influenced modern writers and producers.
See °Theater of Cruelty.
Suggested reference: Antonin Artaud. *The Theater and Its Double,* tr. Mary Caroline Richards. New York, 1958.

1949. Arthur Miller. "Tragedy and the Common Man."
In this brief but significant essay Miller asserts that modern tragedy can be written about the ordinary, middle-class person. Essentially a defense of his own *Death of a Salesman* (1949), this article helped to reconcile the seeming differences between Aristotelian concepts of tragedy and modern tragic writing.
See °tragedy.
Suggested reference: Bernard F. Dukore, ed. *Dramatic Theory and Criticism.* New York, 1974.

1949. Francis Fergusson. *The Idea of a Theater.*
Considered one of the more significant twentieth-century examinations of tragedy, Fergusson's book explores tragic dramas from six different eras, identifying their similarities and the ritualistic patterns that account for their universal appeal.
See °histrionic sensibility, °mythic criticism, °ritual, and °tragedy.
Suggested reference: Francis Fergusson. *The Idea of a Theater.* Princeton, N.J., 1949.

1961. Martin Esslin. *The Theatre of the Absurd.*
Esslin identified and named a significant movement in contemporary theater, calling it the Theater of the Absurd. This book looks at the plays of writers like Adamov, Genet, Pinter, Albee, Beckett, and Ionesco, finding a philosophical outlook common to all of them which marks a distinctive development in modern drama.
See °Theater of the Absurd.
Suggested reference: Martin Esslin. *The Theatre of the Absurd,* rev. ed. Garden City, N.Y., 1969.

Suggestions for Further Reading

Following is a selected list of works on the drama of various periods and on dramatic theory and criticism. These sources both recapitulate and supplement those already cited elsewhere in the handbook, by way of guiding the reader to more thorough discussions of specific topics.

I. Collections of criticism

Adams, Henry Hitch, and Baxter Hathaway, eds. *Dramatic Essays of the Neoclassic Age.* New York, 1965.

Clark, Barrett H., ed. *European Theories of the Drama,* rev. ed. New York, 1966.

Dukore, Bernard F., ed. *Dramatic Theory and Criticism.* New York, 1974.

Gassner, John, and Ralph G. Allen, eds. *Theatre and Drama in the Making,* 2 vols. Boston, 1964.

Hynes, Samuel, ed. *English Literary Criticism: Restoration and Eighteenth Century.* New York, 1963.

Kermode, J. Frank, ed. *Four Centuries of Shakespearian Criticism.* New York, 1965.

Lauter, Paul, ed. *Theories of Comedy.* New York, 1964.

Matthews, Brander, ed. *Papers on Playmaking.* New York, 1957.

Smith, D. Nichol, ed. *Eighteenth Century Essays on Shakespeare.* New York, 1962.

Smith, G. Gregory, ed. *Elizabethan Critical Essays,* 2 vols. Oxford, 1904.

Spingarn, Joel E., ed. *Critical Essays of the Seventeenth Century.* Bloomington, Ind., 1957.

II. General works on the drama

Archer, William. *Play-Making.* Boston, 1912.

Bentley, Eric. *The Life of the Drama.* New York, 1964.

Bergson, Henri. *Laughter,* ed. Wylie Sypher. Garden City, N.Y., 1956.

Brockett, Oscar. *History of the Theatre,* 2nd ed. Boston, 1974.

Brooks, Cleanth, and Robert B. Heilman, eds. *Understanding Drama,* rev. ed. New York, 1960.

Freytag, Gustav. *Technique of the Drama*. New York, 1894.
Gassner, John. *Masters of the Drama*, 3rd ed. New York, 1954.
—— and E. Quinn, eds. *The Reader's Encyclopedia of World Drama*. New York, 1969.
Hartnoll, Phyllis, ed. *The Oxford Companion to the Theatre*, 3rd ed. London, 1967.
Nicoll, Allardyce. *The Theatre and Dramatic Theory*. New York, 1962.
——. *The Theory of the Drama*. London, 1931.
Stuart, Donald C. *The Development of Dramatic Art*. New York, 1928.

III. Greek and Roman drama

Arnott, Peter. *Greek Staging Conventions in the Fifth Century B.C.* Oxford, 1962.
Cornford, Francis M. *The Origins of Attic Comedy*. London, 1914.
Duckworth, George E. *The Nature of Roman Comedy*. Princeton, N.J., 1952.
Else, Gerald F. *The Origin and Early Form of Greek Tragedy*. Cambridge, Mass., 1965.
Harsh, Philip W. *A Handbook of Classical Drama*. Stanford, Cal., 1944.
Kitto, H. D. F. *Greek Tragedy*, 2nd ed. London, 1950.
Norwood, Gilbert. *Plautus and Terence*. New York, 1932.
Pickard-Cambridge, A. W. *Dithyramb, Tragedy, and Comedy*, 2nd ed., revised by T. B. L. Webster. Oxford, 1962.

IV. The medieval drama

Chambers, E. K. *The English Folk-Play*. Oxford, 1933.
——. *The Mediaeval Stage*, 2 vols. Oxford, 1903.
Craig, Hardin. *English Religious Drama of the Middle Ages*. Oxford, 1960.
Farnham, Willard. *The Medieval Heritage of Elizabethan Tragedy*. Berkeley, Cal., 1936.
Young, Karl. *The Drama of the Medieval Church*, 2 vols. Oxford, 1933.

V. Continental drama – Renaissance through eighteenth century

Bruford, Walter H. *Theatre, Drama and Audience in Goethe's Germany*. London, 1957.
Crawford, J. P. W. *Spanish Drama before Lope de Vega*, rev. ed. Philadelphia, 1937.

Duchartre, Pierre L. *The Italian Comedy* . . . , tr. R. T. Weaver. London, 1929.

Herrick, Marvin T. *Comic Theory in the Sixteenth Century.* Urbana, Ill., 1964.

———. *Italian Comedy in the Renaissance.* Urbana, Ill., 1960.

———. *Italian Tragedy in the Renaissance.* Urbana, Ill., 1965.

Jeffery, B. *French Renaissance Comedy, 1552–1630.* Oxford, 1969.

Jourdain, Eleanor F. *Dramatic Theory and Practice in France, 1690–1808.* New York, 1921.

Lockert, Lacy. *Studies in French Classical Tragedy.* Nashville, Tenn., 1958.

Pascal, Roy. *The German Sturm und Drang.* Manchester, 1953.

Rennert, Hugo A. *The Spanish Stage in the Time of Lope de Vega.* New York, 1909.

Schwartz, Isidore A. *The Commedia dell'Arte and Its Influence on French Comedy in the Seventeenth Century.* Paris, 1933.

Turnell, Martin. *The Classical Moment: Studies in Corneille, Molière, and Racine.* New York, 1948.

VI. The drama of England—
Tudor through eighteenth century

Anthony, Sr. Rose. *The Jeremy Collier Stage Controversy: 1698–1726.* New York, 1966.

Bernbaum, Ernest. *The Drama of Sensibility: A Sketch of the History of Sentimental Comedy and Domestic Tragedy, 1696–1780.* Cambridge, Mass., 1915.

Bevington, David M. *From "Mankind" to Marlowe.* Cambridge, Mass., 1962.

Boas, Frederick S. *An Introduction to Stuart Drama.* London, 1946.

———. *An Introduction to Tudor Drama.* Oxford, 1933.

Boyer, C. V. *The Villain as Hero in Elizabethan Tragedy.* New York, 1964.

Chambers, E. K. *The Elizabethan Stage,* 4 vols. London, 1923.

Dobrée, Bonamy. *Restoration Comedy, 1660–1720.* Oxford, 1924.

———. *Restoration Tragedy, 1660–1720.* Oxford, 1929.

Ellis-Fermor, Una. *The Jacobean Drama: An Interpretation,* 3rd ed. London, 1953.

Fluchère, Henri. *Shakespeare and the Elizabethans,* tr. Guy Hamilton. New York, 1956.

Krutch, Joseph Wood. *Comedy and Conscience after the Restoration.* New York, 1949.

Loftis, John, ed. *Restoration Drama: Modern Essays in Criticism.* New York, 1966.

Nicoll, Allardyce. *British Drama*. London, 1925.

———. *History of English Drama, 1660–1900*, 6 vols. London, 1955–59.

Parrott, Thomas M., and Robert H. Ball. *A Short View of Elizabethan Drama*. New York, 1958.

Rossiter, A. P. *English Drama from Early Times to the Elizabethans*. New York, 1950.

Wells, Henry W. *Elizabethan and Jacobean Playwrights*, 2nd ed. Port Washington, N.Y., 1964.

Welsford, Enid. *The Court Masque*. New York, 1962.

VII. *Nineteenth- and twentieth-century drama*

Artaud, Antonin. *The Theater and Its Double*. New York, 1958.

Bentley, Eric. *The Playwright as Thinker: A Study of Drama in Modern Times*. New York, 1946.

Booth, Michael. *English Melodrama*. London, 1965.

Cole, Toby, ed. *Playwrights on Playwriting: The Meaning and Making of Modern Drama from Ibsen to Ionesco*. New York, 1961.

Downer, Alan. *Recent American Drama*. Minneapolis, 1961.

Esslin, Martin. *The Theatre of the Absurd*, rev. ed. New York, 1969.

Freedman, Morris, ed. *Essays in the Modern Drama*. Boston, 1964.

Gorelik, Mordecai. *New Theatres for Old*. New York, 1940.

Lumley, Frederick. *Trends in Twentieth Century Drama: A Survey since Ibsen and Shaw*, 2nd ed. London, 1960.

Matthews, Brander. *French Dramatists of the Nineteenth Century*, 5th ed. New York, 1914.

Miller, Anna Irene. *The Independent Theatre in Europe, 1887 to the Present*. New York, 1931.

Mitchell, Loften. *Black Drama*. New York, 1967.

Quinn, Arthur Hobson. *A History of the American Drama from the Beginning to the Civil War*, 2nd ed. New York, 1943.

———. *A History of the American Drama from the Civil War to the Present Day*, 2nd ed. New York, 1949.

Shaw, George Bernard. *The Quintessence of Ibsenism*. Reprinted, New York, 1959.

Smith, James L. *Melodrama*. London, 1973.

Styan, J. L. *The Dark Comedy: The Development of Modern Comic Tragedy*. Cambridge, 1962.

Walzel, Oskar F. *German Romanticism*. New York, 1932.

VIII. Oriental drama

Brandon, James R. *Theatre in Southeast Asia*. Cambridge, Mass., 1967.
Ernst, Earle. *The Kabuki Theatre*. New York, 1956.
Gargi, Balwant. *Theatre in India*. New York, 1962.
Haar, Francis. *Japanese Theatre in Highlight: A Pictorial Commentary*. Tokyo, 1952.
Keene, Donald. *Bunraku: The Art of the Japanese Puppet Theatre*. Tokyo, 1965.
Kincaid, Zoe. *Kabuki, the Popular Stage of Japan*. London, 1925.
Scott, A. C. *The Classical Theatre of China*. New York, 1957.
Waley, Arthur. *The Nō Plays of Japan*. London, 1921.